Demystifying Police

Strange yet True

Attention Authors

'We Convert Fighters into Writers'. That's the motto of Manas Publications since more than four decades. Our message to the world is that India can win the battle not only by the bullet but also by the pen. There is no dearth of intellectuals in our country, but their knowledge is confined to them only. No sincere effort has been made by any other publisher to channelise their knowledge in national interest. That is why the talent of a large number of intellectuals remains latent. An author transforms his knowledge into a manuscript, and it is our job to spread his/her knowledge by converting it into a beautiful book. For over four decades, Manas has been motivating the intellectuals by publishing their manuscripts and would like to publish your manuscript too. If you or your colleagues have any manuscript ready for publication or are working on it, kindly contact us with detailed synopsis and list of contents. We will transform your work into a valuable publication. If you wish, we can also suggest you the suitable subjects for writing the books related to your area of expertise. Manas is known for its publishing quality and commitments. We take utmost care in production and give wide publicity to the book as well as its author through our national and international distribution network.

Demystifying Police

Strange yet True

Bishwa Nath Lahiri, IP

MANAS

Manas Publications
(We Convert Fighters into Writers)
New Delhi - 110002 (INDIA)

MANAS PUBLICATIONS
(We Convert Fighters into Writers)
(Publishers, Library Suppliers, Importers & Exporters)
4402/5-A, Ansari Road (Opp. HDFC Bank)
Darya Ganj, New Delhi-110 002 (India)
Off: ✆ 011-23260783, 23265523, Res: 011-23842660
Fax: 011-23272766
E-mail: manaspublications@gmail.com
manaspublications@yahoo.com
Website: www. manaspublications.in

2014

ISBN 978-81-7049-480-5

₹ 795/-

Designed at
Manas Publications

Printed in India at
RK Offsets, Delhi
and published by Mrs Suman Lata for
Manas Publications, 4402/5-A,
Ansari Road, (Opp HDFC Bank),
Darya Ganj, New Delhi-110 002 (INDIA)

Introduction

As the very name of the book suggests, it is intended to be a resume of some of my experiences, as a Policeman, over a period of some forty years. It covers, not only an account of crimes and criminals, but also of various happening, likely to be of interest to the average reader. I have left the occurrences to speak for themselves, as I consider this, to be the best way of presenting them.

One thing I have learnt as a Policeman, is that perseverance pays, and so does sincerity of purpose and fair play. Another thing, I have learnt is that life in the Police can be of some fun, if one has the eye for it.

Having joined the police in 1922, I can perhaps claim with some justification, a fair knowledge of conditions, as they prevailed in our country, in pre-independence days. This book therefore gives a glimpse of those conditions, apart from an idea, as to how things were done and how the administration was run. It is said, one lives and learns. This holds good in my case also, although, I happen to be of the proverbial age of seers and then, judging from the present trend of things, a sore point with me, is that while we did tolerably well for some years after independence, as far as the administration of this country was concerned, under the leadership of such stalwarts, as Jawaharlal Nehru, Vallabhbhai Patel, C R Rajagopalchari and Govind Ballabh Pant, to name only a few, we seem to be moving in the reverse gear now, arising from a number of faults that play a dominant role in our national character today.

In spite of their many faults, the British had, by and large, some sterling qualities, such as patriotism, punctuality, discipline, diligence, devotion to duty, which we should do well to emulate, if we wish to make our own mark in the comity of nations.

Should my readers enjoy reading this book, the pains I have taken in its compilation, would be amply repaid.

B N Lahiri

Prateep K. Lahiri
IAS (Retired)

Preface

My father Shri Bishwa Nath Lahiri was born in 1898 and passed away towards the end of 1995, a few months short of completing 98 years of age. His life thus spanned, virtually, over the whole of the twentieth century.

Though he served actively in the U.P. Police for 31 years, he remained till the last day of his life, quintessentially a policeman. He had several firsts to his credit. He was the first Indian to be appointed in the Indian (Imperial) Police (IP), at U.P. through a direct all India competitive examination in 1922. In 1947, after independence, he became the first Indian to head the U.P. Police as the I.G. (the post of D.G. came into existence much later). He was also the first I.G. of the Railway Protection Force, which he was instrumental in setting up, by amalgamating into a Central Police Force various Watch and Wards in different Railways.

The book is not an autobiography in the conventional sense. Shri Lahiri has picked out certain interesting incidents and cases from his experience and narrated them in a way that the book is a page turner. Most of the incidents pertain to the period, he served, in British India, as Superintendent of Police, successively in different districts of U.P. such as Farrukhabad, Pilibhit, Sultanpur, Pratapgarh,

Mirzapur, Unnao, Faizabad and Saharanpur, etc. and he also headed the CID Branch at Lucknow.

Shri Lahiri has narrated numerous cases of criminals, crimes and their detection, which make interesting reading. For instance, the cases relating to apprehending of two brothers, involved in burglary and also of the dacoit Sadho Singh, told in the Chapter: "How I Brought off a Coup" capture the imagination and show how effectively criminals were brought to book and also how speedily cases were investigated and justice dispensed, compared to nowadays when the wheels of justice grind over so slowly.

Chapter 16 "A Case of Mass Hysteria" is a fascinating account of how a communal clash could assume major proportions in a sleepy rural area, situated in the back of beyond. The story of the investigation of the case provides an insight into the travails, undergone in investigating the case and bringing the offenders to book.

The incident narrated in Chapter 17 "An Angry Tiger" takes us back to the days, when a tiger shoot was part of everyday life for district officers, the dangers involved and how tragedy could overtake those, involved in this pastime.

A number of incidents that pertained during British Rule give us a flavour of the times and the oddities of behaviour of some of the British Officers, described very vividly in the book will surely amuse the readers. At least two incidents, related in graphic detail, under the Chapter: "Believe it or Not" and "Shahji of Lucknow", are quite eerie and the happenings narrated, are in the realm of the paranormal.

What comes through clearly, in many of the episodes related, is how the police officers of that era endured extreme physical hardships, while, attending to their duties, in unravelling the crimes committed and enforcing the law. It is difficult to imagine of the S.P. of a district today covering 50 miles on horse back in a single day or going 24 miles on a bicycle, through forest areas, to reach his destination, all in the course of one day. Lahiri Sahib comes across as a true *karmayogi*.

Beginning with incidents, pertaining to the period of British Rule, the narrative has seamlessly proceeded to episodes, which happened in the post independence period. As we progress from 1920s and 30s to 1940s and 50s, we can savour the ending of one era and the beginning of another, with the contrasts standing out, sharp and clear, in the dynamics of the role of the Police in the pre and post independence eras. As the narrative progresses, it is as if we witness history, unfolding itself.

Although, penned many years ago certain descriptions in the book find a resonance in contemporary events. There is an account of the happenings of 1949, pertaining to the dispute relating to the Ram temple at Ayodhya, an issue that remains very much live even today. Similarly, he has written about the need to eradicate corruption in public life, a subject which figures prominently in the current public discourse and at a time, when the Parliament itself is debating the Lok Pal Bill.

I am sure the lay reader will enjoy reading these accounts of the experiences of a Police Officer; they would specially be of interest also to all those concerned with governance of the country and the imperatives of policing in modern India.

In the end I must express my grateful thanks to Shri Shri Ram Arun, a distinguished police officer and former D.G.P. of U.P., for resurrecting the manuscript and helping it see the light of the day.

Prateep K Lahiri, IAS (Retired)

Shri Ram Arun
IPS (Retired), U.P., 1963
Ex-Director General Police, U.P.

My Fond Memories of Mr. B. N. Lahiri
I P - 1922
The First Indian UP Police Chief (IGP)

I had qualified in the written examination for Civil Services and appeared before the interview board of Union Public Service Commission at New Delhi on 14-2-1963. I faced Sri B N Lahiri there, when he was one of the members of the commission. Subsequently, at Central Police Training College, Mount Abu, in 1964, when he came as an examiner of equestrianism before our passing out parade, we saw him mounted erect on a horse back and we were deeply impressed of his riding skills, his age being 65 years. Our batch joined at PTC Moradabad at the end of December 1964, where seniors and other staff members used to discuss very high about the sterling qualities of Mr. Lahiri.

When I was posted as DIG/Chief Security Officer, NER, Gorakhpur, from 1982 to 1985, I learnt that Railway Protection Force was raised by Mr. Lahiri. We were celebrating Silver Jubilee of the RPF, hence we decided to invite Mr. Lahiri, as our Chief Guest, at Gorakhpur, to which he readily agreed. At the Ceremonial Parade, he narrated several anecdotes about RPF. Since then I always remained in touch with him and he too developed a liking for me.

I got promoted in the rank of IGP in 1989 and was posted as IGP, at UP Police Headquarters, Allahabad, where Mr. Lahiri resided at 3 Ponappa Road, Cantt.

During my first calling on him, he said that the serving police officers at Allahabad do not meet each other, therefore, I should do something. I being the senior most police officer at Allahabad then, started inviting all the serving and retired police officers, with spouses at the lawns of PHQ, Guest House every month. This became very popular and Mr. Lahiri used to address us in his usual style. Several such anecdotes of his find mention in this Book.

When I was posted as Additional Director-General of UP, PAC, at Lucknow, we were attempting to write the History of UP, PAC. I thought that who could be a better source of information than Mr. Lahiri. I, along with my wife Shashi and Sri O.P. Tripathi, Commandant IV Bn. PAC Dhoomanganj, Allahabad, went to call on him, in order to discuss about PAC. Earlier, whenever, I went to his residence, I found him well dressed and waiting for me to arrive. This time he was lying on a bed in his drawing room and talked to us in a very feeble voice. After discussion on PAC was over, he gave me a bound copy and some loose typed papers, arranged in chapter forms, which he had written, as and when he could find time and urged that I should get it published in book form. Few weeks later he expired at Allahabad and I attended his funeral. I had decided to get it published early but it took such a long time, for which I really feel sorry.

I have been noticing on the website of 'TOP COPS' that many IPS officers from all over India are inquitive to know much more about Late (Mr.) B.N. Lahiri. I am sure the first hand account given in this book by Mr. Lahiri about Indian Police, particularly about UP, Police, from 1922 onwards, will be of immense interest to readers. My apologies for undue delay in getting this book published.

I am highly grateful to Mr. Prateep K. Lahiri, IAS (Retd., 1959, MP) son of Mr. B.N. Lahiri, for consenting to have his father's book published in this form. He has very kindly written its Preface and also the Profile of the author.

I am grateful to Manas Publications for having agreed to publish this 'Book'.

S R Arun, IPS (Retired)

OBSERVATIONS ON THE POLICE IN INDIA

By Late Dharma Vira, ICS (Retd.)

*(In the context of a book entitled, **"BEFORE AND AFTER"***

Written by BN Lahiri, IP-Retired)

Before independence, the police in India had the task of maintaining law and order, as the servants of a foreign power. Police was the principal tool, used by our foreign rulers not only to maintain law and order but also to ensure that the majesty of the British Crown was held in appropriate awe and veneration by the people of India. The concept that the police was not only the strong arm of the government but also the friend, philosopher and guide of the people had not come into being at all. With the advent of Independence the scene completely changed. From a colonial rule the new Government of India changed overnight into a parliamentary democracy pledged to removing economic disparities and giving a fair deal to the masses of the country. The task of the police in India also got radically changed. From being masters of the people they got converted into their servants. They were no longer required to strike awe in the people to make them subservient to the rulers. They had in the new order to change their ideas completely and from that of rulers to adopt the role of friends and servants of the people.

This would not have been an easy transformation in any case. It was made all the more difficult, due partially to the low level of education of the police force and partially, due to the inexperience and immaturity of the new political masters. The police suddenly found itself in a most invidious position. Whilst in the past, it was generally strongly supported, whether in the right or in the wrong, now it found itself as the whipping dog of the politicians, blamed for every thing that went wrong and very seldom supported, even after having acted correctly.

Shri B.N. Lahiri is eminently qualified to give us the story of the transition in the role of the Police in India, during these times. The story starts from 1922 when Shri Lahiri joined the Indian Police. At that time, the British were firmly entrenched in India and though there was a strong stirring of nationalistic sentiment, independence yet appeared to be a remote dream. From then on, he goes on skilfully to give an insight into the tasks, the attitudes and the status of the police in India and how it changed gradually, and towards the end rapidly, with the advent of independence. The entire narration makes absorbing reading and should be of immense use to students of history and to those interested in an account of the growth and development of the machinery of law and order in our country.

In the concluding chapter of the book Shri Lahiri has expressed some views on the causes of deterioration, in the state of law and order in India and the growth of anti-social crimes, such as corruption. But the fault does not lie entirely with the politicians. The policemen have also to share the blame in a large way. They have not yet learnt that they are the servants and not the masters of the people. Instances of general impoliteness, high-handedness and misdemeanours by policemen are still too numerous to be explained away simply by blaming the politicians. The police in India has still to go a long way, before it can be considered as a worthy custodian of law and order in a democracy.

Dharma Vira

Contents

Chapter 1

My Innings

My innings, in essence, began with my appointment by the Secretary of State for India as an Assistant Superintendent of Police in August, 1922, as a result of the first ever competitive examination held in India for the direct recruitment of Indians to the Indian (Imperial) Police, as the Service was then called—In all, 7 candidates, including myself, were selected, one each from the States of Bengal, Bihar, Bombay (at present Maharashtra), Madras (at present Chennai), Central Provinces, Punjab and U.P. I was selected from U.P.

All my batchmates at the Police Training School in Moradabad, being an Englishmen and the Police Mess there, with its European style of living, being foreign to me, it took some effort on my part to be settle down. One marked thing about my batchmates was their contempt for Indians generally and the Indian way of life. They were also opposed to all political reforms and often tried to sound me for my political leanings. One day, one of them asked me bluntly how

I felt about King George. This was a delicate question, difficult for me to answer. In fact, for all Indians in the Service in those days, it was a case of walking on a tight rope.

My initiation into the mysteries of life in the Police Mess at Moradabad was a novelty for me. At the Mess dinner was in a nature of a parade. While dinner was over, one had to drink for the King's health, ordinarily port or sherry. But for those, like me, who had any scruples against strong drinks, it was permissible to do so in water—One evening as I was about to quaff my drink, it caught the eye of the then I.G. Police, one Mr. L. M. Kaye, who exclaimed to me, "Look, what you are doing. The King will catch a cold. "I am glad, however, I never succumbed to the practice then prevalent of soaking in gallons of strong drinks.

Before Independence, for a Police Officer on tour to cover daily ten to twelve miles on horseback in the countryside was a must. This was possible because each of them maintained a horse. Maintenance of a car, on the other hand, was frowned upon by senior officers. In my own case, I remember how once I got a rebuff from my Range D.I.G., soon after I had bought my first car, a brand new Chev for Rs. 2750/-. One morning as I drove up in it somewhat ostentatiously, to call on him, instead of greeting me with his usual politeness, he looked at me witheringly and pointing to my car and said, "I see, you, too have gone in for that infernal machine."

My record happens to be a marathon ride of 50 miles on horseback which I did during the course of a day, on the eve of Mahatma Gandhi's arrest at Bombay on 4th January, 1932, when, following his return empty handed from the Second Round Table Conference in England, he threatened to give a call for an all-India *Satyagraha.*

If I escaped any trouble as a sequel to Mahatma Gandhi's arrest on this occasion, I had to bear the full brunt of the Civil Disobedience Movement of 1930-31, which took the form of *Satyagraha* of various kinds. I felt that by and large, the best thing to do would be to turn a blind eye on the doings of the participants thereof. In this context I might relate a minor difference I had with my District

Magistrate, an Englishman, one Mr. Wood, over the line of action to be taken against a threat held out by Congress volunteers to plant the Congress flag on one of the public buildings in the station. My reaction to this threat, again, was not to take any notice of it. To this Mr. Wood demurred. I am glad, however, that I gained my point ultimately, although Mr. Wood conceded it only grudgingly.

On another occasion, the subject of difference between us was the Simon Commission Report on Political Reforms. The report by this all-white Commission being unacceptable to most of our political leaders, I did not care to go through it. Mr. Wood, on the other hand, thought it to be admirable. One evening, when he questioned me if I had read it, I said, no, he looked surprisingly and strongly recommended that I should find time to do so. Upon this I blurted out, "What is the good of it, when it is going to be written all over again?" Mr. Wood went red in the face and thereafter, we talked no more of this report, which as we all knew, lies on the dump heap today.

While posted as Superintendent of Police, Faizabad, I took an active part in the rounding up of a notorious outlaw, named Sadho Singh, to earn the Police Medal for Gallantry for myself. At one time later on, as the Chief of the investigation Branch of the C.I.D., I supervised the investigation of a case of Railway Mail dacoity of a purely political nature. The interesting thing about this case is that some 25 years later, when I happened to go to Rudrapur in Nainital District, two of the ex-convicts of this case turned up to greet me. They were cultivating some land granted to them free of rent as political sufferers. I could not help reflecting how the wheel of time had turned a full circle and how those who were treated as criminals at one time were now acclaimed as heroes.

My spell in the Investigation Branch of the C.I.D. from 1940 to 1943 was an arduous one, during which I had to deal with a number of political-criminal cases of prime importance. Most of them having been worked out successfully, I was awarded the O.B.E. in recognition of my service.

During the early part of my service, while posted at Pilibhit, I was once out on night patrol in the city, accompanied by the City Kotwal, both of us being on horse back. While passing through a narrow lane, we stopped opposite a spot where there had been a case of burglary the previous night. Suddenly, I felt the hind-legs of my horse sinking and before I could make out what the matter was, my horse and I found ourselves floundering in water that came up to my neck. I had actually fallen into an open Municipal drain and this made my horse try furiously clamber out. After a brief struggle he managed to do so and so did I, thoroughly shaken by the traumatic experience I had. Fortunately for me, my horse stood stock still in the middle of the lane. I sprang on his back at once and, on my return home the first thing I did was to give myself a thorough wash before going to bed for the rest of the night. It was then 2.00 o'clock by my watch.

Quite unknown to me, this incident, gained me some publicity locally at that time, as I discovered some 20 years later. I was then as I.G. Police attending a party meeting of Congress legislators, at the invitation of the Chief Minister Pt. Govind Ballabh Pant. The idea behind this meeting was to apprise me informally of the complaints the partymen had against the Police generally. I was finding it increasingly difficult to meet their charges, when a Congress legislator from Deoria got up to say in defence of the Police that once at about 1.00 in the night, as he was going home on foot, he came across the local Superintendent of Police, Bal Mukund Sharma, who was then out on night patrol at the sacrifice of his night's rest. I was flattering myself over this turn of events when another legislator, this time from Pilibhit, my old district, got up to say that when he was a child he used to hear that the local Superintendent of Police (meaning me) was in the habit of going out on night patrol in disguise. His point was "why cannot the present day S.S.P. do the same?" The compliment thus paid me not only sounded like heavenly music,but also evoked much goodwill for me.

Soon after independence, I was lucky to be installed as the first Indian I.G. Police, U.P. My problem was that with the retirement of all the British Officers and the exodus to Pakistan of a substantial number of Muslim Officers of the I.P., I was left with barely a handful of officers of this cadre to carry on. Worse still, I had to grapple with an increasingly deteriorating situation on the law and order front, necessitating large scale operations against notorious outlaws.

The situation was further complicated by the influx from both the Eastern and Western Wings of Pakistan of hundreds of thousands of refugees, some of whom indulged in mass killings. Luckily, before long, peace prevailed all over the State.

One signal achievement of those days was the formation in record time of XI Bn of the PAC. Thanks to the great zeal displayed by a selected band of officers headed by late Sri Shanti Prasad, these Battalions were in position within a very short time. Better still, such was the prestige they built up that their services were in constant demand from all corners of India.

In passing, I might mention here that I had the privilege of flagging off a special train by which a contingent of some 1,500 men of the PAC U.P. left for Hyderabad one afternoon, around 1949 or so, in response to a call from Sardar Patel, who was then Union Home Minister and desired a massive man hunt to be carried out against a whole lot of outlaws given to terrorism in this State in those days. They worked in small groups by night and were after the blood of local citizens of particular class, residing mostly in villages.

In all, some 20,000 men of the Para Military Forces from all over India had assembled to carry out this hunt under the over-all command of Mr. Nanjappa, one of the I.C.S. officers who had been appointed Special Commissioner in this connection.

I had an opportunity as a special invitee to go round along with Mr. Nanjappa, the various places where my men had set up their camps and I was very pleased to notice two things. One was the beauty of these makeshift camps in out-of-the-way places, which gave ample proof of their resourcefulness. The other was the way they had won over the hearts of the local inhabitants, who were full of praise for their exemplary conduct. What impressed me most was that as a part-time occupation, they were running classes for the teaching of boys of the school-going age.

Naturally, Mr. Nanjappa was all praise for my men, who he declared were by far the best of all the contingents under his command.

This brings to my mind to had a meeting one day with the Area Commander, U.P., Major General Curtis, to seek his help in men and materials, preliminary to the formation of these Battalions. The very idea of the project struck him as preposterous and he pooh-poohed it by saying. "Don't talk to me in terms of Battalions." General Curtis was among those who were certain of disintegration of this country, the moment he and his friends had turned their backs on it. His attitude was like that of the French Emperor, who is believed to have said on his death bed, "After me the deluge."

The Prime Minister Pt. Jawaharlal Nehru visited Lucknow in December, 1952, for presentation of colours to the U.P. Police and the P.A.C., U.P., it was the crowning event of my career. On the evening preceding the parade, we had a banquet in honour of him at which as host I had to make an after-Dinner speech. I took advantage of it to say that with the partition of the country the necessity had arisen for reorganisation of the Police as a second line Force. The P.M.'s speech in reply was characteristic of him as an apostle of peace and non-violence. He discounted the very idea of making the police into a para-military force. Subsequent events have proved that Pt. Jawaharlal was not clairvoyant—Even so, what can deny his greatness as a man?

The Ceremonial Parade was universally acclaimed to be a great success. One of the dignitaries attending it, went to the extent of mentioning that it was a dream come true. The Prime Minister was also gracious enough to pay a glowing tribute to the UP Police and P.A.C., U.P., for their achievements, apart from complimenting me specially for my part in the game.

Incidentally, one afternoon, soon after this Parade, while we were witnessing various Displays by Police Jawans, I happened to be sitting close to Sri K.M. Munshi, Governor of U.P., and Kunwar Sir Maharaj Singh, who had then lately retired from his exalted office of Governor, Bombay and come to Luckow to settle down there. A thing, I remember with sense of pride is that while the show was on, I overheard Sir Maharaj Singh saying to Sri Munshi, "Look, Munshi, I have been all over India and I can assure you that your Police happens far and away that best of all the Police of India." Then he pointed to the officers moving about on the field in front of us and said, "Just see, how smart they look."

In retrospect, I should say that much of the success of the Force under me was due to the perfect understanding that existed between me and the Government of India in those days, who thought fit to allow me a free hand and abstain from the least interference in the matter of postings and transfers of the officers and men under me, which is, to my mind, the root cause of a large part of the trouble that dogs the Police today.

* * * *

Chapter 2

In Retrospect

My letter of appointment as Probationary Assistant Superintendent of Police of the Indian (Imperial) Police, as this service was then called, came from the Secretary of State for India in England, on a date in August 1922. I must, however, mention it here that it was through sheer chance that I joined this service.

How this happened was something like this. While I was completing my M.A. in English Literature in the Muir Central College at Allahabad, (Now known as Science College of the Allahabad University). I came into contact with one Mrs. Paul Biggane, wife of a senior officer of the Police. Both Mr. and Mrs. Biggane were then living in the same house with Reverend Morton, warden of the Holland Hall of which I was an inmate. Mrs. Biggane happened to be a blue stocking, that is a graduate in English Literature from the University of London. Therefore, a few of the students of this Hostel, including myself, who were then completing their M.A. in English Literature, used occasionally to meet her to discuss it. It was she who came to know from her husband in 1921, that this service was going to be thrown open to Indians for the first time and also that a competitive examination on an all India basis would be held sometime in December that year for admission to it. She was good enough to pass on this information to me, apart from information, also nomination for permission to sit for this examination done by the Deputy I.G., C.I.D. Mr. O'Conor. In all seven candidates were declared successful from all over India in which I happened to be one, And Uttar Pradesh had been allotted to me.

On receipt of my appointment order I reported to Mr. (Later Sir) Robert Dodd, Principal of the Police Training School (now College) at his residence in Moradabad. Mr. Dodd gave me a letter of introduction to the senior most Probationary Assistant Superintendent of Police undergoing training, named George Reeves. I then went over to the Police Mess and found this gentleman busy tinkering with his travelling machine, a T model Ford, in a posture that made any communication with him difficult. For, he was then lying on his back under the chassis of his car. I had therefore, to bide my time till he came out of his hide out. When he did so, he looked quizzically at me, since I with my brown skin and black hair was as much of a novelty to him as he with his ginger hair and ruddy face was to me. He then took me inside the Mess where I noticed about a dozen officers, all Englishmen, having their breakfast. Reeves introduced me to them in acknowledgement of which they simply nodded their heads before carrying on unconcernedly with their meal. The quiet that prevailed was oppressive and I felt very awkward till Masit, the Mess *Khidmatgar*, made a place for me at the table and served me my breakfast.

Once, the breakfast was over, I adjourned to the then Mess President George Parkin's room. He was a lad of 19 or so who initiated me into the mysteries of life in the Mess. One thing I learnt was that dinner at the Mess was a ritual at which one had to turn up in regulation kit. Also, that it was heralded by bugle call at 8.00 in the evening. George Parking took it upon himself to fit me out right and proper with the help of a local *durzee* within 24 hours of my arrival. He also engaged for me a personal servant known as bearer, at Rs. 25/- per month. His name was Sukhan, a Muslim by religion.

A man of few words, Sukhan was god-send who made for me an ideal batman whom I admired greatly for his quiet efficiency. But there was one thing about him which I dreaded, although it stemmed from his extreme solicitude for my comfort. For instance, he would not allow me to dress by myself, much as I hated the idea of some one else assisting me to do it. This resulted in a regular battle of wits between the two of us. For my part, the strategy I employed to escape his notice was to try and tiptoe into my dressing room. But so sharp was his ear that he generally caught me out and rushed in either to help me with the tucking in of my shirt or with the tying up of my Sam Browne belt. Sukhan was of a class that has become extinct now with the departure of all officers of foreign extraction. Mostly Muslims by religion, they were adepts at their profession which they carried on from father to son. They were extremely faithful to their masters who were, by and large, attached to them, in their turn. I have known of an Englishman, namely Mr. S.G. Dunne of the Muir Central College, who once came all the way from England after his retirement from service, to put in a word with our Vice-President, Dr. Radhakrishnan, for the rehabilitation of his bearer, a Muslim, who had made the mistake of running away to Pakistan from India for a while and had thus forfeited his right to the owner-ship of certain immoveable property, which he had acquired with the money, left him by his old master. Instances of this kind of mutual regard between a British master and his Indian servant can be cited in galore.

This was one side of the medal. But there was another side to it in so far as it was not at all uncommon for Britishers to make free use to their boots to chastise their servants. Some of my companions at the mess openly declared that they were here in India to rule. They also made no secret of the fact that they had been attracted to service in India by the infinite variety of *shikar* that could be had here for the asking. Except for some honourable exceptions, they had no use for Indians generally and were very critical of their ways of life.

Here I will quote an incident that left a deep impression on my mind. I was being driven back to the mess one day by one of my companions who, in common with most others of his nationality, suffered from a superiority complex that made them obnoxious at times. It so happened that on our way we went past a country bumpkin who, while he took good care to give us a wide berth, missed to make the customary *salam* to my companion. This enraged him to such an extent that with the help of the choicest Hindustani swear words, which he had learnt by heart, he gave him a ticking off so as to admonish him for his grave delinquency.

I might mention here that if my companions took kindly to me, it was simply because they viewed me as one of their batch-mates and not as an Indian. In fact, out of their regard for me they nicknamed me Bill. One thing that went in my favour was that I was not in the habit of chewing pan or of smoking through a hookah, which they called a hubble-bubble or of playing Indian records.

It is indeed no exaggeration to say that every Tom, Dick and Harry who had any pretensions to foreign extraction looked upon himself as a superior being, entitled to homage by all Indians. They were commonly known as Anglo-Indian who in those days made a clear sweep of all the upper subordinate services under Government, such as the Railways, the Posts and Telegraphs and the Ordnance.

In the Police, for instance, there is a post of Reserve Inspector who is in immediate charge of what is known as the reserve Lines in each and every district. This post was in the past invariably held by an Anglo-Indian. As Superintendent of Police at Sitapur in 1925 I had an unpleasant experience with my Reserve Inspector named Bacon. Something in his bearing gave me the impression that he resented having to work under an Indian. Nor was I happy with his general conduct, although he was clever enough not to give an opportunity for me to make an issue of it. Anyhow, I thought it best to try and get rid of him and wrote to my Deputy I.G., who was an Englishman, to this effect. But, much to my disappointment, the answer I got from him was that it would take yet some more time for persons of Bacon's class to adjust themselves to the changed circumstances, implying thereby that I should hold my patience till then.

It is almost unbelievable today that there was a time when all our Railway passenger trains had a third class compartment marked 'for Europeans only' reserved for such of the so-called Europeans who were unable to travel by first or second class.

To revert to my experience at the P.T.S., I could not, while I was there, resist the feeling that I was a second class citizen and as such subject to certain disabilities *vis-a-vis* my companions. For instance, I was not considered eligible for the office of president of the mess which held in rotation by all my companions. This discrimination against Indians, in fact, continued till the grant of our independence, particularly in the matter of posting to what were known as plum districts.

I have alluded to the drill and discipline that went with dinner at the mess. They assumed a special character on our guest nights with the premises transformed into almost a fairy land, the dinner table artistically arranged and making a brave display of all the silver ware the Mess had. Being the only Indian present among a host of Englishmen, I was at times oppressed by a feeling of loneliness which made me wonder whether I was on my native land.

I remember that there was practice current in those days of drinking to the health of the King Emperor. The drill laid down for it was something like this. When dinner was over, the Mess President made a gentle tap on the table. This was a signal for every one to rise, drink in hand. The next thing he did was to call out "Mr. Vice the King". The Vice-President in his turn called out "Gentlemen, the King Emperor," whereupon the Band played the first bar of the National Anthem and the entire company partook of their drinks, saying "God bless him". Those who were teetotallers had the option to drink the toast in water. It so happened that one evening while I was drinking for the King Emperor's health as usual in water. It caught the notice of the I.G. Police, Mr. L.M. Kaye who was present there. This led him to exclaim jocularly "Lahiri look what you are doing. The King will catch a cold".

Much of the drill and discipline of the mess, I noticed, was gone when, some twenty five years later, I had occasion to visit it in company with the Home Minister U.P., Sri Lal Bahadur Shastri. For one thing, while the practice of sounding a bugle call for dinner was still in vogue, many of the guests for the occasion turned up late. Nor was there any question of dinner being served on the dot. At another time within my knowledge, what amounted to an outrage against the old traditions of the mess, was committed when the personal servant of the Chief Minister, Pandit Govind Ballabh Pant, sneaked in, to have his meal with the rest of us. This was indeed democratic socialisation with a vengeance.

One thing I learnt while I was under training was attention to details, about which the Principal of the school was very particular. Another thing I learnt was a type of grim discipline, unknown to most of us.

The Police Officers' Mess at Moradabad was for me like a territory carved out of and yet quite distinct from the surrounding area, with an invisible wall separating them. Within this territory everything was spick and span. The mess servants looked spotless in their milk white liveries and seemed to add to the lustre of the whole place. Access to this area being restricted, it looked more or less like a small corner of Britain where one was expected to conform to the European style of living.

On the grounds of the Police Training School there stood another building tenanted by officers of the State Service under training. But such was the unwritten law in vogue at the time that it was not open to them to mix with officers of the Indian Police on terms of equality or friendship at any time. Nor to enter the sacred precincts of the mess. Here was a case of class distinction of a type unknown today.

The insularity that characterised the Police Officers' Mess at Moradabad was only in line with the aloofness and rigidity which our British masters studiously observed in their relations with Indians generally, at least in the later years of their rule. In the result, they remained like birds of passage till the last. For them Indian manners and customs like eating with the fingers or squatting square legged on the floor, was the height of crudity. At the same time, so far as our language was concerned, most of them felt that it was no business of theirs to learn it sufficiently well to the able to speak it fluently or without an accent.

Another trait of British character I marked was the riotous gaiety of which they were capable at times or the surplus energy that they possessed which explained their fondness for manly games, such as polo, pigsticking and hunting to which they were accustomed to devote most of their spare time.

To proceed. The business of correct observance of the English etiquette was something that no Indian was able to master fully. In my own case, I remember how I once tripped up when I went round dropping cards on the married couples of the station. The list given to me included the names of Mr. and Mrs. Craker and Mr. and Mrs. Baldock. When I called on the Crakers I found that while Mr. Craker was out, Mrs. Craker was in. All I should have done was to drop two cards on them and then vanish. But since Mrs. Craker was in. I remained standing outside their house till she came to me, more or less under duress. On the other hand, when I called on the Baldocks, both of them were out, So, instead of dropping two cards on them, as I should have done, I made the blunder of dropping one only, since the not-at-home box outside their residence had the name of Mrs. Baldock only painted on it.

This reminds me of an error which one my friends, an Indian, who had joined the Police after me, made when he dropped his cards with all his academic qualifications printed on them, on Mr. and Mrs. Walten, Mr. Walten was then District Magistrate of Moradabad. He sent these cards in a closed cover to the Principal of our school to see. For, it was in bad form to flaunt one's academic qualification on one's visiting card, unless one was a professional and was making a call on a business errand of his own.

Before I close this chapter, I will mention one more incident which is also interesting. One day one of my batch mates who had some doubts in his mind about my loyalty to the British Crown, asked me abruptly, "Bill, how do you feel towards King George?" This was a difficult question for me to answer for the simple reason that I had no feelings of any kind towards a man who sat on his throne some four or five thousand miles away. But in my position as a Government servant, I knew it would be a folly on my part to say so bluntly. I therefore, found myself on the horns of a dilemma and ultimately blurted out. "After all, he is our Kind Emperor". I am not aware to this day whether my interlocutor was satisfied or not with my answer. But I felt thankful to him for abstaining from putting me any further questions on this subject by way of cross examination on me.

* * * *

Chapter 3

Freddie Young of the UP Police

Freddie Young of the UP Police was a name to be reckoned with at one time. This was because he had made a name for himself as a Giant Killer through the liquidation of many an outlaw of great notoriety, such as Sultana of Uttar Pradesh and Pir Pagaro of Sindh, among others. One distinctive feature with him was his bulk which was enormous, almost double the average, if not more.

I made Freddie's acquaintance in the autumn of 1923, when he was posted as officer on Special Duty for the apprehension of Sultana. During those days he used to come occasionally to Moradabad and stay at the Police Mess in a guest room next to me. I had thus an excellent opportunity to observe him at close quarters.

On one occasion when Freddie was staying at the Mess, he had, as usual, a busy programme throughout the day, with a stream of visitors, who, I guessed, were from among his informers. Some of them were even women in *'burqas'*. In the evening he had his dinner and then adjourned to his room to have another round of talk with his officers. This went quite some time and thus kept me awake till late in the night. It was only after they had gone that there was a lull and I dozed off.

After some time, when I was half asleep, half awake; I seemed to hear a peculiar sound emanating from Freddie's room. It went something like "Kring, Krang, Kring, Kring, Krang". Soon I was fully awake. I wondered what this sound was due to. At one time I even felt like shouting "murder" and calling for help. But before long it dawned on me that Freddie's spring bed, made for ordinary mortals, was giving way under his superior weight. My suspicion was confirmed when I heard a thud indicating that his bottom had landed on firm ground. I said to myself how very awkward it must be for him to lie in bed with part of his body on ground and part in mid-air. But I didn't have to keep thinking for long. I heard him lift himself and make his bed on the floor to snatch what little rest he could. Thereafter, it didn't take me also long to all fast asleep.

At the sound of the morning bugle, I got up to dress for parade. The moment I came out of my room, Freddie also, dressed in his pink pyjamas and with a beaming face like that of the sun-god himself, emerged, as large as life, discomfort he might have caused to me during the night. I was greatly touched by his solicitude for me, a mere probationer, and have cherished his memory with fondness ever since.

* * * *

Chapter 4

Sheer Force of Habit

In October 1923 on a date, that His Excellency Lord Reading, Viceroy and Governor General of India and Lady Reading were slated to pay a visit to Lucknow where he was to hold a *darbar*, among his other engagements. I was then under training at Moradabad and received an order of my deputation to Lucknow on a special duty in that connection and so did all my batch mates, numbering six in all. Great was our jubilation on receipt of the order for we felt that it would help to relieve the monotony of our life at the Training School (now College) and at the same time, prove beneficial for us before starting our career as regular policemen.

On our arrival at Lucknow, we were required to arrange for our own billets, which we did. Thereafter, we discovered that our duties were to be of a purely supervisory character. In the first instance, we would have to check up whether or not all the men detailed for street lining or patrolling or security duty in our respective charges, were in position and in the second instance, whether or not they were sufficiently alert at their posts. We were also given a horse each raised from a local Artillery unit, to carry on our duties.

Those were the days when in UP there was no para-military force (PAC) for emergent duties. Therefore, some 850 men had been drafted in for the occasion from various districts,in batches ranging from 20 to 50 according to the size of each of these districts. They were all quartered under Chapman who was one from among us and was specially suited for the job, having a background of service in the Army for several years before he joined the police.

Now, I will come to the horse allotted to me. It happened to be some 16 'hands' in height and as such I used to have some difficulty in mounting on him. But that was not so much of a problem for me to tackle, as was the habit he had of swerving so abruptly the moment he saw an elephant, that I ran the imminent risk of being thrown off his back. Unfortunately for me, it so happened that a fairly large number of prize elephants had been requisitioned for the occasion from the Maharaja of Balrampur to give the Viceroy a salute. The drill laid down for them was that they were to stand in the form of an arc on a ground specially marked off for the purpose on one side of the *Darbar* tent. The Viceroy on his arrival, before going to the *Darbar* tent would stand at a marked spot in front of the elephants, After given them signal, the elephants would lift their trunks in salute to him- although this made a brave show, yet it lasted for barely a minute or two which made me think of the toil and trouble, apart from the cost involved in it, merely to titillate the vanity of a potentate who ruled over the destinies of an entire subject nation, as it was then.

What really I wanted to explain, is that with such a large number of elephants knocking about here, there and everywhere, I had constantly to be on the alert to avoid any mishap to me and learnt the trick of almost automatically turning away the head of my mount the moment I espied an elephant at a distance, so much so, that this had become almost a second nature with me and I did not have to think twice about it.

I will now relate some of the amusing incidents that came to my notice on the day of the *Darbar*. One thing I noticed was that under each of the ornamental trees that stood on the grounds of Kaiserbagh, one could see a plain clothes man on duty, making a vain effort to hide his person. This gave me some cause for amusement as did the sight of another plain-clothes man crossing the road in front of me. He was walking with such short and minding steps and at the same time shoulder, I could at once spot him as a plain-clothes man of the CID on duty, who seemed to labouring under the false notion that he had donned the magic cap which made him invisible to other.

One such other incident occurred upon with the arrival of His Excellency, Sir William Marris, Governor of UP, exactly five minutes ahead of Viceroy. As he arrived, his chauffeur, after parking his car on one side of the road got out to stretch his legs, leading the Governor's pet dog, a deschund by its leash. Thereafter, when a foolish constable on duty challenged him to show his identity card, it was most amusing to see how with an air of supreme indifference mixed with a touch of insolence, he pointed his index finger at the dog by way of his answer.

To revert to the story of my mount during the period of the rehearsals, on a Sunday, which was the off-day for all of us, it so happened that I was peddling along merrily on my bicycle towards my abode, when I noticed a number of elephants being given a shampoo by their *mahouts* in a tank off the road. The moment I did so, such was the force of my habit acquired since my arrival at Lucknow, that I abruptly turned round the handle-bar of my bicycle to find myself wheeling away in opposite direction which, when I realised it, gave me much cause for mirth at my own cost.

* * * *

Chapter 5

Viceroy's Special

Winter in parts of Uttar Pradesh can be pretty severe at times, the temperature dropped to a few degrees within freezing point. As luck would have it, it was on one of these intensely cold nights in the month of January 1925, that I happened to be detailed for special duty at Railway Station Khurja for the Viceregal Special, which was due to pass that station at about 4.00 in the morning, on its way to Delhi from Calcutta. Since I was posted as Assistant Superintendent, Meerut, in those days, I had to travel by rail from there and thus arrived at the other end at about midnight.

The usual drill laid down for such occasions provided, among other things, for a search being made of the station premises of any suspicious persons that might be hiding themselves. But once the search was over, and all the men detailed for specific duties were in position, there was nothing left for me to do, except cooling my heels till such time as the train was due to arrive. I might add here that who have had to wait and keep a vigil like mine, will be able fully to appreciate the tedium of such waiting for some four hours, particularly on a frosty night with hardly anything to engage one's attention.

Anyhow, to while away the time, I kept walking up and down, up and down the platform times without number and, while I did so, I had a sense of companionship with the bright stars over my head, which seemed to be watching my movements, "With their eternal eyelids apart". on occasions like this, man feels humbled by the thought of his insignificance in face of the great scheme of things which envelops him. Various questions to which there is no answer, arise in his mind and then fade away.

After a lapse of what seemed to be an eternity, I was suddenly brought back to the immediate present, by a perception of some hurry and bustle among the station staff, thus heralding the approach of the "special", which made so much work for countless persons, in its passage from one end of the country to the other. It was so, because no precaution against any possible danger to the life of the Viceroy, what soever remote it might be, was too great to be taken.

Actually, a pilot engine which was running ten minutes ahead of the special, was first to arrive. Thereafter, as soon as it had gone, everybody seemed to hold his breath in expectation until the special steamed in quietly and then came to a halt without making a sound or a murmur. This being a watering station, the engine was drawn up by the side of the water column and, as it stood there drawing water, the hissing caused by its steam, was the only sound that broke the silence of the night.

The question arose in my mind instinctively was, what might the great potentate, who ruled with an iron hand, over the destinies of over three hundred million souls of India, might be doing at that moment? Most likely he was fast asleep, quite oblivious of the vigil that had to be kept by so many souls on his account.

There stood the train in front of me, with all its shutters down, looking in the enveloping silence, more like a hearse than what it actually was. Presently, the engine was heard sounding a short blast, next, its wheels started moving, ever so slowly and noiselessly, and soon enough the train was again swallowed up in the surrounding gloom from which it had made its appearance only a short while ago, leaving not a trace behind. Naturally, I felt like asking myself, "Am I awake or asleep?"

A thing that calls for mention here is that while the train as passing by and I was looking at it like one entranced, I noticed some light streaming from a compartment of which the window shutter was up. Inside that compartment, as it flashed past me, I noticed a buxom South Indian woman, apparently a handmaid of the Viceriene, brushing her long tresses, opposite a mirror, which fell in cascades down to her hips, while a young man, apparently a personal attendant of the Viceroy or of one of his staff, was gazing at her with lovelorn eyes, both of them having a smile on their face. I could never imagine even that I would be a chance witness to a scene of this romantic nature, flashing past me to be lost for ever in the folds of time. This made me reflect how the Viceroy's entourage, down to the level of his personal attendants, were lucky enough not only to travel in such luxury, but also to be able to carry on their amours on the quiet, if they chose to do so; while I, a poor policeman, was, on the other hand, fated to keep a vigil by night in intense cold, to ensure the safe passage of his special train.

* * * *

Chapter 6

A Long Long Way to Indergarh

My first posting as a Probationary Assistant Superintendent of Police was at Farrukhabad in Uttar Pradesh. I arrived there on the morning of 16th December 1923 from the Police Training School at Moradabad and planted myself in one of the rooms of the Dak Bungalow at Fatehgarh, a suburb of Farrukhabad. Thereafter, I made it my first business to call on Mr. (Later Sir John) Nott-Bower, my would be boss. It so happened that he was then away in camp at a remote Police Station named Indergarh. To get there, I discovered, that I had first to go to Kannauj by rail and from there to Indergarh by a metalled road for part of the way and by an unmetalled one for the rest of it. Before setting out on my journey, I had taken the precaution to ask the Station Officer Kannauj to make suitable arrangements for my trip from Kannauj to Indergarh and back. Later, when I arrived at Kannauj one morning at about 4.00, the first person to greet me there, was the Station Officer Kannauj, whom, I noticed, was a tall and handsome young man, fully dressed in his uniform. As it was still quite dark, I thought fit to pass my time at the Railway Station itself till day break, which was not much of a pleasure since the cold was intense and the place had no amenities to offer.

At about 7.00 A.M. in the morning, the Station Officer Kannauj informed me that all was arranged for a carriage-and-pair belonging to the Raja of Tirwa to take me as far as Tirwa and an elephant from there to Indergarh. Everything was then new for me and I was impressed to see the stately carriage by which I was to travel as far as Tirwa and its equally striking coach-man who with his two attendants in livery made a trio hard to beat. Having never before in my life had an opportunity to ride such a smart turn out, I must confess, I was filled with a sense of my importance that was hardly compatible with my status. All went well as far as Tirwa, where I found an elephant, also belonging to the Raja, waiting to take me to Indergarh. He had a thick pad on his back and I somehow managed to camber on to it and so did my orderly, who had accompanied me all the way from Fatehgarh.

While I had seen many an elephant before this in my life, I had never had the occasion to ride on one. Huge as he looks, he is a clumsy animal, as compared to a horse. This was the first experience of my life and he shuffled along and my body alternately tilted forward, backward and sideway, with every step that he took, a thing that was far from comfortable for me. Anyway, for the first mile or so, I did not mind it very much. But as the day advanced I felt increasingly tired, besides losing my patience. All the same with a big hulking animal like an elephant, there is nothing one can do. In brief, in spite of the best efforts of the *Mahaut* to make him go faster, he ambled along in his own slow and stately way. Consequently, when we reached Indergarh, it was past 2.00 o'clock in the afternoon and, worse still, I found that Mr. Nott-Bower had left for the Police Station, a mile away, where I had a brief interview with him. He struck me as a very amiable sort of man, full of life. My halt at the Police Station had necessarily to be cut short as I was anxious to get back to Fatehgarh by the same evening, having brought no change of clothes or bedding with me. I was also feeling starved as I had not taken any food or drink since the previous evening, a fact which I foolishly kept back from Mr. Nott-Bower when I met him.

Indergarh, as I was told, was ideal for its duck shooting. Mr. Nott-Bower was camping there for a longer spell than elsewhere through his desire to combine work with pleasure. As I came to know later, he was an extremely good shot, apart from being very good at pig sticking and such other manly games. This reminds me that my batch mates as the training school used to tell me that one of the attractions India had for them was the scope it held out for *Shikar* of all types. Incidentally, one could easily indulge in it in the past, when cartridges could be bought for a song and when there was no ban against the shooting of wild animals at that time. It will perhaps be news to many that the Maharaja of Bikaner used to arrange annually a duck shoot in his territory for the Viceroy and his party, at which the bag totalled more than a thousand birds. Likewise, the Raja of Payagpur in Uttar Pradesh used to arrange annually in his territory, a shoot for the Governor and his party at which the person with the highest tally of birds to his credit, was declared to be "the man of the match". I am aware that once Mr. G. Waddell of the Police, with a tally of 93 birds, won this distinction.

To revert to the account of my return journey from Indergarh I had to cover some 30 miles on elephant-back in a day which was an experience in itself. As before, my elephant ride back to Tirwa was a bone shaking affair. When I got there, I found the Raja's car, a Sunbeam Talbot, waiting to take me to Kannauj, my train for Fatehgarh had already left. The railway track from Kannauj to Fatehgarh runs parallel to a metalled road. The race that now began between me and this train, was thrilling. The advantage, however, lay with the train, for, every time I overtook it. I was held up at a level crossing which I found closed. This happened three or four times, much to the enjoyment of the passengers of the train, who missed no opportunity to boo at me, whenever the train overtook my car. Ultimately, when I got to Gursahaiganj, I found my train still standing there and I lost no time to board it with the utmost alacrity. Finally when I arrived at Fatehgarh, thoroughly tired and ravenously hungry as a wolf, (for I had no food or drink for more than 24 hours) it was well past 9.00 in the evening, what a day!

This was the first experience I had of my service in the police, which taught me how one has to take the rough with the smooth.

* * * *

Chapter 7

First Ever Visit to a Police Station

I remembered a *thana* inspection of Police Station Kaimganj in Farrukhabad district which I want to mention here. I visited for the first time in company with Mr. Nott-Bower (later Sir John) early in 1924. I was then a probationary Assistant Superintendent of Police and had just come out of the Police Training School (now College) at Moradabad Mr. Nott-Bower wanted me to learn how a *thana* inspection was to be done and had, therefore, invited me to join him as his guest at Kaimganj where he was camping at that time. Till then I had never been in camp and the prospect of living under canvas in the countryside thrilled me.

On the appointed day, I set out for Kaimganj on horseback, the distance to be covered being roughly twenty miles. Those were the days when all Police Officers were required to maintain a horse. So I had one of my own, whom I had named Pratap.

The ride was uneventful except that at one place where the road passed through a ravine and the surrounding countryside wore a dreary and deserted look, I noticed two wild animals, whom I took for Jackals, dogging the heels of my horse. But as they were not very large of size, I paid little attention to them till I discovered that they would not leave me. At this I felt a little alarmed and dug my heels into the aides of my horse, so as to speed him up. Later, when I learnt that they were really wolves and not jackals, I thanked my stars for having escaped them without a mishap. Truly, I have at still a vivid recollection of their ferocious look and their lolling tongues.

During my stay in Farrukhabad I came to know of several cases in which wolves carried of babies up to five years of age at night, while fast asleep. When I reached my destination, if was about 5.00 in the afternoon when Mr. Nott-Bower was on the point of going out for a little partridge shoot in the neighhouring fields. I then joined him, only to watch the fun. In fact, it was indeed marvellous for me to see the way he shot the game birds down with unerring accuracy. By the time we closed in, he had dropped a dozen or so birds and a hare in the bargain.

My bearer had in the meantime found out from Mr. Nott-Bower's bearer that he dined with his dinner dress on. Fortunately, I had my dinner suit with me. So both of us dined in style as was customary in those days.

In the afternoon of the next day Mr. Nott-Bower was scheduled to pay a visit to the Police Station for his annual inspection and I accompanied him on horse back to see how it had to be done. After we had gone some distance, the Station Officer, Mohammad Siddiqu, also on horseback, joined us. From there onwards rows and rows of paper bunting tied to stakes on both sides of the street were to be seen without a break, I came to know that they had been specially put up in honour of S.P.'s visit and so had the triumphal arches with the word, "Welcome" superscribed on them in letters of gold.

At the entrance to the Police Station, there was an even more colourful display of bunting and banners which lent a festive look to the whole place and attracted the townsfolk in their hundreds. As we entered the courtyard of the Police Station, we saw the entire staff in their best uniforms drawn up in two rows for kit inspection. When kit inspection over, Mr. Nott-Bower proceeded to check up the *thana* records, which I noticed had been neatly arranged with paper coverings of all imaginable colours, red, blue, yellow, green and so on, their titles written on the back in Urdu calligraphy of the finest style. This amused me not a little. But, what was still more amusing was the look of the office table and the chairs meant for the two of us. The table had spread on it a rich velvet cloth with heavy gold embroidery, while both of the two chairs, were in the shape of thrones, one had a gold and the other a silver plating on it, the gold one meant for the S.P. and silver one for me. I found it difficult to suppress my laughter at the sight of this entire splendour. But Mr. Nott-Bower seemed to accept all this with supreme indifference, without even once batting an eyelid.

By way of a footnote to the foregoing account of my first ever visit to a Police Station, I wish to point out that to make a *thana* inspection purposeful, it is essential, in the first place, to verify if all forms of crime have been duly registered or not, In other words, that no attempt has been made at suppression or minimisation of crime, a weakness common to most Station Officers. This can be done only through a free and frank discussion with the persons assembled there. This will also help to establish the desired rapport between the inspecting officer and the common man which is an important thing to aim at.

The next thing calling for attention in the degree to which the surveillance of bad characters or suspects has been carried out. It was a common practice in the old days to arrange a parade of the history-sheeters before the inspecting officer. Incidentally, once I discovered that a couple of harmless persons had been brought on history sheets at the request of a bigwig who had a grudge of his own against them.

Thirdly, an endeavour should be made tactfully to ascertain whether or not the conduct of the *thana* staff in their dealing with the village folks has been above board. Needless to say, serious notice should be taken of any high-handedness on their part. The inspection report should be pithy and business like and should not run to inordinate length.

Before I close, the chapter let me recall a meeting of all the District Officers at Unnao in 1938 or so, which was addressed by Pt. Govind Ballabh Pant, the then Chief Minister of U.P. in the following pregnant words:

> "Gentlemen, I am aware that you are accustomed to go round on tour of your district to the accompaniment of much pomp and show. But let me tell you that you will be failing in your duty when you go to a village, unless you care to sit for a while in the village *chaupal* and feel deeply the bad lot of its inhabitants."

* * * *

Chapter 8

An Early Lesson

The ensuing narrative will show how early in my service I learnt that never to take things for granted. I was then posted as A.S.P., Meerut and so was George Parkin, my batchmate. Both of us were Probationary Officers at that time and had to obtain what was then known as a "Practical Certificate" to qualify for a district charge. Our D.I.G. at that time was Mr. Robert Dodd (later Sir). He had been Principal of the Police Training School (now College) when we were there under training and it was he who as our Range D.I.G. was to give us this certificate. At one evening during the course of his visit to Meerut on his inspection tour, he invited both of us to dinner at the local Inspection House and said he would give us a test to see if we were fit for this certificate.

With this object in view, Mr. Dodd got off the mark, by narrating to us the facts of a case of rioting combined with murder in Etah, which has ended in acquittal owing to its bad handling by the local Police in the initial stage of its investigation. But the manner in which he related them was so rambling (at least for me) that I failed to make head or tail of it. This was also partly because I was feeling nervous all the time, not knowing what his question would be like.

At long last when he came to the end of his story, after a lapse of what felt like ages, he looked at me and said, "Now, tell me what you would have done in that circumstances, if you had been S.P. Etah? This question was indeed a difficult one for me to answer, for the simple reason that I had not at all been able to follow the story. In my confusion, therefore, I blurted out, " Sir, the first time I would have done is to go to visit the spot myself to ascertain the facts of the case. "Upon my telling him so, he cried out, "Exactly. This is what Swift failed to do. "In the result, I got through the test with flying colours and so did George Parking who shared with me the honours of the answer I gave on this occasion.

I am sure Mr. Dodd had not the foggiest notion that my answer was only a random one in the predicament in which I found myself. I might add that ever since then, it had been my practice in the course of my service, to make a spot enquiry, whenever I felt the need for it instead of relying on the reports of others.

It is indeed a great pity that most officers are now-a-days inclined to pass on a complaint to their subordinates for enquiry and report as a routine measure, which is wrong. An enquiry can prove useful only if it is a prompt one and is made without giving time to the parties concerned to concoct the evidence.

I have also noticed that now-a-days it takes section 7 Proceedings a long time for their disposal. If they are important ones, then they should be handled by the Supdt. of Police himself and not allowed to gather dust.

Another lesson which I learnt early in my service was to beware of anonymous letters. There hangs a tale by it. One fine morning in the year 1924, while I was officiating as Superintendent of Police, Farrukhabad, I received a letter through the post, stating that there was handsome young girl in particular locality of the town, who had lost her husband and was now carrying on with a young man of her acquaintance living in the same locality as herself. Her elder brother had therefore removed her to an unknown destination with the intention of getting her murdered to save his family from disgrace. The sender of this letter had signed himself as a philanthropist and letter had ended it with a fervent appeal to me to get an enquiry made into this affair, failing which the murder of the girl would be on my head.

I knew there was a catch in this letter and therefore took no notice of it, But it was followed up by another letter the next day and still another the day after, each of the more and more frantic of tone. I was still cogitating what to do in this case when another letter of a like nature was forwarded to me by the District Magistrate, Mr. A. P. Collett, with the remark, "Here is an opportunity for you like a knight-errant of old to rescue poor helpless girl of Sweet Sixteen." I then felt compelled to refer the case to the City *Kotwal* Mr. Ayub for enquiry and report. Soon after he came to me and explained how the author of the anonymous letters received by me, was the very person with whom the girl in question had contracted intimacy and how she was perfectly safe, in proof of which he showed me a letter written by her to her elder brother. There was nothing more to be done now, I filed the papers in this case.

It so happened, that some three or four months later, while I was having discussion with a friend of mine, Ayub whom I thought to be quite an efficient and honest officer, but my friend thought otherwise and came out with a story that took me by surprise. According to him, Mr. Ayub had threatened the elder brother with an open enquiry into the allegation made in the petition received by him unless he (the elder brother) was prepared to cough up a substantial sum as hush money. The latter had then sent for Mr. Dube who happened to be a relation of her and sought his intervention in this case.

This is Mr. Dube's account in his own words of what had passed between him and Mr. Ayub "I called on the *Kotwal* for an amicable settlement of the matter and when I explained my mission to him, his lips parted in a smile and he said, I am not one of those fellows who would beat about the bush. Frankly speaking the occasion demands a greasing of the palm. In reply to this homily of his when I made him an offer of Rs. 50/- he burst into a fit of laughter and said, what, do you expect me to abandon my principle not to accept anything less than hundred rupees in a case like this? To make a long story short, I finally gave him Rs. 75/- in settlement of the case."

Mr. Dube's narrative served like an eye opener for me and I was extremely careful thereafter in dealing with all anonymous petitions, which are sometimes engineered by members of the Police themselves.

* * * *

Chapter 9

A Memorable Bicycle Ride

Among various adventures of my life, I remembered bicycle ride which I had by day from Biswan to Sitapur over a distance of some 24 miles, on the 29th of May 1925, and which proved to be the hottest day of the year with its maximum temperature touching 117 Fahrenheit. It was because of a case of murder at Biswan, which I wanted to look into. I arrived at Biswan by rail from Sitapur on the morning of this date and my work was over by 10.00 o'clock in the morning. I then discovered that my return train for Sitapur was not available till some time in the evening. Some how, I did not feel inclined to spend the whole day at Biswan as a guest of its Station Officer. At my request he sent a man to Kutra to get a car for me, if possible, from the Raja of Kutra. But his car being out of order the latter sent a carriage and pair which I thought was useless for my purpose. I therefore, decided to push off on a bicycle lent to me for the occasion by the Station Officer Biswan, which was perhaps a foolish thing for me to do.

By the time I left Biswan, it was past 11.00 in the morning when the sun was riding high in the sky and the heat was intense. The road in front of me looking like a white ribbon which lost itself in the horizon. The entire countryside provided a deserted look but for the roadside trees here and there. I was then wearing a thick Sola hat. Even so, I began to perspire profusely before I had covered a mile or two. The sweat trickling down my dark eyeglasses obscured my vision and I had to wipe them dry again and again. I was riding with one of my hands in my trouser pocket and the other, wrapped up in a handkerchief, on the handle bar of my bicycle. At one stage, the thought of a cold bath in a tub full of water at the end of my journey, served to fill me with renewed vigour and kept me going till I had covered some 6 miles.

And now, I said to myself, I must make a halt to have some rest. There was a shady mango tree ahead of me by the side of the road. So I dismounted and sat down under it with its trunk as my backrest. I felt like sitting there for a millennium. But my will to get back home without delay seemed to reassert itself and I got up to hit the road once again. At that moment my eyes caught sight of some mangoes hanging from the tree. Starved as I felt, having had nothing from the previous evening to fill my stomach except for a bottle of lemonade at Biswan, I lunged at one of them to pluck it off its stem. I then dug my teeth into it, but, alas I, found it to be too sour for me. So I flung it away with disgust and mounted my bicycle once again with a grim resolution to cover another 6 miles—which would mean for me winning half the battle.

The sun now riding the sky at an angle that was increasingly uncomfortable for me. To my amusement I was reminded of Tennyson's lines, "Half a league, half a league, half a league onwards". For was this also not a case of my charging into the very jaws of what had the alarming features of death, an unrelenting sky with a burning sun looking like an inferno? And what is more, there was not a soul to keep me a company. But here I am losing myself in poetic fervour, for I did encounter some bullock carts with their drivers fast asleep. On such occasions I wondered how it was that they did not mind the sun and the heat in the least, while it was a case of blood, toil and sweat for me?

Near the twelfth mile from Biswan, my eyes caught sight of a Persian wheel which was being worked in a well by the roadside. The temptation of it was too great for me to resist. I made a beeline for it and thereafter drenched my parched body with its refreshing water which fell in cascades from the well. I repeated the process more than once and then felt ready once again to face the elements. By now it was close on 1.00 o'clock in the day and I kept shutting my eyes to escape the unrelenting glare from the light that seemed to envelop both the earth and the sky. At one time my energy seemed to be ebbing away. Still, I went on pedalling doggedly through sheer will power and every mile post I passed, seemed to infuse more vigour into me. In this way I reached Khairabad, where there was a police out post by the side of the road and where I had made up my mind to make my next halt.

I had by now covered 18 miles and my legs did not feel at all steady. I somehow managed to enter its office room and lower myself all in a heap, into the only chair that stood there, a broken one at that. On their part the outpost staff having been taken by surprise by me, disappeared into the recesses of the outpost and I could spy one of them tying his putties frantically round his legs so as to be fit to appear before me. At this moment of my agony, how amused I felt at this spectacle.

It was the Head Constable writer of the outpost who was the first to come up to me from his hide-out. When he saw me in the state I was in, he at once picked up a thickly bound outpost register to fan me frantically with it. For a while no words were exchanged between the two of us but I saw in his eyes that marked concern for me. Then when I was in a fit state to speak out I asked him in a hoarse voice to get me some water to drink. Such was his solicitude for me that he begged me to wait for a little while, as otherwise I might have a heat-stroke. Thereafter, when he had brought me a *Lota* full of water with lots of ice in it and I had fully quenched my thirst with it, I again set out on the last lap of my journey. My feelings at that time were, perhaps, not far different from those of a marathon runner who is nearing the winning post and whose one and only aim is to complete the course ahead of the others. He is not conscious of what is going on around him, nor of the shouts of the people cheering him. Half dazed he struggles on till he is within sight of his goal and calls forth every ounce of the energy still left in him to rush forward in a supreme effort to breast the winning tape ahead of all his competitors.

I vaguely remember that as I entered the outer gate of my house, I started ringing the bell of my bicycle frantically for some one to come and take charge of it. But as there was no response to my signal I pushed my bicycle away from me went staggering like a drunken man into my bed room where I flung myself into my bed, dressed as I was, to be there motionless until I was in a position to take an interest in the things around me. I have no idea as to how long I did lie there like that. The only things I was aware of was the old time pull *punkha* swishing to and fro over my head of which the breeze felt like zephyr to me and gradually helped to bring me to life.

Then when I felt some what refreshed, I got up, though still feeling exhausted, and plunged into a tub full of cold water, to lie there indefinitely. Such was the bliss I was feeling, that I would not have cared to leave it, if it were not for the announcement that my food was on the table. When my meal over, I lay down once again on my bed and slept like a top till late in the evening. Oh! what a horrible day.

* * * *

Chapter 10

Merit by Proxy

For the very novelty of my experience on the occasion I have cause to remember a ride I had, on horseback, while posted at Sultanpur in the year 1926. It was a bright November morning with the sun bathing the entire countryside in its golden light. In front of me lay miles of cultivated fields which with their soft freshly ploughed up surface and their crops still in a nascent state, made a cross-country ride like mine, a sheer joy. The sky had the appearance of an immense dome of intense blue, superimposed upon the ground below. The atmosphere was crystal clear, while drops of dew on the ground sparkled like bits of diamond.

In these idyllic conditions I was going along in a slow canter, comfortably cushioned on the back of my horse, without a care in the world, when my attention was drawn to a man standing stock still under a *babool* tree. There was something so unusual about this posture that I instantly reined in my horse to see what he was doing. On a closer examination of him I noticed that his eyes were fixed intently on a solitary sparrow perched on a branch of the tree, while he was stealthily advancing towards it a telescopic bamboo rod he held in his hand. It had a fork like thing smeared with gum at its extreme end with the help of which he soon managed to drop the bird he was after. The next thing I noticed was that he had a cage by his side, containing scores of birds of the same species.

This looked odd to me, for I had never seen sparrows being either sold in the market or kept as pets. So, I asked his, "What on earth do you propose to do with these birds?" In reply he said to me, there are persons who deem it an act of piety to get birds released. So I shall take them to the village market and charge an anna for the release of each of these birds. I said to myself what a queer way of earning one's livelihood and then cantered away.

My cross-country ride in the month of November 1926, while I was posted at Sultanpur, is memorable for the novelty of my experience on the occasion, another ride I had while posted at Sitapur is equally memorable for my experience of quite a different kind, verging on the traumatic.

What had happened something like this which I wanted to mention that when. I visited to the scene of occurrence in a case of murder in the district which lay at a distance of some 14 miles, from Kamalapur by *Kuchha* road, After some thought, I decided to go as far as Kamalapur by my car and to cover the rest of the distance on horse back. I knew the Raja of Kasmanda, Thakur Suraj Baksh Singh, who lived at Kamalapur and owned many horses. So, I thought of borrowing one of them for my journey for the rest of the way. On my arrival at Kamalapur, I was joined by the Station Officer of Kamalapur, Sub-Inspector, Mohammad Faiyaz, who took me directly to the Raja Saheb. The latter was good enough to take us to his stables where I saw a string of some two dozen horses of the best breed, each of which looked like a prize-winner. The only snag about them was that they did not appear to have been ridden for some time. This was evident from the fact that they looked much too fresh and started stamping and neighing the moment they saw us. I left the choice to the Raja Saheb, who pointed to two of the horses there, Ablakh and Tablak as being the best of the whole lot.

Ultimately, the Raja Saheb ordered Ablakh to be taken out.

But apparently, this was not to the liking of Ablakh and it needed a good deal of effort on the part of his keeper to coax him out of his habitat. Therefore, when he was made over to me, saddled and bridled, I found he would not let me get on to his back. With his neck arched and his eyes looking menacingly at me, he shied away from me whenever I attempted to do so. I patted and patted him, but all in vain. Meanwhile, a crowd had assembled at the spot to see the fun. My prestige as a rider being at stake, I thought of a strategy that might work. I led the horse by his reins for some distance alongside a low field embankment and at a suitable opportunity vaulted on to the saddle, much to the annoyance of my mount, who tried his level best to throw me off his back. To gain this end, he played all the tricks he was capable of. He reared and bucked alternately. But for my part, I stuck to him till he calmed down a little to give me an opportunity to slip in my toes into the stirrups that hung loosely by his side. Having done this, I felt like a topdog. Thereafter, I made him do a few circles at the canter which helped to subdue him still further. I carried out all this operation in full view of the onlookers, whose number had now swelled considerably and who seemed to appreciate my skill at horsemanship fully.

I then dashed off at a gallop towards my destination in what I might call a cloud of glory, leaving Mohammad Faiyaz behind to follow me on his horse. For me it was now like sitting on a cushion, while all the hard work fell to the lot of my mount. After sometime he slackened down to a walk which suited me to the hilt for which I was anxious to hear from Mohammad Faiyaz details of the case which I was out to investigate. But it was sometime before he was able to draw level with me.

It was the month of December with a clear sky and a bright sun over head. After my vigorous ride, I was enjoying myself thoroughly and was listening attentively to all that Mohammad Faiyaz had to tell me about the case in question. We were riding side by side with barely any space separating the two of us. Suddenly, without giving me any kind of notice whatsoever, my mount with the speed of lightening swerved his neck to the right to catch by his teeth Mohammad Faiyaz's hindquarters. For a moment, I felt flabbergasted. Thereafter, I was witness to a tug of war, of a kind I had never seen before, during the course of which Mohammad Faiyaz was letting out a piteous cry that rent the skies, and at the same time digging his heals into the sides of his horse to make him move off. But the odds lay on the side of my mount, who held on to his victim with his teeth like a vice. I went on tugging at his reins as hard as I could and making a free use of my riding stick on his thick neck, but all in vain. Fortunately, for Mohammad Faiyaz, in the course of this uneven struggle, the leather girth of his back snapped which made him fall down on the ground, freed from his captivity.

This seemed to enrage my mount beyond measure. With bloodshot eyes and a vicious look on his face, he made repeated attempts to catch me by my legs. But I was careful enough to withdraw them sufficiently from his reach, whenever he made a lunge for one or the other of them. I also made him go again at a gallop which helped to put him right for the rest of the time he was with me.

On my return to Kamalapur I was glad to make him over to his rightful owner, ironical as it may sound with my thanks. And this was the last I saw a good old Ablakh whose memory still lingers in my mind like a bad dream.

* * * *

Chapter 11

How I Brought off a Coup

At a small village lying in a remote corner of Pilibhit district, there lived two brothers, named Hari Ram and Gopal Ram, who were generally believed to be notorious characters. But since there were no specific charges that could be brought against them, they were free to carry on their depredations on the quiet. In the meantime, reports of road robberies in the neighbourhood of their village, came pouring in and the local police were at their wit's end to trace the offenders. News was also received of a scrious burglary at Gola Gokarannath in a cloth shop within a close range of their residence.

One day it so happened that a man was caught red-handed in a case of burglary not far from where Hari Ram and Gopal Ram lived. He was put up before me for interrogation before being sent to the lock-up. This was done in pursuance of a standing order issued by me to all Station Officers to this effect; for I knew that such a thing might prove profitable. In this case, the moment I enquired of the man put up before me, what he had to say for himself, he came out with a grievance that while the small fry got caught, the big fish managed to give one the slip. This was intriguing and on my further interrogation he told me that the principal culprits in this as well as a number of other cases were Hari Ram and Gopal Ram. He also offered to assist me in recovery of the stolen property from their residence. I then immediately drew up a plan of action and decided to make a raid on their houses at the same night.

The nearest rail head for the village where Hari Ram and Gopal Ram lived happened to be Puranpur. I left for this station in a closed carriage by a night train and arrived there at about midnight along with a handful of my men in plain clothes. Our next step was to try and collect some more men for the intended raid. With this end in view, we then walked over to the nearest village in quest of its headman. We found him fast asleep in the open along with a number of others. What was funny was that when we were trying to wake them up, they took us for dacoits and that some of them felt so scared that they could hardly raise their voice beyond a pitiful croak. But when they realised their mistake, they went all out to raise some 50 to 60 volunteers for us, all of whom followed me in a single file. I was then mounted on a pony raised locally for me by the headman, more was a quaint procession made up of an odd variety of men, armed to the teeth and full of excitement at heart in anticipation of the raid we were going to carry out. No one spoke a word, as if under the influence of a spell. It was a day in the month of August close to full moon. Flocks of clouds sailed across the sky in an uninterrupted procession, throwing dark patches on the ground below, while frogs of all sizes kept up a din that drowned all other sounds. There was water, water all around and it shone like molten silver.

After we had covered three miles or so, we halted in a mango grove close to the village where Hari Ram Gopal Ram lived and divided ourselves into small parties, with a team leader. I chose to head the party detailed for the raid on Hari Ram's house and it was close 4.00 o'clock in the morning when we all set out to throw a cordon round this village and wait till the first signs of dawn before proceeding any further.

As soon as there was sufficient light for one to be able to distinguish faces, a dashing young man of my party vaulted on to the roof of Hari Ram's house with the help of his staff and having done so, like an acrobat, he jumped down into its courtyard below, to open its main door and thus to let us in. We found Hari Ram fast asleep on a *charpoy* in his courtyard. Quick as lightening, another member of my party, who was particularly of a strong built, fell upon him to pin him down. Upon this, Hari Ram woke up and gave him such a violent jerk that he fell sprawling on the ground a few feet away. In the twinkling of an eye Hari Ram whipped out a dagger from under his pillow and brandished it furiously in the face of all of us. But the moment he realised that he was far out-numbered he composed himself and stood still.

We then started a search of Hari Ram's house. To begin with, we went through the contents of all the boxes in his house, but of no purpose. We then turned our attention to a corner room stacked to the ceiling with fodder and here our labour soon crowned with success. Hidden under the straw we found bundles of cloth with their trade marks intact. This was encouraging for us and, as we delved deeper and deeper, more and more things came to light, including a large collection of silver ornaments turned grey with rust, and, most important of all, an unlicensed single barrel breach loading gun.

Meanwhile, Hari Ram, handcuffed, sat with a sullen look on his face, in one corner of the house, while the rest of the members of his family sat huddled up in another, looking the very picture of misery except for a child of three years or so who toddled up to his father to clasp him round the neck. This was indeed a pathetic sight, made still more pathetic, when the latter told the child in a choked voice to go back to his mother and then two large drops of tears coarsed down his cheeks.

The search of Gopal Ram's house proved to be equally fruitful and yielded a mass of stolen property of the nature of cloth goods and silver trinkets. All the articles recovered by us from the search of these two houses were later identified by their owners including the cloth dealer of Gola Gokarannath.

News in our country travels fast. This was borne in on me when on my return journey by rail, there were scores of men to be seen at all the wayside stations waiting to felicitate me on the success of my mission, which fully made up for the toil and trouble I had to undergo over it.

In the sequel, Hari Ram and Gopal Ram were both sentenced to rigorous imprisonment for 7 years, which led to much rejoicing in the locality to which they belonged.

In retrospect, I flatter myself over the little tete-a-tete I had with the man put up before me for interrogation as a matter of routine, but for which, I am sure, these two rogues would have continued to reap a rich harvest indefinitely from their nefarious deeds.

Another coup I managed to bring off successfully, relates to the liquidation of Sadho Singh, a notorious, outlaw who had learnt his trade from one Sanchit. There was a time when the very name of this man struck terror into the hearts of all residents of Gonda, Bahraich and Basti districts. A common practice with him was to let off his gun indiscriminately whenever he raided a village by night and at the same time to strike his chest to announce in a stentorian voice, *"main Sanchit hun"* (I am Sanchit). He became such a menace in the thirties in these districts that a special force had to be detailed for his liquidation.

Sadho Singh was one of Sanchit's gang fellow who followed closely on his heels after his death in these very districts and used like him to strike his chest to say loudly, *"main Sadho Singh hun"* (I am Sadho Singh) before letting off his gun, whenever carried out a raid on a village at night.

The first time I came to know in of this man was when sometime in 1938, Mr. Bolom my counterpart at Gonda informed me that Sadho Singh might extend his operations to my district namely Faizabad. It so happened that soon after that I came to know that Sadho Singh had been seen at a spot lying within my jurisdiction in the riverine area of the Sarju, I then decided to carry-out a raid against him the same night with the help of some two dozen men. The bed of the Sarju where it flows past Faizabad is some three miles in width. The river being in spate, we had to cross it in a country boat of large size moored at Guptar Ghat. This was a thrilling experience by itself, with the moon bathing the entire countryside with its bright light. But when we got to the other bank of the river we found we had drifted for a mile or so downstream from our destination. We then had to trudge upstream through a difficult terrain full of wild growth and infested with snakes, worse still when we got to our destination, we found much to our disappointment, that Sadho Singh was nowhere to be seen. It was then about 1 o'clock in the night and when wc got back home, thoroughly tired and crestfallen after our fruitless raid, it was almost dawn.

As luck would love it, within a fortnight or so of this wild goose chase of ours, information was received by me one night, of a case of that murder by gunshot of a diabolical kind within close range of Faizabad proper, in which the victims were one of the Raja of Ayodhya's *Ziledar* and the *Ziledar*'s peon. From the very face of this case, it appeared to be the handiwork of a hired assassin, our suspicion in this connection fell on Sadho Singh and one Jang Bahadur Singh, a sworn enemy of the Raja of Ayodhya. We then brought some pressure on Jang Bahadur Singh as a result of which he offered to give up Sadho Singh, on condition we gave him a man of our choice who would act as a decoy.

Later a drama followed in which Head Constable Sher Bahadur Singh of Kotwali Faizabad played a major role. One night, Jang Bahadur Singh took him in the guise of a fugitive from the yaw, to thicket which served as a hide-out for Sadho Singh to introduce him to the latter. Sadho Singh came out of the thicket, with a gun in hand. The moment he saw Sher Bahadur Singh, he asked who this man was and was satisfied about his identity only after a thorough cross-examination of him, for which he had already been tutored by us.

The understanding between me and Sher Bahadur Singh was that on an appointed day, Sher Bahadur Singh would ply Sadho Singh with some drinks after his midday meal and thereafter when the latter was sound asleep, he (Sher Bahadur Singh) would walk over to a spot where I would be waiting for him along with my men disguised as a wedding party. But this plan misfired in that Sadho Singh refused to do the bidding of Sher Bahadur Singh and made himself scare after his midday meal. As a result of this, when Sher Bahadur Singh turned up in a nervous state where we were waiting for him and told us of the situation that had arisen, I had to do some quick thinking I knew that to make a raid, on Sadho Singh's hide-out, would be like looking for a needle in a hay stack. I then had a brain wave and asked Sher Bahadur Singh to discuss to Sadho Singh that the Police were after the two of them and that the best thing for them to do would be to run away to Bombay the same night. For our part we planted ourselves after dusk around a culvert on the road close-by, which led to the railway station at Faizabad. This trick worked and the moment the *tonga* carrying Sadho Singh and Sher Bahadur Singh reached this culvert, I held it up. Quick as lightening Sadho Singh jumped off the *tonga* to fire his gun in the direction of some of my men who were hiding there. But his shot went wide, while the one fired simultaneously by S.I. Jamuna Prasad hit him in the chest, resulting in his death on the spot.

Sadho Singh, I noticed, had a vicious countenance. He was dark skinned and pock pitted with protruding teeth. He was wearing a belt of cartridges across his shoulder and had a 12 bore gun and a five cell torch by his side. As for his identity, we were left in no doubt, as he had his name tattooed on his right forearm.

By way of a sequel to this case, Sher Bahadur Singh was awarded the King's Police Medal for gallantry, while S.I. Jamuna Prasad and I were awarded the Indian Police Medal also for gallantry. The liquidation of Sadho Singh at a time when he had made a menace of himself was an achievement which, I am glad to say, was of no small order.

* * * *

Chapter 12

A Misadventure by Night

My story relates to an incident that took place when I was posted as Superintendent of Police at Pilibhit in 1926. During this period, I was out one night in the month of August on night patrol in the town along with the Station Officer, Kotwali Sub-Inspector Imtiaz Ahmad. Both of us were on horse back and as we were passing through a narrow lane, he pointed out to me a hole dug on the previous night into a wall by the side of this lane, I then reined in my horse to look at it closely. It had been raining till a late hour that night with the result that all the water courses of the town were running full to overflowing. All of a sudden, I felt the hind legs of my horse sinking and before I knew what the matter was both I and my horse found ourselves floundering in water that came up to my neck. What had actually happened was that we had fallen into a deep municipal drain. My horse then struggled furiously to clamber out and in the process his hind Legs went on hitting the rear wall of this drain with the force of a sledge hammer. Instinctively, I sought the cover of his belly to save my head from being reduced to pulp. After a brief struggle my horse managed to climb out, leaving me behind to fend for myself. Thereafter I, too, managed somehow to retrieve myself from what might have proved to be my watery grave. All this while, Imtiaz Ahmad looked on aghast and speechless and it was only after I had come out, that he was able to open his mouth and repeatedly say, "*Ghazab ho gaya, Ghazab ho gaya*". I do not blame him for it, because in the circumstances of the case, it was but natural for him to feel dazed.

My anxiety now was to get back home as soon as possible for I was stinking badly from the ducking I had. Fortunately for me, my horse in the meantime stood stock-still by the side of this drain, as if waiting for me to mount. I then sprang on his back and made him go at a fast trot. To my great good luck, the rain came down in cascades about this time which helped to lessen the foul odour I was exuding for all the pores of my body. On my return home, the first thing I did, was to plunge into a tub full of water and give myself a through rub with a cake of carbolic dog soap, before turning in for the night. It was then close on 2.00 o'clock by my watch.

Quite unknown to me, I believe this incident earned for me some publicity locally as I discovered some twenty years later when I was holding the office on I.G. Police, U.P. This I did at a party meeting held by the Chief Minister Pt. Govind Ballabh Pant one evening in the Council House at Lucknow, at which I was present by special invitation. The idea behind this meeting was to apprise me informally of the grievances his party men had against the Police generally. As was to be expected they stood up, one after another, to reel them off to me. All I could say in reply was that the police were still in the making and that they should give me some time to enable to do my bit. In any case, it was becoming increasingly difficult for me to meet their charges, when an M.L.A. from Deoria, Thakur Ram Dhari Singh, got up to say how late one night as he was going home on foot from the Railway Station, he came across the local S.P. Pt. Balmukund Sharma out on patrol, at the sacrifice of his night's rest. I was flattering myself over his unsolicited tribute to the Police, when another M.L.A., this time from Pilibhit, my old district, got up to say something like this. "When I was a boy I used to hear that our local S.P. who happened to be our Chief of Police to-day, used to go round the town at night on patrol, in disguise, I wanted to say is, why can't the same thing to be done to day by the Superintendents of Police." The compliment he thus paid to me, not only sounded like heavenly music, but also evoked much good will for me, which helped me in my task to tone up the Force under my command, suitably.

* * * *

Chapter 13

Story of a Love Potion

Long time ago, I had a Reserve Inspector named Henderson under me at Pilibhit. He was a Londoner, who had joined the U.P. Police as a sergeant after his release from the Army around 1920. One afternoon when I passed his house on my way to home, I noticed a non-descript crowd assembled there. This was unusual and what was still more unusual was the presence among the crowd of two mullahs dressed in their all white loose garments. So I discreetly asked my orderly Ahmad Hussain, if he know what was going on. With a flicker of a smile playing on his lips he said to me, "Doesn't *Hazoor* know that the Line Sahib is getting married to a Muslim woman? The *Mullahs* have come to perform the *Nikah*." This was news to me, for Henderson had a wife and five children who, I knew, had gone to Agra for a change.

The situation was one calling for quick action on my part. I sent for Henderson to my house and enquired of him if what I had heard about his prospective marriage was true. With his eyes downcast, face averted, he murmured, "Yes, Sir," I then reminded him that he would be liable to a charge of bigamy if he failed to change his mind. Upon this he said, "But then, Sir, how can that be when I am going to embrace Islam?" This was another piece of news to me. I said, "What is wrong with your own religion that you have decided to quit it?" To this, he said in reply, "Sir, I have thought deeply over this question and have come to the conclusion that as compared to Christianity there is much to commend Islam."

I then felt that it would be futile to argue the case with the man any more. So I left him sitting in my office room and sent for the Subedar, a man next in command to the Reserve Inspector, who appeared to be mainly responsible for what had come to pass. I gave him a scolding and ordered him to clear out the rabble assembled in Henderson's house. I also ordered the city *Kotwal* over the phone to make sure that the woman in the case left the station by the next available train.

Having taken all due precautions against the impending catastrophe, I took Henderson out with me for a long walk and I must say to his credit that he uttered not a word in protest. In the evening I let him go home and ruminate in solitude over the happenings of the day.

Some weeks later when Henderson's wife and children had rejoined him, I asked him casually how it was that he had decided to enter into a second marriage. To this, he said in reply, "Sir, I was introduced to the woman in question by the Subedar and used to pay her frequent visits. She once gave me a *pan* to eat which I suspect contained a love potion, potent enough to turn my head."

All is well that ends well. So there was nothing more for me to do in the case.

* * * *

Chapter 14

A Thing of Beauty is a Joy Forever

In the month of March, 1927 on one fine morning at about 11 or so, I was returning on horseback to my headquarters at Pilibhit from Bisalpur, a Sub-Divisional town some twenty-four miles away. I was doing this journey in slow canter and after I had covered approximately half of the distance, I noticed that my mount was sweating profusely. Intending therefore, to give him a breather, I halted him opposite a mango grove on the roadside and dismounted. By the side of this grove there was a dry ditch which suited me as a resting place. Holding the reins of my horse in one hand, I stepped into it and, thereafter, stood in a reclining position with my back on its side wall. I was wearing a pair of brown leather riding boots, a pair of Khaki breeches, a Khaki coat and a thick sola pig sticking hat, apart from a pair of dark glasses.

There were no pedestrians on the road, and the grove was empty except for a couple of village urchins who were tending their goats whom I failed to notice. But it so happened that they noticed me.

I also suspect that in my attire and with my face gone red with exhaustion, I must have struck them as strange creature, unlike any they had ever seen before. In order therefore, to satisfy their curiosity about me, slowly and hesitatingly they advanced step by step in my direction before coming to a halt some ten paces away from me. It was then that I noticed them for the first time. Both of them were stark naked and while one of them looked like five or six years of age, the other was slightly older. I also noticed that the latter held an empty *Chilam* in his hand which he had most likely picked up in the grove. After a time when they had taken the measure of me fully and assured themselves that they had no cause for fear from me, apparently they felt some pity for me in my state of exhaustion. The elder one of the two taking courage in both hands stepped forward to come closer to me and holding up the *Chilam* chanted in a sweet piping voice, *"Piyabo?"* meaning "will you have a smoke?" quite unmindful in his innocence of the fact that it had neither any tobacco nor any cinders in it. I felt so moved by this kind gesture of his, that I felt sorry to have to say, "No, thank you."

The incident which I have thus related happened nearly seventy years ago. Still, to me it is as fresh as ever. Was it not Keats who wrote, "A thing of beauty is a joy forever?"

* * * *

Chapter 15

The Vanishing Trick

In the year 1927, the Government of India decided to transfer to the Andamans such criminal tribesmen, who were willing to settle there. Arising from this decision, I was required in the month of January of the following year, to escort by rail as far as Howrah, a large party of them, men, women and children, from the settlements at Najibabad, Moradabad and Bareilly.

I had arranged for a bogey being attached to the Dehra Express at Najibabad for accommodation of the party and all went well till we came to Bareilly. Here I took over the charge of a number of families, mostly *Bhatus*. By then, it was past mid-night. The time at my disposal being limited, it was a job getting them seated, the more so, because they carried with them every conceivable form of household article, such as *charpoys*, mill-stones, spinning wheels, pots and pans of various sizes, which they felt they might need in their new home. All the same, I somehow managed to pack them all in along with their chattels by the time the train was to leave and having done so, walked over to my compartment in another carriage. After a while, when the train was on the move, I heard a frantic cry from a woman of my party, who had boarded the train at Bareilly. She was repeatedly shouting "Mir-Chania, Mir-Chania, Mir-Chania," like one demented and the sound of her voice was echoed back from every single building we passed as the train gathered speed, till it was lost in the void, I wondered what the matter was. But there was nothing I could do, till our next halt.

Mir-Chania, I discovered, was a grown-up unmarried daughter of the woman who had been calling out her name. She did not want to accompany her parents to the Andamans, having lost her heart to a young man who was not going there. She therefore cleverly managed to give them the slip in the confusion that prevailed at the time of departure of our train and this explained the frantic cries of her mother.

The next day, when we reached Varanasi at about noon, I noticed a great rush of passengers there. The train being full to capacity, they moved about helplessly from one carriage to another. Noticing that the carriage reserved for my party was not quite so full as others, they sought my permission to squeeze themselves into it. Reluctantly, I granted their request, little realising what was to follow.

Once these passengers had got in, they deposited their luggage wherever it suited them to do so. But soon they found some of their stuff missing. This led to heated arguments between them and others. The moment the train came to a halt, the aggrieved persons surrounded me to seek my intervention. I heard one Bengali girl say to her brother, "Dada, I had my handbag by my side and I saw that woman there slip it under her skirt."

From the account I had from these people, it looked as if their missing articles had been spirited away. I pleaded with the men and women in my charge to surrender them, but in vain. Later when we reached Howrah, I had arranged a search parade to be carried out. But again, we failed to succeed. And how could it be otherwise, considering that I was conducting some of the worst criminals of this country, who had raised their profession to a fine art?

* * * *

Chapter 16

A Case of Mass Hysteria

There is a village named Machi, about sixty-four miles to the south-east of Mirzapur. A number of mud huts, some thatched, others tiled, all huddled together on a patch of level ground, a sluggish stream with a rocky bed for the most part dry-girdling it on its three sides, a scrub jungle interspersed with sal saplings, making a ring in the form of an outer circle round it and, some low hillocks for a background, made up this insignificant little village, where life generally would appear to have come to a sudden halt. Who could ever imagine that this veritable sleepy hollow of a place at the back of beyond, would one day provide the scene for one of the most tragic events on record in this district and thus would hit the headlines.

In Machi people of many communities, lived them the most numerous of them being Kharwars, a backward but peaceful tribe, mostly cultivators by profession. Among others there were two Muslim families, one headed by Mohammad Baksh and the other by Mohammad Hussain, apart from a Brahmin family headed by two brothers named Tapeshwari and Bindeshwari. All these people lived as one family and, at least outwardly on terms of perfect amity and friendship born out of generation of mutual dealings; so much so, that they addressed, one another as *Chacha, Mama, Kaka,* etc. But despite this surface cordiality, there existed an undercurrent of animosity between Mohammad Baksh on the one hand and Tapeshwari and Bindeshwari on the other, arising from a litigation of some sort between the parties. Such in fact, was the background against which the ensuing episode has to be viewed.

One day it so happened that Mohammad Baksh, while out hunting in the jungle around his village with his Muzzle-loader, came across the remnants of what he thought to be a deer. Most of it had been devoured by some wild animal or animals and there was only a leg left over. It being strictly forbidden for all true Muslim to partake on any game not slaughtered in the orthodox fashion, Mohammad Baksh, in all innocence, had it sent to his Kharwar ploughman. On his part the latter on seeing it, suspected it to be the leg of his bull-calf which had been missing for some time. He then sought the advice of Tapeshwari and Bindeshwari, who found in this incident an excellent opportunity to harass their arch-enemy and declared that Mohammad Baksh had slaughtered the missing bull calf and made a present of its leg to him in order to defile his caste.

Therefore, on the advice of the two brothers, a secret meeting of the local Kharwars was held at which it was decided to invite all the members of this community residing in and around Machi, to a tribal *panchayat* at this village. Accordingly, a brief note was scribbled by Tapeshwari, charging the recipient of it to come to Machi positively on the following Friday and at the same time on pain of dire calamity, to write four such messages for despatch to his friends and relations.

In fairness to Tepeshwari and Bindeshwari, it must be acknowledged that prior to this action of theirs they had a petition sent to the Tahsildar-Magistrate at Robertsganj, seeking redress for the outrage committed in this case and that it was only when no notice was taken of this petition that a decision was taken in favour of calling a tribal *panchayat*.

In consequence of a chain message on these lines, received by them, hundreds of Kharwars from far and near, armed with their crude weapons, assembled at Machi on the Thursday afternoon, in anticipation of the *panchayat* fixed for the following morning. They then dispersed themselves in small group all along the stream flowing past this village to make a halt for the night. According to eyewitnesses when they started cooking their meal, they looked like an invading army bivouacking for the night. But the only person somewhat frightened over the arrival of these men, was Mohammad Hussain, the doyen of the village, who approached Tapeshwari and Bindeshwari to seek their advice. For their part, they gave him an assurance that so long as they lived, they would not allow a hair on his person to be touched. It was thus that Mohammad Hussain abandoned the idea of quitting the village for safety.

With nightfall silence reigned all over the village and everybody, friend and foe alike, surrendered himself to sleep. When the day broke, preparations were made for a *panchayat* being held in front of the local primary school building. Sheets of cloth were spread on the ground and all the elders of the village were invited to participate in it. Mohammad Baksh some how sensed danger and thought it prudent to stay away from it. Emissary after emissary was sent to secure his attendance, but in vain. As time were on, feelings ran more and more high till some one gave a call to set fire to Mohammad Baksh's house, soon bedlam was let loose and the gathering, almost to a man, in the name of Mahatma Gandhi led an assault on it, to the accompaniment of drums and set it ablaze with the help of lighted faggots.

Due to Friday a number of Mohammad Baksh's friends and relations had assembled in his house to participate in the *Juma* prayers that were to be held in a local mosque. Being unable to stand the heat from the raging fire any longer, as they emerged from this house one after another, the crowd outside it, which had by now turned into a shrieking, gesticulating and frenzied mob, chased them with their *lathis* and other crude weapons and battered them to death like rats. In this way as many as six men were killed.

At about this time, an itinerant pedlar, a Muslim, who seated on a pony used to visit this village occasionally with his merchandise, turned up quite unaware of the happenings. He too met with a similar fate at the hands of the rioters and so did Mohammad Hussain who had shut himself up in his house along with his wife and his children and was made to pay the penalty for his obstinacy, in the eyes of his adversaries.

The only thing that can be said in favour of the rioters is that they did not harm any of the women and children of either Mohammad Baksh or Mohammad Hussain's family, on the ground that such were Mahatma Gandhi's instructions. On the other hand, they made them sit at one spot as helpless spectators of the orgy of bloodshed that was being enacted before their eyes.

Mohammad Baksh all this time remained hidden in the ruins of an adjoining house and thus escaped detection. But such was the state of his mind that he did not venture out of his hide-out till long after the rioters had dispersed and night had set in. Almost instinctively, he first went to his maternal uncle Mohammad Ibrahim's place at village Raiya to acquaint him with the happenings as an eyewitness. Thereafter, he moved on to Police Station Pannuganj to lodge a report.

When Muhammad Baksh tired and worn-out arrived at the Police Station the next morning, he was hardly in a position to give a coherent account of the whole affair. The Head Constable writer at the Police Station, in the absence of the station officer, prepared a First Information Report of the case and had a cryptic message sent by canal wire to the Headquarters asking for help. It was received by the Reserve Inspector Mohammad Siddiq, in my absence and he promptly arranged to send an armed guard of one and four to the scene of occurrence and at the same time passed on the message to my residence.

I had gone to Lucknow at that time to attend a farewell dinner held there in honour of the Inspector General of Police, Sir Robert Dodd, on the eve of his retirement from service and returned home at about 11 in the night. I thought it would be useless for me at that late hour to leave for Machi and, therefore, decided to go there early next morning. Meanwhile, I arranged to send another armed guard of one and eight under Inspector Sheo Nath Singh, to the spot. One thing that troubled me was that the message sent by the Head Constable writer at Pannuganj was so vague that I was not quite clear in my mind as to what to make of it.

To revert to my account of the happenings at Machi, the first flush of their excitement being over, the rioters began to reflect upon the consequences of their mad act and finally decided to do away with the dead bodies. With this end in view they collected men of the depressed classes and made them carry the corpses suspended from sticks, for a distance of over a mile into the interior of the forest close by, two men acting as bearers of each corpse.

There being in all eight bodies to be disposed of, the procession was a long one as it wended on its way to its destination. It was escorted by a few of the stalwarts from among the rioters, who being in no hurry, fell well behind the corpse-bearers. This proved to be a blessing in disguise for one of the victims who had been taken for dead but was actually alive. Realising that this only chance of escape lay in rousing the sympathy of his two bearers, he appealed to them in a whisper to save him. Upon this, they quietly stepped aside—unnoticed by others and when safe from observation, they let him go. Thus there were now only seven bodies left to be disposed of. These were put in a heap inside a ditch and then cremated with the help of some dry wood cut from the forest.

This part of the episode being over, the attention of the ring leaders once again turned to Mohammad Baksh, who was believed to have sought asylum in Raiya at the house of his maternal uncle, Mohammad Ibrahim. The latter was another well-to-do man, who had for some reasons become an eyesore to the residents of village Raipur of which Raiya was a hamlet. Tapeshwari and Bindeshwari soon joined hands with these men and in consequence both men from Machi and Raipur made a concerted attack the next day on the house of Mohammad Ibrahim at Raiya. It stood all by itself, in a corn field and Mohammad Ibrahim resided in it along with his large family inclusive of his sons, his brothers and a host of women folk and children.

The inmates of this house on seeing the mob, advancing towards it, hastily armed themselves with whatever weapons came handy and stood ready for the fray. Then followed a day-long battle between the two parties, unevenly matched as they were, which dragged on for hours. During the episode, Mohammad Ibrahim being fairly advanced in years, remained in the background, while his sturdy brothers and sons took up position at various vantage points and brandished their swords against all those who came within close range of them. A rioter then thought of an ingenious plan to outwit his opponents. He bored a hole into the wall at the back of the house to let in his Muzzle-loading gun. But since his quarry took good care to move away from the line of it, his strategy failed. But another rioter managed to get on to the roof of the house and knock down one of Mohammad Ibrahim's brothers by an open fire.

In another part of the house, one of the inmates having completely lost his nerves, made a bid for escape by rushing out of it, only to be knocked down by his pursers.

By the afternoon the house had been reduced to a shambles and its few remaining survivors had lost all hope of saving their lives. They had even embraced one another to say good bye before meeting their end, when the police party under Inspector Sheo Nath Singh was sighted at a distance. Such was the magic effect of it that the rioters then and there began to melt away, leaving only the stragglers among them to be rounded-up.

Inspector Sheo Nath Singh found Mohammad Ibrahim and the rump of his party in a state of complete nervous prostration. But when the first shock of their surprise was over, they wept for sheer joy and acclaimed the Police as their deliverers. In all, some seventy men were rounded up by Inspector Sheo Nath Singh and marched to the Police Station at Pannuganj. This had to be done very tactfully as he had no handcuffs with him and also because they far outnumbered the escorting party.

Let me now switch over to an account of my personal role in the drama. The rioting at Machi took place on a Friday morning in the month of March 1930, when I was on my way back from Lucknow. It was early in the morning of the next day when I set out by my car for Police Station Pannuganj, where I arrived at 9.00 o'clock or so. I found Mohammad Baksh sitting there, but he was in such a state of mind, that I was unable to get from him a coherent account of the happenings at Machi the previous day. I then decided to go there, but this time I had to foot it all the way, over a distance to some 14 miles through a countryside largely made up of scrub jungle. My journey was uneventful except for some *Neelgais* and deer's that I saw passing by. Later on when I arrived at Machi at about 3.00 in the afternoon, I found, much to my surprise, not a soul stirring there. Not only that, I noticed quantities of ashes heaped here and there and, worse still, Mohammad Baksh's entire house burnt down to the ground. The village, in short wore a look that had something uncanny about it.

While I was thus engaged in my inspection of this village, I saw a Chaukidar coming in my direction in sheer haste. He told me that he had been sent by Inspector Sheo Nath Singh from village Raiya where a great killing had been going on since morning. Tired, as I felt after my trek to Machi from Pannuganj, it was no welcome news to me. However, I decided to set out at once for Raiya in company with the Chaukidar who had come to fetch me.

Our track again lay through scrub jungle intersected at places by minor streams with rocky beds, over a distance of approximate three miles, when we came within sight of Raiya, I noticed it lay at some distance below us, the ground suddenly dropping a couple of hundred feet or so, to merge into a plain, which being covered with ripening corn as the eye could see, looked golden in the setting sun.

Like Machi, at Raiya also no life was to be seen. Wisps of smoke, here and there spiralling their way to the sky boded ill. My guide took me straight to Mohammad Ibrahim's house where I was faced with a pathetic sight of some dead and some dying. The whole place was littered with brickbats and broken pieces of tiles, used against the victims of what appeared to be instance of mob violence of an unprecedented kind.

Since it was getting late in the evening, I decided to proceed to the Police Station at Pannuganj, without loss of time, taking along with me the six corpses that were found lying at Raiya. Luckily for me, I managed to raise some depressed class men locally to carry them. By now it was almost nightfall and so having collected a couple of lanterns to light our way, I set out at the head of a procession of a most dismal kind. The track this time lay mostly through a forest and, worse still, we had to ford a wide stream which lay in our way. To cut a long story short, it was around 11.00 in the night when we reached Pannuganj.

On my arrival at the police station, I first got busy sending telegrams to various quarters asking for assistance in the shape of armed guards, mounted police and supply of various kinds, including handcuffs and my own clothes. I then went around to see how the seventy and odd men arrested by Inspector Sheo Nath Singh were being guarded. I saw them huddled up in the none too spacious courtyard of the police station, some dozing others fully awake, but one marked thing about them was that one and all, they seemed to be supremely indifferent to the goings all around them. Indeed, they presented a strange spectacle with the light from four incandescent lamps, striking upon them and an equal number of sentries with their fire arms at the ready, mounting guard over them.

Thereafter, I helped myself to some simple food cooked for me by my fellow policemen assembled there. This I needed badly because I had nothing to eat since early that morning. It then occurred to me for the first time that I had meantime covered on foot about thirty miles across country. I then got busy interrogating the men under custody to ascertain the facts of the case which were till then a mystery to me. This went on for almost day break, when I left for Machi once again on foot.

As the culprits came up before me, one after another, the only thing which tried to impress upon me was that they were guiltless in that they had acted merely in the vindication of their faith. I camped for about a week, at Machi, during the course of which several contingents of the police including a troop of sowars (Mounted Police) from Varanasi joined thus transforming the one time sleepy hollow of a village into a veritable hive of activity. During my stay there, I was engaged in a day time recording the statements of witnesses to the case and in the night ferreting out the culprits involved in it, most of whom remained in hiding during the day in the neighbouring forest. The strategy employed by me to collar them was to leave Machi quietly at the dead of night to throw a cordon round one or other of the villages involved, preliminary to carrying out a house to house search at dawn. It was quite an experience for me keeping a vigil by night and watching the slow march of the stars till they faded away one by one. As a result of these nocturnal raids, we were rewarded each time by a catch of weapons seized and above all our joy knew no bounds one morning, when we were able to lay our hands on Tapeshwari and Bindeshwari, the two arch offenders in this case.

The case investigated by me summed up with a result that the rioters charged with murder and arson, a charge sheet was filed in court against some 200 accused of whom, after a protracted trial in the court of the Sessions Judge at Varanasi lasting for several months, 19 were sentenced to death including Tapeshwari and Bindeshwari, while some 50 others sentenced to various terms of imprisonment including transportation for life, thus bringing to a close my endeavour to book the offenders of a most extra-ordinary case within my knowledge of mob fury, arising from merely a confusion over the identity of a leg of meat. I have also cause to remember this day for the endurance test it provided me during the course of my investigation of it.

* * * *

Chapter 17

An Angry Tiger

In a small township of Mirzapur district which is in a close range of Robertsganj, there lies a fairly thick belt of forest that used to be good for *shikar*. I was then new to the district and had no particular interest in big game shooting. All the same, the moment of my winter tour in 1928, the officer in charge of the local police station, Sub-Inspector Baldeo Singh, brought me news that there had been a "kill" in the forest nearby and requested me to get ready for the hunt that he had arranged for me.

It had been a tradition with my predecessors in office to combine business with pleasure while out on tour. Therefore, in making arrangements for a tiger shoot by me in anticipation of my visit, Sub-Inspector Baldeo Singh had done nothing unusual.

The technique for the hunt is quite simple. Inside the jungle there are certain tracks that a tiger generally follows on his night rounds in quest of his prey. At various points of these tracks, young he-buffaloes are tied to serve as bait. In case a tiger comes along and feeds on one of these animals by night, he then generally carries off the carcass or what is left of it, to a safe place to have a second helping by day. So, if a drive or what is commonly known as *hakwa* is intended against the beast, the most appropriate time for it is midday, when the tiger is likely to be resting, if not fast asleep.

The actual drill for this drive is something like this. If you are the person wishing to "bag" the tiger then you sit on a *machan* rigged up at a strategic point that the tiger is most likely to pass in his attempt to get away. The "stops" spread out in fan shape in the direction of the tiger, forming two sides of a triangle with you at its apex, while the beaters are ranged in a line facing you to make a stop on the third side of the triangle.

The duty of the "stops" is to see to it that the tiger does not break away from the triangle. They are seated on trees, usually with small axes in their hands and as soon as they notice any indication on the part of the tiger to do so they gently tap the trees on which they are seated, thus producing a sound that makes the tiger turn inwards.

When all is set, the beaters move forward at a given signal from the leader of their party, making as much noise as possible with the aid of an odd variety of instruments, they carry for the purpose such as drums, gongs, cymbals, flutes, trumpets and even *cannisters* and tin pots. The din thus caused is deafening and it compels the tiger to get up and move away from the beaters towards the *machan,* provided, of course, the "stops" carry out their part of the job effectively. Then when the tiger comes within his view, the hunter takes aim and fires. It happens, however, that luck plays a great part in these shoots, and notwithstanding the most careful arrangements, the tiger may get away.

A great excitement caused in my camp when Sub-Inspector Baldeo Singh brought news of the "Kill". Word was immediately sent to the nearest villages for beaters, who soon turned up in large numbers. They were made to sit in rows for the distribution of small paper tokens which they were required to exchange at the end of the shoot for two *annas* each (corresponding to 12 *paise*). Today this sum may seem to be ridiculously small as wages for a day's work.

But in those days, it was alluring enough to attract a host of beaters, who came as much for the sake of the money as for the fun of the game.

In this context an old man, reminded me a rather miserable specimen of humanity, who sat among the beaters with a wooden flute in hand. Except for a slip of cloth around his loins, he was naked from head to foot, a sight that made me feel sorry for him. I asked him in a friendly manner, "Old man, what do you think you are going to do with that flute of yours?" By way of his reply he made a vigorous motion flutes with his fingers, to point towards the inside of his flute and declared with supreme assurance, "*Sasura ehi me be to niksi*" (meaning—why? the blighter is going to issue forth from the bowels of this very flute).

Distribution of the paper tokens over, all the assembled men were formed into parties, each in the charge of a leader, and after detailed instructions as to what each party was to do, they were told to march off. I was given in charge of a man who took me quietly to a *machan* set up on the top of a tree. For the benefit of those who have not seen one, I might explain that it is usually made of sticks fastened to the fork of a tree, and is so camouflaged that it is not easily discernible. It has a loophole in front which serves both as peephole and as an opening for the barrel of one's gun or rifle to pass through.

After I had been comfortably seated on my *machan* it was the turn of the "stops" to take up their seats on tree tops in both flanks Mcanwhilc, thc bcatcrs had sprcad out in a linc facing mc at some distance.

The preliminaries being over, it was now time for the beat to commence. At the word "go" from the leader of the party, the beaters swung into action. Now was the time for me to sit up, and with my eyes and ears straining to look out for the beast movement or for the slightest noise, such as might give me warning of the approach of my quarry.

As time passed and as the beaters advanced slowly but surely, the tension within me kept mounting till it became almost unbearable.

Suddenly I heard a footfall, a very soft one. With my ears pricked up I looked in the direction from which it had come. But except for the loud pounding of my heart, I could hear nothing.

After a brief spell, my ears picked up the same muffled footfall. This time there could be no mistake. Thump, thump, it went, till I noticed an object moving forward through the brushwood in front of me. It had a dark shaggy coat and every now and then it stood up on its hind legs to make sure that the coast was clear. Soon enough, my doubts were resolved. The mysterious intruder was a bear trying to escape from its pursuers. Purposely I desisted from firing at him, for I knew that if I fired at him, the tiger would break away, so I let the bear pass.

After a brief interval, again, it was the same muffled sound of approaching feet, the some cautious movement culminating in the appearance of a second bear again, I let this one, too, go, for the sake of the tiger I was after.

The beaters had by now advanced within a hundred yards or so of the spot where I was seated and I could even see one or the other of them emerging from a thicket only to disappear again from view. Surely, I said to myself, there could not be any tiger in the area of the beat or he would have put in an appearance by now?

And while I was cogitating like this, what should I hear again, but the same muffled sound of a bear's footfall, But this time I was not going to let him pass. So, as soon as he broke cover, bang went my rifle and the animal dropped dead a few yards away from me. I then stood up in my *machan* to make it known that the bearers might close in. The shot fired, my rifle was no longer ready. It hung loosely by my side.

Suddenly, without any reason I turned my eyes towards a *Semal* (silk cotton) tree standing some yards in front and saw a tiger, large as life, emerge from his cover for quite some time. I looked at him, disbelief in my eyes. He looked at me with a menacing gaze as if to say commandingly, "How dare you?" Thereafter, with his head raised upwards towards me, he delivered himself of two blood-curdling roars before bouncing forward like a ball of fire. Automatically, I lifted my rifle and fired at him—once, twice and then in the heat of the moment lost my balance. I was about to fall off my *machan*, but somehow managed to hold on to it. Meanwhile the tiger disappeared into the bushes in my rear, like a streak of lightening.

It has taken me much longer to relate this incident than the time that was taken in the enactment of it. At any cost it was then known to everybody that I had twice fired at the tiger, whether I had hit him or not. To make sure I carefully went over the ground on which he had been standing when I first fired at him. Initially I could see no signs of any damage done to the beast. But, after a minute examination of the ground revealed faint trace of blood and, what was more important, small piece of bone smeared in blood.

This was proof enough that the tiger had been hit. An examination of the course he had followed in his wild flight revealed more traces of blood and these became increasingly marked as I advanced in the direction in which he had fled. The occasion demanded a council of war. We all knew it would be folly to proceed any further, for there might be few things more dangerous than a wounded tiger. So, it was unanimously decided that we should come the next day and carry out combing operation with the help of a herd of buffaloes.

A wounded tiger if he has not been so incapacitated as to be unable to move, is sure to retaliate. As such, the best thing to do is to go after him the next day with a herd of buffaloes. The buffaloes as soon as they spot him, start snorting and with their horns lowered and menacingly pointed at him form a solid phalanx in the shape of an arc facing him. The rest is simple. The hunter is then provided with an opportunity to fire at him behind cover as it were, and thus give him the quietus.

To take up where I had left off. Some of my companions, whose number had now swelled considerably and who had in the meantime spotted more blood further up, invited me to come up and have a look. The invitation was one I could not resist and on my walking up to the spot, I was told of the existence of many more traces of blood further up. In this way, little by little and without any conscious exercise of the will, I must have advanced some fifty yards or so in the direction in which the tiger had fled. Judging from the speed that had marked his mad rush past my *machan*, I felt sure he had gone a considerable distance before coming to a halt, so that there was no cause for worry.

All of a sudden, one of my companions shook me by the shoulder to say "there he is". At first I failed to grasp the meaning of what he was saying It was soon, however clear.that he was referring to the tiger, for he was pointing to a spot some thirty yards to the right of us. I strained my eyes hard to place the animal. But it was not at all easy to do so because the light and shade effect of the surrounding trees blended nicely with the black and tan of the beast's head lying flat on the ground, with his eyes glowing like two red lights. This discovery did not unnerve me in the least. For, at the back of my mind was the reassuring thought that the tiger had been mortally wounded and was unable to move little did I realise that the position of his head was a sure sign that he was crouching for a spring.

Unmindful of the imminent danger to which I stood exposed, I started calculating what I should have to do next. But the tiger was is no mood to wait for my convenience. With a terrific roar he flung himself into mid-air with the force of a projectile. Not being prepared for such a sudden assault. I was taken aback and a thick layer of haze seemed to spread before my eyes and I felt as if I were in a trance.

Nevertheless, I fully realised that it might be end of my life, which struck me as rather funny. I said to myself, "Here I stand, a sure prey to the tiger whom I had set out to kill." Yet when I woke up in the morning, little did I know that such would be my fate before the day had run out. I thought of my people at home—of how they would grieve over their loss. These and similar other stray thoughts flashed past on my mind's curtain as I stood rooted to the spot, with the tiger still poised in mid-air.

Somehow, it did not occur to me to fire. But even if I had done so, it could have been worse than useless, considering that to try and stop a charging tiger with a light sporting rifle such as the one I held, is like attempting to stave off a tidal bore with one's bare hands. Instinctively I stepped aside to dodge the beast, which move, I am sure, saved my life, for to turn and make a headlong flight would have been suicidal. Next, to save myself from falling into the tiger's clutches, I scrambled up a nearby *babool* tree unmindful of the pricking I had from its thorns. My numerous companions were also seen dangling precariously from every tree, big or small, that stood around.

Now began a count of heads to make sure no one was missing. Soon after, it was discovered that constable Basawan Singh of our party, who had been missing, was lying prone on the ground at the spot where the tiger had landed following his spring into mid air, but it was not possible to render any help to him, with the tiger sitting within close range of him and giving vent to his rage by a deafening roar at intervals. Our discussion to one another across the trees seemed to provoke him all the more. So we lapsed into silence which seemed to appease him somewhat. Unluckily for me, he was not visible from where I was perched. But one of the men of my party, who had chanced to climb up the very tree under which the tiger was seated, was able to watch his movements.

Time was running out of our hands. Yet, to descend on the ground, meant coming face to face with the beast By and by, his roars became less and less frequent and this emboldened me to come down quietly and climb up another tree from where I could command a good view of him, Simple as this operation was, it gave me a rare thrill. From this other tree I could see the tiger sitting with his head up, looking rather morose and meditative. Probably he sensed that his time was up. On my side I felt there was no time to lose, for it was past 4.00 in the afternoon and the sun was fast receding. I took careful aim and fired, hitting him in the neck. This made him getup and walk in my direction without showing the least signs of distress.

At that moment, the tiger looked very majestic indeed, with the light from the setting sun playing upon his body. A thing that I noticed particularly was that as he walked, his hind quarters dragged, thus indicating that his spine had been broken. I at once knew that this had been caused by my second shot, fired as he was passing under my *machan*. This also explained his subsequent conduct in not fleeing further away. But majestic as he looked, I did not hesitate to fire another shot at him, hitting him in the head this time, with the result that he fell in a heap, and dead.

After this, the first thing I did was to run up to the spot where Basawan Singh lay prone. The tiger had evidently given him a terrific blow from behind with his paw—thus breaking his spine—and then dug his teeth in—a few inches below the nape of his neck. I had him turned over whereupon he did something that I remember to this day with some pride combined with compassion. As soon as he saw me standing by his side, he raised his right hand in salute, an act that greatly moved me. I stood there grief stricken while a stretcher was being rigged up. When this was ready I had him removed as expeditiously as possible to the hospital at Robertsganj, where he was given the best medical attention available at that time. But alas he quietly passed away in the wee hours of the night.

Much distressed by this tragic occurrence I thought the best thing for me to do would be to report it personally to the Inspector General of Police, Sir Robert Dodd. So, I rushed off to Lucknow by the first available train. There I met him at his residence and the first thing I told him was, "Sir, I have come to you in some distress." Thereafter, when I finished relating to him all the facts of the case in detail, he said to me by way of his reaction, "Oh, I see, it is not as bad as I had thought. I had thought you had inadvertently shot someone dead." The next thing he did was to call out to his wife and say to her some what jubilantly, "Do you know, Lahiri has shot a tiger and a bear in one and the same beat?" Upon this I felt greatly relieved and returned to Mirzapur as a changed man.

This brings me to the end of an episode of my life which I have reason to remember with some emotion. It so happened that Basawan Singh had no father, no mother, no wife, no children to mourn his loss. He had been brought up by a woman of another caste whom I paid some money as a compensation.

* * * *

Chapter 18

All about Christmas Camp of Yore

My mind goes back to the year 1930, when I organised a Christmas camp at Hathinala, a remote spot, which was at the south of the Shone, in the forests of Mirzapur with my Range D.I.G. Mr. Rowland Bell as my chief guest. Apart from myself, our party consisted of Mrs. Bell and their infant son, Mrs. Grant and her infant son, Mrs. Grant's younger sister, and Miss Murphy, Mr. Bruce and Lt. Wright. We travelled as far as Chopan by car. But since the track from Chopan to Hathinala was not motorable, I had arranged for an elephant for Mr. and Mrs. Bell, Mrs. Grant and Mr. Bruce, a riding horse each for Lt. Wright and Miss Murphy and a palanquin for each of the two infant sons and their nannies, while I had my own horse to carry me.

By the time we left Chopan, it was past 4.00 o'clock in the afternoon and all went well till sunset when Lt. Wright and Miss Murphy forged ahead on their horses, followed by Mr. and Mrs. Bell, Mrs. Grant and Mr. Bruce on the back of their elephant. Thus leaving me behind in charge of the two infant sons and their nannies. At this stage I found myself in a quandary, because I noticed, that the palanquin bearers, who happened to be weaklings were floundering under the load they were required to carry. To add to my woes, it became pitch dark before we had gone very far. I tried to persuade the two nannies, who were much above the average weight, to get down from their perch and thus give a chance to the palanquin bearers to put up some speed. But the two of them had at my request hardly walked a hundred yards or so, when they declared it was impossible for them to go on like that any further, and crawled back into their respective palanquins. The fact was that they had never before walked through a forest and that, too, after dark. So they felt frightened beyond measure for which I don't blame them.

I felt pity for the palanquin bearers, but there was nothing I could do beyond dismounting and keeping company with them on foot. In order to put some heart into them I repeatedly cried out, *"Shabhash, Shabhash"* and started counting their steps—1, 2, 3, 4, 5, 6, 7 and so on. That is how I kept chanting. Even though, they felt compelled to lay down their loads on the ground at brief intervals to have a little rest. For me, therefore, it was like an eternity before we spied the lights of our transit camp at Mahof and in response to our shouts, heard the shouts of all those who had already arrived there, far ahead of us. It was nearly 10.00 o'clock by then and needless to say, Mrs. Bell and Mrs. Grant were beyond themselves with joy at the sight of their babies, whose behaviour all through, I must say, was exemplary, for I did not hear them crying even once. I may add here in all modesty that by common consent, I was declared to be the man of the day.

At the ensuing reunion each of us recounted his or her experiences and in this rehearsal Lt. Wright and Miss Murphy easily scored over the rest of us. According to them what had happened was something like this. In the prevailing darkness they happened to lose their way. Thereafter, when they saw the light streaming from a fire burning at some distance from them, they decided to go there and enquire which way they were to go. Both of them having come fresh from England were not at all conversant with the local language. Later when they got there, they saw a girl, barely nine or ten years of age, warming herself in front of the fire. Lt. Wright then with some difficulty coughed out the words, *"P-A-R-A-O, K-I-D-A-R"* (which way to the camp). Now imagine an innocent little tribal girl, who had never previously set her eyes on the face of a European, being suddenly accosted at night by two such persons, each astride a horse and dressed in quaint clothes, emerging from the surrounding gloom and saying something of which she could not make head or tail of and then imagine what her reaction would be like. Naturally, she took them for *jins* come up from the underworld and after crying out *"Are maiyya re maiyya"* (oh mother) bolted from the site, head over heels. In other words, as fast as her legs could carry her, leaving her interlocutors agape and without any answer to their query. Such was the story Lt. Wright and Miss Murphy told us. Plausible as it was, some of the doubting Thomas's from among us, were inclined to take with a pinch of salt for reasons which I had better leave untold. By way of a hint, however, I might mention here that both Lt. Wright and Miss Murphy happened to be in their early twenties.

At Mahof Mr. and Mrs. Bell, Mrs. Grant and Miss Murphy were accommodated in a tin shed, while the remaining three of us were accommodated in a small single fly tent each. Unfortunately, there was a heavy downpour of rain that night, so much so, that but for the heroic efforts of our camp attendants to build up an earthen ridge all around our tents with the help of spades, we would have found ourselves floating on water and drenched to the skin, at least shivering with cold, the time of the year being mid-winter. But by dawn, the sky became cleared and when we got up in the morning, we were greeted by a glorious sun bathing the countryside with a refulgence hard to describe. Shelly once wrote that, "If winter comes, can spring be far behind?."

On our arrival at Hathinala in the afternoon, the first thing that caught our eyes was a red banner spread over the entrance to the camping ground, with the words, "Welcome to Hathinala camp", superscribed on it in big bold letters of the colours of gold. Incidentally, I had left the arrangements here in the hands of Sub-,Inspector Shamshuddin, Station Officer Dudhi. The entire landscape looking picturesque with a stream flowing past in front of us. Across it lay a glade flanked by Sal trees. Down the glade there was a pathway spread over with powdered brick and having bunting tied up stakes on either side of it. At the other end of this pathway stood our tents. Here and there on the camp site, we noticed green branches of trees, planted in the ground, with apples, oranges, pears and bananas, hanging from them by way of decoration of the site. Inside the tents there were thick Mirzapur carpets spread over the entire floor, while outside there were a dozen or more gas lights hung from poles which when lighted at night, illuminated the entire area like day.

The arrangements so far appeared to be perfect. But it was the commissariat that worried me. On my enquiry as to what Shamshuddin had done about the supply of eggs, meat and milk, he first took me to a shed where I saw a huge pile of eggs arranged in the shape of a cone. He then took me to a courtyard where there were some two dozen heads of young goats, huddled up and, finally, he took me some distance into the forest and pointed to a pen with some cows in it. These he said, had been rounded up from the surrounding area where they had been left by their owners, to graze.

By now my admiration for this officer knew no bounds. But there was still another problem that gave me some cause for concern, namely, what about the beaters for out daily hunt, when the nearest village lay some twelve miles away? To set my mind at rest, Shamshuddin took me to yet another part of the forest, where I saw an army of men cooking their food. He said he had collected them from the nearby villages and that they were going to stay there for the entire period of our camp.

Incidentally, these were not the only surprises this officer had up his sleeve. In the evening when we sat round an open air camp fire, he had invariably some entertainment which were ready for us, One evening he had arranged for a folk dance by tribals, on another day, a display of fireworks with a particular type of wood which when ignited blazed away so fiercely that it looked almost like a display of an imitation, if not of real fireworks. In fact there was no end to Shamshuddin's resourcefulness. For instance the day Mr. Bell shot a tigress we saw the words "Welcome to Hathinala Camp" substituted by the words, "Congratulations, Sir" on the banner standing at the entrance to our camp. He had a similar surprise reserved for us on New Year's day, when the first thing that greeted our eyes when we woke up, was a banner with the words, "Happy New Year Sir" in front of each of our tents.

Shamshuddin exemplified a type of officer not to compare with anyone. Now, when I look back upon this camp, I cannot help feeling how conditions have changed since then and how most of our fellow countrymen were treated like dumb driven cattle in those days. My conscience also pricks me for at least some if not all the doings of Shamshuddin behind my back, on the occasion to please me and my D.I.G.

* * * *

Chapter 19

A Novel Satyagraha

The year 1930 will always be remembered for the wave of popular enthusiasm that swayed this country of ours, following the call given by Mahatma Gandhi for Civil Disobedience. During this period, one afternoon while I was posted as S.P., Mirzapur. I received a telephonic message from the Station Superintendent there informing me that a batch of some 200 school boys, most of whom appeared to be minors, had arrived by rail from Chunar and were not prepared to pay the fare due from them. As such he wanted to know what he should do with them. This was news to me, for so far the Police did not have to combat with ticketless travel carried out in an organised manner. Promptly I hurried to the Railway Station where, I found a huge crowd assembled to see the fun, if nothing else. As soon as they saw me they rent the skies with cries of *"Mahatma Gandhi Ki Jai, Motilal Nehruji Ki Jai, Jwaharlalji Ki Jai"* besides surrounding my car in a body.

I felt myself in a difficult situation, for I knew that the police were then like a red rag to the masses. I also felt that the best thing for me to do would be to keep smiling and humour the crowd which had the desired effect. Thereafter, when with great difficulty I managed to clamber out of my car I went over to the Station platform to come face to face with the erring boys. I noticed that they were drawn up in a double file as if on parade with their leader holding aloft a Congress flag in their hands. On my questioning them as to what they wanted, they kept mum. Obviously enough, they were there to court arrest. What was amusing was that they were students of primary school of Chunar and had come by rail without tickets to Mirzapur, at the behest of their class teacher.

I then made up my mind to whisk them away to the District Jail close by, before coming to a decision about the line of action to be taken in this case. To detain so many persons for trial would mean overcrowding the jail and was therefore not advisable. I had them drawn up in a line to pick out for detention such of them as might be over sixteen years of age. But as soon as they saw through my design, they came up before me, one after another, to declare that they were over sixteen. Even so excepting the leader of the party, I had them packed in a motor bus and sent to a spot outside the city, before their release. This, I said to myself, would serve as a punishment for them. But my plan misfired, for, soon enough they walked back to the city, where they were feted before being given a hearty sent off.

I then thought my trouble was over. But I was sorely mistaken in my assumption. The next day, a similar batch of *Satyagrahis* of tender age, turned up at an identical hour to court arrest. I had therefore once again to make my way though a milling crowd, fully defiant and at the same time busy raising shouts of *Mahatma Gandhi Ki Jai, Motilal Nehruji Ki Jai, Jawaharlal Nehru Ki Jai* which rent the skies. This time also I found it expedient to take the same action as I had taken on the previous day.

Thereafter, when yet another batch of a similar type turned up by the same train on the third day, I was almost ready for that. At the same, way I managed to face my ordeal with all the fortitude at my command and, what was more, got into touch with the Divisional Railway Superintendent at Allahabad who arranged, at my request, for a party of ticket collectors to be sent to Chunar, so as to stop the boys from boarding the train there. Meanwhile, instructions from the Congress High Command at Allahabad were conveyed to their partymen at Chunar to make it known that ticketless travel was not on their programme. Consequently, there were no more instances of this kind after the third day and I felt greatly relieved.

The agitation, however, continued in different shape throughout the year, causing no end of trouble for the Police. They had to deal with the *Salt Satyagrah,* the picketing of cloth and liquor shops, among other forms of agitation that appeared to have caught the imagination of the masses from one end of the country to the other.

* * * *

Chapter 20

My One and Only Tiff with District Magistrate

My one and only tiff with any District Magistrate relates to one Mr. C.F. Wood who was my contemporary at Mirzapur in the year 1932. He represented a type of Englishman who honestly believed in the myth of the white man's burden. This was brought home to me one day through an unguarded statement of his to the effect that, according to his calculations, (over which he had apparently taken great pains) his posting to this district made a difference of two pies only per head of its population, compared with the cost involved in the posting of an officer of the local breed, meaning an Indian.

Now, to revert to the story of my tiff with him, it centred round a tournament in the nature of a regatta, held annually at a site where a tributary of the Ganga which is known as Ojhla Nala, flows into it. When it started, the idea behind this tournament, was to give a boost to the *Mallahas* (boatmen) of Mirzapur who were much helpful to the British army during the First World War in the training of the river Euphrates, which now marks the boundary line between Iran and Iraq. In my time, the regatta used to be patronised by all the Europeans of the Station, including some of the heads of the two leading carpet factories of Mirzapur. What may sound somewhat ridiculous today, is that while most of the money for running this tournament came from the Indian gentry of Mirzapur, they were relegated to a secondary position in the seating arrangement made for the occasion, to view the tournament. On the particular day which I have in mind, while I was talking to the then City *Kotwal*, Mohammad Sayeed, at one spot of the ground there, Mr. Wood suddenly came charging into us to tick off the City *Kotwal* for his bad management. I had not the least idea at the time of what the cause of his displeasure was. So when I asked him, what was matter, he brusquely said to me, "I call it a bloody *bandobast",* and then walked away in a huff. Later on, my enquiries revealed that he was feeling annoyed over the fact that during the tea interval, some from among the Indian visitors to the show had the audacity to walk over to the tent reserved for the Europeans of the station, to occupy for a little while some of the vacant seats in it.

Mr. Wood's behaviour on the occasion rankled in my heart. So when I returned home in the evening, I sat down to compose an epistle which, far from being a love letter, ended up by demanding an apology from him, for his misbehaviour. On his part, Mr. Wood wishing to catch me on the wrong foot, showed this letter to Mr. Panna Lal, Divisional Commissioner, who was on a visit to Mirzapur and staying as his guest. Mr. Panna Lal then asked Mr. Wood to inform me that I should see him at 10.00 o'clock the next morning. This I did with a fluttering heart, because, in the first place, Mr. Wood happened to be miles senior to me besides being a member of the ruling race and, in the second place, because Mr. Panna Lal was at the time staying with him as his guest. In any case he listened to my version of the case, during the course of which I also told him how Mr. Wood looked upon himself as a Lord, Almighty or a God, and how he was inclined to be rough with Indians generally. Upon this he had a discussion separately with Mr. Wood and on his return from his meeting with him, he told me that Mr. Wood felt very sorry if he had unwillingly given me any cause for offence.

Finally, as a result of Mr. Panna Lal's mediation, the two of us shook hands together and became good friends once again.

I must say to the credit of Mr. Wood that after that episode, I found him a changed man. He not only showed me the utmost courtesy during the rest of my tenure at Mirzapur, but also took a leading part in a Citizen's farewell given to me, on the eve of my departure from Mirzapur on transfer, besides throwing a dinner party at his residence in honour of me and my wife.

* * * *

Chapter 21

A Social Event

In the year 1931 or so, when I was posted as Superintendent of Police at Mirzapur, I had asked the Mr. and Mrs. Wood to have a dinner at my place one evening. Mr. Wood was then posted as District Magistrate, Mirzapur. Apart from them a number of other European couples graced the occasion. Such exchange of civilities among the favoured few, was a common feature of life in Mufassil stations in the days gone by. For me, being an Indian, it was incumbent to observe this custom, if only to keep pace with the times. My wife being away, I had to play a dual role and was anxious that the event should pass off without a hitch.

As, it was customary in those days, I had a retinue of domestic servants, including a *Khansama* and a bearer, a *Khitmatgar* and a *Masalchi* among others. The dishes had been prepared by the *Khansama,* named, Khuda Baksh, while the table had been laid by the bearer, Ram Lal. My guests sat at the table strictly according to the protocol. Mrs. Wood being the senior most lady present, there, sat on my right.

The dinner started with soup. It was first served to the ladies and, thereafter, to the men. I kept a strict watch over the proceedings with a keen eye to make sure that nothing went wrong. Each of the guests had a small salt cellar at hand to be able, if at all necessary, to help themselves to some of the stuff from it.

As my eyes fell on Mrs. Wood, I noticed her taking out a pinch of salt and mixing it with her soup. But what gave me some sense for surprise was that the moment she did so, tiny little bubbles came to the surface of her soup to form a ring along in periphery. She, however, kept quiet to save me from any embarrassment and so did I in my state of utter confusion over the happening. For, which I had never known table salt to effervesce like this. Barring this small misadventure, all went well and the party dispersed sometime after the dinner was over.

For my part, being keen on unravelling the mystery of the fizz I had noticed, I asked Khuda Baksh if he could think of a possible cause for it. Upon this, he knitted his eyebrows for a while and then came out with an explanation that took my breath away. According to him, what had happened was that my bearer Ram Lal, who had laid the table, mistaking a bottle of Eno's fruit salt for one of table salt, had incorrectly filled the cellars with this stuff.

The mischief had been done and I could do nothing to retrieve it. For did I have the guts to ascertain it from Mrs. Wood, when I met her next, the aftermath, if any, of her dinner with me.

* * * *

Chapter 22

All in the Day's Work

Around the year 1930 or so (when I was posted as S.P. Mirzapur) there was a case of dastardly murder of one Jagannath Singh on the outskirts of Vindhyachal which clearly indicated the hand of a hired assassin in it. At about the same time, a notorious outlaw, named Dhiraj Singh, who was wanted in a number of cases of the same nature in and around Allahabad and there was a reward of Rs. 5,000/- on his head, had gone underground. It was therefore surmised that most likely it was he who had been responsible for the commission of this murder.

Partly because of this reason and partly because Mirzapur happened to be a neighbouring district of Allahabad, it had been put on the alert. Thereafter, it so happened that a man identical to the description of Dhiraj Singh, was seen with a revolver in hand, walking for a distance along the railway track that lies behind Vindhyachal. The informant in this case, when put up before me by S.I. Sayeed Ahmad of Kotwali Mirzapur, further revealed that this man had been seen disappearing into a small house that stood by the side or the railway track close to Vindhyachal.

The house was found to be one of a cluster of similar buildings belonging to a *Mahant* of Vindhyachal, all of which mostly remained vacant. The *Mahant* himself lived in a stately house in the same compound. On one side of this compound, there was a metalled road and on the other a railway track, both connecting Vindhyachal with Mirzapur.

I then held a council of war with my Reserve Inspector, Mohammad Siddiq and S.I. Sayeed Ahmad of Kotwali Mirzapur. At this council we decided that the best thing for us to do, would be to keep an unobtrusive watch on the suspect in this case. As a result of it was observed he mostly kept indoors and came out once in the morning for his bath at a well close by and again, once in the evening, for a stroll alongside the railway track behind his abode.

Having thus made sure of his movements, we decided one evening to carry out a raid on this man's hide out, the next morning at 8.00 o'clock. With this end in view, we set out from Mirzapur at an appointed hour in a bus hired for the occasion. Our party consisted of some 30 officers and men, including Inspector Mohammad Siddiq, S.I. Sayeed Ahmad and myself. On our arrival at our destination, the first thing we did, was to throw a cordon round the house in question and thus seal it off. It then occurred to me that we would do well to have the *Mahant* also with us in our raid. So, I walked over to his residence to collect him. It was thus accompanied by Inspector Mohammad Siddiq, S.I. Sayeed Ahmad and *Mahant*, I was the first to enter the place through a door in an enclosure some 10 feet in height which shut it off the house from the rest of the compound. This place in fact, in the form of a fairly wide courtyard with vegetation of a man's height in it.

Opposite this courtyard, there lay a two-storied *pucca* building, each storey consisting of three rooms, with a verandah some eight feet wide in front of them. The entire place presented a dismal look. Having crossed the above noted courtyard, we entered the middle room with bated breath, only to find that it was empty, but for a string cot on this floor, with a pillow on it which had visible signs of its having been slept on till a few seconds earlier, a copy of

Hanuman Chalisa and a white cap with some 455 bore cartridges in it. On the very face of it, the man we were after, had precipitately moved off to hide himself somewhere in the vicinity. The situation was indeed alarming, for the man might fire at us any moment we all had a revolver in hand including, Inspector Mohammad Siddiq, S.I. Sayeed Ahmad and myself. Then we rushed from room to room in a bid to corner him before he was able to shoot at us. But all in vain. There were no signs of the man on the ground floor. We then inferred that he must have fled up the staircase to get to the first floor.

This was even worse for us, for, now we thought our adversary had a distinct advantage over us. But advantage or no advantage, we could not very well give up the chase. The only thing for us to do in the circumstances of the case, was to rush up the staircase, come what may. All the three of us, in fact, did so with throbbing hearts and without giving ourselves time to think.

I distinctly remember how during this process, I was expecting each moment a bullet from our adversary's revolver to hit any one of us. But, again, much to our surprise, we drew blank. He was nowhere to be seen on the upper floor also.

Thereafter, while we were cogitating over what the matter was, we heard a loud report coming from the courtyard below. We then rushed to the terrace overlooking it and saw a thin wisp of smoke floating in mid air above a spot where the undergrowth was the thickest. The next thing we did was to surround this spot and to call on our adversary to surrender. Thereafter, in the absence of any response from him, we led an assault on him to find that he was lying stone dead, prone on the ground, with his revolver pressed under his chest, which had a neat hole in it with blood oozing from this hole. He was well built and looked like an athlete, but except for a loin cloth he had nothing on.

Later from this man's finger impressions it had been confirmed that he was one Kunj Behari Singh of Raebareli who was an ex-serviceman convicted in a petty case against him. But beyond this scanty information about his antecedents, we failed to find out anything significant about him. Nor were we able to get much out of the *Mahant*, who had probably been harbouring him for some nefarious purpose of his own.

This brings me to the end of my story with a lot of froth in it, but little doubt is there.

I am not aware to this day, if Dhiraj Singh of Allahabad was ultimately run down to earth or not. But I regret to say that the murder case of Jagannath Singh remained unsolved.

* * * *

Chapter 23

All about a Marathon Ride on Horseback

Horse riding by police officers has unfortunately become a thing of the past. But there was a time when it was not at all unusual for a Police Officer on tour to cover 15 to 20 miles daily on horseback. A District Magistrate, well known to me—an Englishman, who owned four horses and through a system of relays, occasionally covered as much as a hundred miles in a day. But in my case, I can claim to have covered some 52 miles on horseback without any relays in some ten hours. This was my marathon ride for which I earned much credit. It took place early in January 1932, when following the breakdown of the Second Round Table Conference in England, the Government of India took a firm decision in favour of the arrest of Mahatma Gandhi on his return to India. The date fixed for it was the 4th January 1932 and Government's instructions were that no processions or public meetings were to be allowed on the occasion.

A copy of these instructions was passed on to me by my District Magistrate Mr. C.F. Wood, which reached me late in the evening of the 2nd January. I was then camping at a place named Kuldumri which lay at a distance of a little over a hundred miles from my headquarters at Mirzapur. It stood in the heart of a forest and my problem was that to get to the nearest road-head at Robertsganj, I had to cover some 52 miles which one was ordinarily expected to do in easy stages of 10 to 12 miles a day either on horseback or on the back of an elephant.

Incidentally, this is no longer the case to-day when a state highway runs all the way from Robertsganj to Rihand (the site of the famous second highest concrete dam in India having this name), and when there is a concrete bridge over the Sone at Chopan which took hours to cross by boat in the rainy season. But now gone are the fauna and the flora which used to give a sylvan look to the entire country side between these two places. To mark the march of time and to mar this look, a number of factories with their tall chimneys belching smoke and their ancillary settlements have now come up at places enroute, thus changing the scene beyond recognition.

To revert to the story of my ride, I was fortunately able to borrow a horse from the Rani of Singrauli as well as the services of a *Sowar* to accompany me.

We left Kuldumri at about 8.00 in the morning of the 3rd January and I found the conditions ideal for a ride. A clear sky with the Sun's rays glittering off every leaf and every pebble wet with the morning dew, a soft breeze with a nip in it, blowing in my face, a long undulating pathway through lovely forest country and a mount that responded to my least suggestion, besides being light footed, left nothing to be desired.

I went on and on at a slow canter, smoothly and effortlessly, followed close behind by the *Sowar* and in the process lost all count of time or of distance. A thing that attracted my notice was that here and there by the side of the pathway, lay loose stones heaped in the shape of a pyramid. My curiosity about them being aroused, I was told by a passer-by much to my surprise, that each of them marked the spot where an unwary traveller had fallen a prey to a man-eating tiger. Initially, the deceased's friends or relations had heaped some loose stones on it in the belief that the deceased's spirit would keep wandering unless care was taken to keep it properly pressed down. Thereafter, whosoever passed by it, placed some more stones on it, thus building up in course of time, a heap in the shape of a pyramid, which was locally called a *Baghaut*. I must confess that I was filled with a sense of terror at the sight of each of these so-called *Baghauts*, whenever I passed by it.

At the time of my setting out from Kuldumri, I had planned to make a bid for Obra, a halting place some 20 miles away from it, but I found the going so good that when I arrived there, it was barely midday. I was also agreeably surprised to see the Station Officer of Chopan, Sub-Inspector Yadunandan Pande who had come there in anticipation of my visit, tethering his horse to a tree. I then decided to proceed to Chopan after a brief halt, seeing that the day was still so young. On his part, Pande at once got busy in arranging some fodder for my horse and some refreshments for me. He also had a string cot laid for me under a mango tree by the side of the river that flow past Obra. I then lost no time in flinging myself on the cot to give myself some rest for an hour or so.

Half asleep and half awake, I then went once again in my mind over my experience of the morning, the smooth flowing movement of any mount, mile after mile, and the sight and sound that assailed my senses during the course of my journey, uphill and down-dale, through forest country that made it all the more interesting. While I thus lay motionless, I was also conscious of the rustle of the leaves that spread their canopy over my head, the chatter of the birds that relayed from tree to tree in a spirit of gay abandon, the occasional back of a *cheetah* or a *sambhar* announcing its presence in some cool spot nearby, and finally, the sweet murmur of the river that flowed majestically by my side in its onward course to join the Sone some 15-20 miles down-stream. For me a brief respite like this was the height of bliss. But bliss or no bliss, I knew I must be up by 1 o'clock sharp to hit the road once again and this sub-consciously acted as a thorn in my side.

Therefore, as per my schedule, the moment it was 1 o'clock by my watch, I got up, ready for the fray. Now that Pandey was there to accompany me, I dismissed the *Sowar* with instructions to return to his place at his convenience. And now began my ride to Chopan over a distance of some 14 miles. Accompanied with Pande by my side, I had some one to talk to, whenever I felt like it. My journey, again lay through Nelly forest country, but this time interspersed with patches of lovely green fields here and there. I occasionally passed heads of cattle let loose in the jungles to graze. I was told they mostly came from neighbouring districts were there was a scarcity of pasture. The journey was on the whole uneventful and by the time I got to Chopan, it was a little past 3.00 in the afternoon.

Incidentally, during the course of my journey from Obra to Chopan I noticed a man jogging along ahead of me. There was fresh wound some six inches long on the nape of his neck. I then could not resist the temptation of asking how he had come by this wound. In reply to my question, he told me that he used to suffer from severe headache, therefore on the advice of a man he knew he had the nape of his neck cauterised with a red hot rod of iron and thus got rid of his ailment. I then said to myself "Good God, what a cure?"

As I had yet another 14 miles to go, to get to Robertsganj, I thought I must change my mount and so kept waiting at the Police Station, while Pandey tried to raise one for me locally. But in spite of his best efforts, he failed to do so. This put me in a quandary. It was then the afternoon. The alternatives open to me were, either to spend the night at Chopan or, cruel as it might seem, to go ahead on the back of the same horse that had brought me so far. Somehow the idea of staying put at Chopan for the night did not appeal to me and I decided to proceed on my journey.

To get to Robertsganj from Chopan, I had, in the first place, to cross the Sone which I did by fording it. But by the time I was on the other side of the river, it was close on 5.00 in the afternoon. From here my track again lay through thick jungle for part of the way. But since the terrain was flat and the ground soft, I meant to give my horse his head. I, therefore, let Pande go back to his Police Station. But I soon realised my mistake. Before I had gone half a mile or so, I saw the sun disappearing fast behind the trees that stood in a solid block on both sides of me, I felt a little alarmed by this and dug my heels into the sides of my horse to make him put up speed. But the poor beast, was feeling dog tired and did not have the energy to go beyond a slow trot. After a while I found he was unable to go even at this pace. So I let him go at a walk, which too, was not to his liking. He whinnied and neighed to express his distress and from time to time, he made a right about-turn to give me an inkling of his mind.

My plight at this stage can better he imagined than could be described. By then it was quite dark. So much so, that I could hardly distinguish anything beyond a few paces from me. The only light, feeble as it was, came from the stars that peeped at me through the narrow strip of the sky overhead, open to me. Seeing the pitiable condition of my horse, I dismounted to lead him at a walk by his reins. My only thought at the time was to seek some refuge for the night. But, also none was within sight. Nor was there a soul to be seen anywhere. The silence was expressive and the only sound that penetrated my ears came from our own footfalls.

The forest through which I was now passing was known to be infested with animals of all types, particularly bears. My apprehension was that I might be accosted by one of them and made to pay the penalty for my trespass into his domain at a time when I had no business to be there. With my eyes and ears straining and my heart throbbing, I groped my way as best as I could for another mile or two when through God's grace I noticed what I thought was a stockade by the side of the road. Although I could see it very indistinctly, it looked like a stockade which it actually turned out to be on my close examination. Inside the enclosure I saw scores of cattle huddled together in all poses, some standing, some squatting. I said to myself something is better than nothing and decided to spend the night inside the pen. It had a small thatched cover at one corner which I thought would come in very handy for me and my horse at a time of the year when the cold was at its height.

With this idea of passing the night inside the pen, I was about to undo the catch fastened to its gateway, when I heard a faint jingle of bells. This made me prick up my ears and I felt intrigued as it became more and more distinct.

It also carried with it the sound of footfalls approaching in my direction. I waited with bated breath till I saw a man emerge from the surrounding gloom. He carried on his shoulder a stout staff mounted with a spearhead at its extreme and having a bunch of bells tied to it. There was large sized canvas bag slung from his staff. The first thing I did on his arrival within close range of me was to stop him and ask him who he was and where he was going. On his telling me that he was carrying *Kaptan Saheb's dak,* I said to myself God is great and my joy knew no bounds. I felt like meeting a long lost friend and told him that he should now escort me as far as Robertsganj which he did.

This man was a village *Chaukidar* engaged in one of his routine duties for which he was paid at the rate of *six annas* or forty paise per day. Such was the devotion of these *Chaukidars* that they seldom faltered in the discharge of it, although at times they had to go through a thick forest to get to their destination. Winter or summer, sun or shower, one could depend on them to do this allotted task to the best of their ability for which I take my hat off to them.

To go back to the account of my marathon ride, it was plain sailing for me from the time I met the village *Chaukidar* mentioned above to the time I arrived at Robertsganj over lap of some 7 to 8 miles, which I did partly on horseback and partly on foot. When I saw the twinkling lights of Robertsganj from a distance, my heart was delighted such as I had seldom known. Fortunately for me, on my arrival at Robertsganj, I found the last bus for Mirzapur still waiting. I promptly boarded it after bidding good bye to my two inimitable companions namely, the horse that had carried me all the way from Kuldumri to Robertsganj and the *Chaukidar* who had proved to be god send for me.

Concurrently with my departure, Sub-Inspector Baldeo Singh of Robertsganj flashed a message about it to Mr. Wood at Mirzapur who, in his turn, relayed it to my household staff there. In the result, when I got home, close on midnight, fully tired and aching all over, not only for my marathon ride on horseback to Robertsganj, but also from my bus ride from there to Mirzapur, I was served with food that was piping hot.

Next morning when I met Mr. Wood, he congratulated me over my performance, besides making a hero of me. Later I also got a pat on my back from my Range D.I.G. Mr. A.G. Phillips which made up for the trial and trouble of my journey.

Luckily for me, Mahatma Gandhi's arrest on the 4th January caused little stir so far as Mirzapur was concerned.

* * * *

Chapter 24

A Penitent Husband

A man stood there in front of me, balanced on one leg and with folded hands, he looked like any other villager, simple and submissive, and somewhat nervous. His very demeanour announced that he had something to confess. This happened one fine December morning when, with a newspaper in my hand, I was sitting on an arm chair and enjoying the sun, in the front *verandah* of my house at Unnao. How he managed to evade my orderlies, I cannot say. But there he was, looking the very picture of penitence. I felt some pity for him and asked what he wanted from me. But instead of giving me a straight reply, he said, "*Hazoor*, I want you to sentence me to death or to inflict any other punishment you may deem fit."

"How can I do so?" I replied. "You have not told me what you have done to earn any punishment at all." By way of answer, he took down a piece of cloth from his shoulder and after squatting on the floor proceeded to undo a small knot tied on one corner of it. He was taking his own time over the process which made me all the more inquisitive. At long last, when with quivering hands he held out the stuff he had with him, I could not at all make out what it was. Nor did the man seem to be in a hurry to clear the mystery. I looked hard at the thing and was able to discern a bit of flesh gone dry, with a silver ring, the size of a four *anna* piece, attached to it. I felt puzzled and said, "What is this stuff you want to show me?"

"Hazoor", he said, "This is the tip of my wife's nose." The announcement he made was like a bomb shell for me. For a while I looked on without being able to utter a word. Then after I had regained my wits, I said, "And what have you to say about the tip of your wife's nose?"

"I Just sliced it off with a sickle" was his plain and simple answer.

"And, why did you do so?" I enquired of him after some hesitation. Upon this he got up and said with folded hands, *"Hazoor,* I am a poor villager. I have a field at some distance from my house with a crop of barely standing on it. It has been my practice to keep watch over it by night. Last night, when I got back home from my field, it was still dark. But when I went into my room to lie down for a while, I was amazed to find my neighbour fast asleep by the side of my wife. I saw red and felt like killing both of them. But the man bolted. My wife stood in front of me looking guilty. I took hold of a sickle and, before she could do anything to defend herself, sliced off the tip of her nose which is here before you. Now you may please order any punishment for me which in your superior wisdom you may think fit."

Startling as this confession was, it was made very simply. The only course open to me was to send the man to the *Kotwali* under escort to be locked up. The law, I said must be allowed to run its course. And so it did in that he was ultimately sentenced to two years rigorous imprisonment.

* * * *

Chapter 25

Lalloo of Pansaria

Lalloo of Pansaria, a village in police circle Achalganj in Unnao district, was a notorious bad character, given to much high-handedness. That the local police were unable to account for him, was a sore point with me. But they were not much to blame, because of the difficulty of getting evidence against him for his prosecution under section 110 of the Cr.P.C. Anyway, nemesis soon overtook him and he had to pay the extreme penalty for his sins. Here is an account of how it came about.

One winter evening a little after 10.00, as I was about to retire for the night, I received a special report from Police Station Achalganj. Contained in a red cover the arrival of a report of this type always gave me the jitters, as did this one. On going through its contents I learnt that Lalloo of Pansaria and his brother Hari Ram, along with some twenty other men, had led an assault in broad day light against Ram Nath and Sukhram of Jeonathpur and shot them dead. This they had done following a dispute over the ownership of a dead tree. I also learnt that they had spirited away their bodies.

In a case like this, I was expected to take a hand in its investigation. So I was off to the scene of occurrence in my car within some fifteen minutes of receipt of the report. As a precautionary measure, I took with me the armed guard posted at my residence as usual for sentry duty. On my arrival at the spot the sight that greeted my eyes was heart-rending. The old mother of Ram Nath and Sukhram lay prostrate with grief, while the other inmates of the house looked dazed. There were bloodstains to be seen on the roof of the house where the deceased had fallen before breathing their last. From my preliminary enquiries, I came to know that the deceased were *Kachis* by caste who owned a few acres of land between them and lived quite comfortably. Their only misfortune was that they were an eyesore for Lalloo. The tree which made the bone of contention in this case had been standing within a few feet of their house and they looked upon it as their property. Lalloo, on the other hand, claimed its ownership in his self-accredited position as an overlord of the village in a vague way. On the day of occurrence Ram Nath and Sukhram were having the tree felled to bring it in for their own use. This was too bitter a pill for Lalloo to swallow. He collected a few of his sturdy henchmen, numbering twenty in all and along with these men as well as his brother Hari Ram, proceeded to the spot, along with a gun in his hand, to teach them a lesson.

On their arrival, Ram Nath and Sukhram look frightened. They hurriedly shut themselves up inside their house and from the comparative safety of their position on their roof top, hurled some brickbats as well as abuse at their adversaries. Lalloo felt greatly enraged at this open challenge to his supremacy and, that too, in full view of all the village folk. He aimed his gun at Ram Nath and fired, thus dropping him dead with a shot in the temple. Lalloo's brother Hari Ram likewise took aim at Sukhram and fired, thus killing him outright.

Having in this way done their worst, Lalloo and his brother, Hari Ram decided to whisk away the two bodies, so as to escape the consequences of their misdeed. Therefore, they got hold of a ladder to climb to the rooftop. There they found that while Ram Nath was still gasping for breath with his head resting on the lap of his mother, who was trying in vain to revive him by pouring some water into his mouth, Sukhram was stone-dead. Lalloo, heartless as he was, snatched away Ram Nath's body and threw it down the ground below, thus snuffing out whatever little life was still left in it. Hari Ram likewise pushed Sukhram's body over the edge of the roof, to make it fall to the ground below. Then they set out to commandeer a bullock cart locally and after they had done so, they had these two bodies put in it and hidden under a heap of straw, preliminary to the cart being sent under a heavy escort, to a spot in the Ganga some miles away. These proceedings were being watched by scores of men, but they did not have the courage to raise a little finger in protest. Lalloo took the additional precaution of posting a guard at the village to prevent any communication with the Police Station at Achalganj, before the bodies had been safely disposed of.

After making my preliminary enquiry at Jeonathpur, I went over to village Pansaria in quest of Lalloo and Hari Ram. The time then was close to 10.00 o'clock in the night. I expected them to have gone into hiding. But I was mistaken for this because, I found them waiting to receive me in their best garments and without a trace of anxiety on their faces. I had known Lalloo for some time. Therefore, he greeted me with the affability of an old acquaintance and, thereafter, when I shamed him for his inhuman conduct, he had the audacity to tell me that the allegations against his brother and himself were false. He even went to the extent of telling me that the bloodstains I had noticed, were all fixed ones. To make a long story short, I arrested them and sent to the Police Station without any further ado.

Having thus secured the arrest of the two arch offenders in this case I set up my headquarters at Jeonathpur, both for the purpose of pursuing its investigation and for organising a hunt for the two dead bodies. I had several small parties of men dispatched in all directions in quest of them. After a lapse of some three days, during the course of which I recorded the statements of numerous witnesses to the occurrence, I had definite news that the bullock cart had been seen going up to a spot on the bank of the Ganga, I noticed that its wheel tracks were clearly visible up to this spot. The thing to do now was to have a search for the dead bodies carried out in the river bed close to it. This was done on time and again under the supervision of the Station Officer, but we were not succeeded.

I then decided to have a supreme effort made on the following Sunday in my presence. I also had arrangements made for some fisherman from Gangaghat (opposite Kanpur) to assist in the search with the help of their *Mahajals* (fishing nets of super size).

The operation began early in the morning and I watched them with keen interest. But the men engaged in the search had not succeeded for hours. At about midday, one of our party noticed a float made of *gharas* tucked away at one spot of the river bank close-by. Apparently it was meant for use as a ferry to get to us opposite sand bank where there was a melon field. Our next step was to get hold of the owners of this float. But when they were asked if they had seen anything of interest, they flatly denied having done so. This time another member of our party a Muslim had a brain wave. At his suggestion these men were made to stand in the river and then swear by mother Ganga whether or not they had seen anything of interest. Put to the test they broke down and testified to what they had seen. According to them they saw a week or so previously, a bullock cart come to the edge of the stream opposite their melon field. There were some half a dozen men with it of whom one had a gun with him. Two of these men successively took two bodies out of the cart and flung them into the river. One of the bodies failing to drop clear of the shallows, they pushed it with a *lathi* to make it float down the river. Then they went away. Later on, after a close examination of the site, they (the witnesses to this incident) noticed the water there stained with blood. Then they decided not to breathe a word of what they had seen, lest they should also get into trouble.

The information these men gave us had a magic effect. To our great delight the men engaged in the search were able to recover, a few yards downstream, the remains of the two bodies about the identity of which there could be no doubt. One of them had on it a key tied to a sacred thread which fitted into a lock used by the deceased Ram Nath. It also had a hole in it in the region of the left temple, marking the spot where he had been hit by a gun shot. The other body could be identified by a *dhoti* Sukhram had been wearing when he was shot dead. I sent the bodies to the mortuary at Unnao for safe custody till the next morning when the Civil surgeon Dr. Brahma Gupta would be carrying out a post-mortem on them.

Being particularly interested in this case, I kept watching the post-mortem when it was being done. Much as I abhorred it, I hung on to the last in spite of the foul odour that filled the room. My interest in the proceedings rose to fever heat when the ward boy sawed open the deceased Ram Nath's skull to reveal the presence inside the brain matter, of some lead shots flattened out by their impact with the skull. I thought all would be plain sailing after this. I had a jolt, therefore, when I saw Dr. Gupta putting down the age of the deceased as 13. On my asking him for his reason for doing so, he cited as his authority a book of medical jurisprudence by his side. When, however, he actually referred to it at my request, he had to acknowledge his mistake and correct the entry made by him, to make it 21 which was more in accord with Ram Nath's age.

To sum up, Lalloo and Hari Ram along with their associates were sent up for trial on a charge of murder-cum-rioting and they finally met with their deserts in that both the brothers were sentenced to death and the others to various terms of imprisonment by the Chief Court at Lucknow, the entire population of Achalganj were much to the joy at that time.

This case is illustrative of the tremendous difficulties the police have to encounter in their tussles with notorious criminals. It also shows how they have, at times, to do it on all fronts. Another lesson to be learnt from it is that perseverance always pays.

* * * *

Chapter 26

Love's Labour Lost

One evening in the year 1937 or so (when I was posted as S.P. Unnao), a man from Kanpur informed me that a certain gang of dacoits from there had planned to loot a wedding party that night from Kanpur which would be camping for the night in a mango grove outside a village close to Maurawan in my district. The information he had given me was so specific that I had no reason to doubt its authenticity. Therefore, I vested no time to draw up a plan of action in consultation with some of my officers.

In those days the Police personnel had no vehicles of their own, except for a prison van which had been provided in each district. We, therefore, had to commandeer a privately owned passenger bus to carry some fifty policeman to our destination, while I decided to go there by my own car. We set out on our journey after the day became dark and by the time, we got to the other end of it, it was close on 10.00 o'clock. During this journey, needless to say, we felt fully buoyed up by the prospect of bringing off a coup that would hit the headlines. Our party consisted of some fifty policeman and we parked our vehicles a mile or so short of Maurawan. Thereafter, we footed it to a point within close range of the grove in question and proceeded to throw a cordon round it. This we did with the utmost caution, so as not to give the least inkling of our presence. Once our cordon had been completed, there was nothing for us to do but to wait for developments. To recapitulate the scene, while we stood there in a circle, motionless as a rock and armed to the teeth, those who provided the cause for all this concern on our part, lay fast asleep. With the light from a number of gas lamps playing on their faces, quite unmindful of the danger hanging over them and of what was going on all around them.

For the first hour or so of this wait, we felt fully keyed up. Every little movement, every little sound, the sigh of the winds or the rustle of leaves, sent a rush of blood through our veins. As time passed and the measure of our hopes dropped by degrees, signs of dawn, which were heralded by just a suspicion of paleness in the sky, we seemed to wake up and thereafter, it was a delight to watch the night merge slowly but surely into day. But the loveliest vision that greeted my eyes was the sight of the police with their red turbans on, their rifles in hand, standing motionless at intervals a few yards apart, which made them look like a garland of red poppies.

Simultaneously with the advent of day, the men in the mango grove got up to answer the call of nature and as *lotas* in hand, they set out for the outer fields, they had the shock of their lives when they came up face to face with their overnight sentries, who made them sit down, Unique as this spectacles was, now that there was no prospect of the dakcoits from Kanpur, about whom I had been forewarned, turning up any more to oblige us, I gave a signal for my men to close in, preliminary to our departure for Unnao after our fruitless vigil for a whole night. This, I thought, was certainly a case of love's labour lost, a thing that all policemen are destined to experience. No wonder that on my way back I felt extremely miserable and, what is more, equally sleepy.

* * * *

Chapter 27

My Brush with a So-called Neta

Pt. Bishambhar Dayal Tripathi, a budding lawyer of Unnao, managed to get elected to the Legislative Assembly of Uttar Pradesh following the general elections of 1936 or so. Those were the days when the Congress had assumed office in the State of U.P. with Pt. Govind Ballabh Pant as Chief Minister. This gave Tripathi the opportunity to throw about his weight and make nuisance of himself. He also felt foul of me, because, I refused to toe the line with him. He made a grievance of it and complained against me to Pt. Pant, who gave him an assurance that he would look into the matter on his next visit to Unnao.

Thereafter, when Pt. Pant came to Unnao on a date towards the close of 1937, I had an opportunity to meet him for the first time. He had then been in his saddle as Chief Minister for a short time only, yet his reputation as a man of outstanding ability had travelled far and wide. It so happened that while he was slated to arrive at 10.00 in the morning, he actually turned up at 5.00 or so in the afternoon.

Thus, being behind time by some seven hours, he had to rush through his engagements including a public meeting at which Tripathi did his level best to malign me.

When the meeting over, Pt. Pant adjourned to the local canal inspection House to address the senior officers of the Station. After he had done so, just as the officers assembled there, were going to disperse, he signalled to me for waiting. I knew that Tripathi had carried tales against me to him. So, I was at the time seething with a sense of righteous indignation against Tripathi. Then when the coast was clear, Pt. Pant asked me softly to sit close to him, on doing so, he said to me "Conscientious as you are, how is it that you are not able to get on with Bishambhar Dayal Tripathi?" Owing to the conciliatory manner in which he put me this question, I felt encouraged to say. "Sir If it had been any one other than Tripathi who had made any complaints to you against me, I would have felt hurt. But knowing him as well as I do, it makes not the least difference to me." Then I explained to him how he wanted to be boss over the entire police organisation of the District and how he was at daggers drawn with me for failing to toe the line with him.

Pt. Pant listened to my point and replied, "I know, I know." At the same time he suggested to me that I should try and make up with him, for, in a democracy one had to make certain concessions for an elected representative of the people. Upon this, I told him how it was too late in the day for me to do so, for I had already done four years at Unnao and was expecting a transfer. He then asked me, "How many years service have you put in?" I answered, "Sixteen Years", he appeared to be taken by surprise and quickly remarked, "I will remember it." This brought to an end my meeting with him. I mention this episode as showing how knowledgeable Pt. Pant was and how one could depend on him to give his full support to one, if necessary.

I will now relate how as a sequel to his meeting with Pt. Pant, which was not of my seeking, I was lucky enough to be posted to Faizabad, a plum station which had hitherto been the preserve of Britishers only.

Soon after Pt. Pant's visit to Unnao, I called on Mr. Horton, I.G. Police to have an inkling, if possible, of my next posting. He said he was thinking of Sitapur for me. I told him that Sitapur would not suit me, he said, "What is your idea?". Then I mentioned to him successively, Faizabad, Shahjahanpur or Gorakhpur. He said he had already made up his mind about these stations. Upon this I gave up my case as lost and came away crestfallen. Against this background, therefore, when I received the order of my posting to Faizabad, I had a shock of delight. The most interesting part of this episode is that later when my Range D.I.G. Mr. Hugh Inglis (later Sir) came to Faizabad, he told me how I had missed my posting to Agra which I could not ever dream of. According to him, Mr. Horton had, in putting up his proposals for some of the important charges nominated Biggie who was two to three years junior to me, for his posting to Agra. Pt. Pant, on his part, had deleted his name and mentioned my name in its place. Mr. Horton had then rushed to Pt. Pant to explain him that he had given me Faizabad on my choice. Upon this Pt. Pant had said, "Well then, let Lahiri go to Faizabad." I have mentioned all this if only to show how anxious Pt. Pant was to break the tradition of Britishers only being posted to plum districts.

Pt. Govind Ballabh Pant was a rare type of man with a towering personality. Even the British officers of his time acknowledged his superiority as an administrator of the first order. One characteristic of him was his prodigious memory. Massive of built and slow of movement, he was like a man mountain unruffled and standing four square to the winds. He had sharp penetrating eyes that made people fight shy of him. Although generally very suave of manners, he had a quiet and decisive way of choking off anyone who chose to enter into any argument with him. He could also be caustic at times. Here is a classic example of it. Mr. Marsh Smith (then Food Commissioner), had applied for leave preparatory to retirement on the understanding that on his application being turned down, he would be entitled to post retirement leave on full pay for six months, Pt. Pant saw through the game and since he was not favourably disposed towards Mr. Marsh Smith for his ruthless suppression on the so-called Congress rebellion of 1942, he noted on this case, Mr. Marsh Smith has been working so hard all his life, that I cannot in all conscience refuse him the leave asked for".

Pt. Pant had no caste or communal prejudices. Nor had he any provincial bias, as is borne out by the fact that at one time during his regime, there were as many as seven Bengalees, including me among the Heads of Departments in the State.

He never chose to interfere with the law taking its own course. Nor did he ever allow any extraneous considerations to influence his decision in the matter of postings, promotions and punishments.

A man of few words, he appeared to be somewhat distant and stiff. In short, there can be no doubt that he was a giant of a man, born once in a century, who lived for his work and died a martyr to it. His death can be said to have been heroic. He was then Union Home Minister. One day while he was making a speech in the Lok Sabha on an issue of some importance, he had cerebral haemorrhage and sat down abruptly. Thereafter, when he was brought home, he sent for Mr. P.C. Sen, Law Minister, to dictate some points of the debate to him and while he was doing so, he lost consciousness, which he never regained and finally died.

* * * *

Chapter 28

Believe it or Not

When I was posted as a S.P. Unnao, one Sunday afternoon, I heard a hubbub outside my bungalow which stood opposite the Reserve Police Lines there, with a metalled road separating the two, this was something unusual and so I came out to see what was up. I then saw a recruit constable named Subh Karan Singh running fast, up this road, chased by a number of others. He had a long stick in his hand and his *dhoti* was trailing behind him. He was also ceaselessly uttering a loud wail which sounded something like, O, O, O. But it was not long before he was overtaken by his pursuers and pinned down to the ground. We all thought that he had suddenly gone stark mad. To cool him down, several, bucketfuls of water were poured over his head and at the same time I had a word sent to the Civil Surgeon, Dr. Brahm Dutt to summon him.

Finally, the man became quieter and seemed to improve further with the application of some ice to his head. But the wild look in his eyes was disturbing and so I had him removed to the police Hospital for further treatment. At 8.00 o'clock the same evening, the man again turned violent and on my arrival at his bed side, I found five or six men holding him down. Dr. Brahm Dutt gave him some injections which seemed to make little difference, as he continued to have violent convulsions. At one time it was thought he was suffering from hydrophobia. But the convulsions gradually subsided and the man regained consciousness after some time when he complained of a chill. He had another attack at 2.00 A.M. and, thereafter, the fits came at intervals. In any case, it was clear that it was not a case of hydrophobia, both because he had at intervals been fit enough to take some nourishment and because he denied having ever been bitten by a dog.

On receipt of information of his sickness, Subh Karan Singh's relatives arrived on the following morning. They were convinced that it was a case of visitation by an evil spirit. Hence, they sought the permission of the Civil Surgeon and me to send for a sorcerer (*Ojha*). This man was named Janki who arrived the same evening at about 8.30 or so. When I visited the Police Hospital to see how Subh Karan Singh was doing, I noticed both the Civil Surgeon, Dr. Brahm Dutt, and the Reserve Inspector, named Hayhurst, present there. I also found the *Ojha* trying to appease in some what flattering terms, the alleged spirit who was believed to have descended on Subh Karan Singh. At that time the latter was in the throws of a violent fit, with his eyes upturned, frothing at the mouth and all the muscles of his body taut with exertion.

Now ensued one of the most remarkable scenes that I have ever witnessed. After Janki had been at his job for quite some time, it seemed as if the spirit in answer to his entreaties was making an effort to articulate some words which were far from distinct. But soon we were able to make them out. They were spoken in a deep gutteral voice suggestive of some one vastly different from Subh Karan Singh. Such was my wonder that my hair stood on end and I could hardly believe my ears. The words gradually became more and more distinct and here is a verbatim account of the regular colloquy that went on between the spirit and Janki.

> **Janki:** I have been entreating you for quite some time now to reveal your identity. Do have pity on me and tell me who

you are and why you are harassing this man. I also implore you to have mercy on him and leave him to himself.

Spirit: *Tumhi batao* I will not do so. You may do your worst. I am not an ordinary man. I understand you are a *"neotiha"* (meaning a sorcerer who has come by invitation) now try your skill on me.

Janki: Pray, do not be angry with me. I am no *"neotiha"*. I am a simple rustic. Whosoever you may be, a Muslim or a Hindu, I salute you.

Spirit: You pretend to be a *"Johri"* (one who deals in precious stones and can tell a genuine from a spurious one). So find out for yourself who am I. I am not going to tell you.

Janki: I am not a *Johri* I am merely a simple rustic, I beg of you, again and again, to reveal your identity to enable us to pay our homage to you.

Spirit: I am a *Brahm* (the spirit of a dead Brahmin).

Janki: Well and good. I touch your holy feet. Now, tell us what do you want and how this man has given you cause for offence.

Spirit: He used to swear at me. I will not leave him.

Janki: I entreat you with folded hands to leave him. He has suffered much and paid for his folly. Tell us what we must offer to appease you.

Spirit: I want nothing.

Janki: Here we are all waiting to hear your pleasure. Do please oblige us.

Spirit: I want you to offer me milk, water, *Khatia* (a string cot), sandals and rice.

Janki: Very well. We promise to do so. This very man will take the things to you. But do please let us know your name and abode.

Spirit: I am known as *Bhari Baba.*

Janki: But where do you live?

Spirit: Don't you know me?

Janki: As I told you, I am ignoramus. Do you live somewhere near this man's house?

(In answer to this question the spirit was heard to utter something which sounded like—*Iske ghar se teen kos purab*).

Janki: Do you mean *teen kos* to the east of this man's house?

Spirit: No, no. (This he said somewhat petulantly.) I mean *teen khet* (field) to the east.

Janki: Very well. This very man will go and make the offerings to you.

Spirit: Well, let him do so first next Saturday when I shall leave him.

Janki: I implore you once again to have pity on him. I make a solemn affirmation in the presence of the Kaptan Sahab, the Civil Surgeon Sahab and the Line Sahab who are here, that the offerings you have asked for, will be duly delivered to you.

Spirit: All right.

Janki: Please say this three times.

Spirit: Must I say this three times? Don't you trust me?

Janki: No, no. It is not so.

Spirit: I leave him, I leave him. I leave him.

Janki: Now, will you set this man up on his foot.

(As Janki said this, he patted Subh Karan Singh on the head three times and asked him to get up, which he did.)

Incidentally, the time taken by these dialogues were much longer that would appear from the account of it. In fact, Janki had very often asked the same question repeatedly before he could elicit an answer to it. Another noticeable thing was that when Subh Karan

Singh got up at Janki's command, he looked dazed and much the worse for the trance he had gone through.

Arrangements were promptly made according to the promised offerings taken to *Bhari Baba* at Subh Karan Singh's village in Bahraich. Thereafter, so far as I am aware, his fits did not recur. It so turned but, however, that after some time once in a fit of depression, he attempted to cut his throat with a razor which made me dispense with his services.

Being a non-believer in spooks, I have been unable to understand this, to fathom the mystery behind this most extraordinary episode or to find a rational explanation for it. I can only make a guess in this connection. Was it a case of auto-suggestion which Subh Karan Singh's material body (if there be one) played a leading role?

I am able to recall another incident deserving of mention here, only because of the novelty of it. This is how it goes. One morning in the year 1929 or so, when I was seated in the office room of my residence at Mirzapur, I had a visitor. He was a young man of some 20-25 years of age and fairly well dressed. From his looks and demeanour, I could gather that he probably belonged to a respectable family—I could however see that something was troubling him. On my enquiry as to what I could do for him, he kept mum, but took out a piece of brown paper from his pocket and placed it before me by way of his answer to my query. On scrutiny of this paper I found that it was merely a summons from a court of Law for his attendance on a particular date, as a witness for the prosecution in a petty case of theft. I could at once see that he was needlessly upset over it through his ignorance and so told him soothingly that he had no cause for worry. Thereafter, when I noticed that he was still in some doubt about it, I gave him an assurance that if ever he found himself in trouble he could come to me for help. He went away and I forgot all about him.

It so happened that on the very next day, while I was seated in my regular office, I noticed the same man sitting outside it, with a little boy by his side and from time to time, yelling *Bam-m-a-h-a-d-e-o* in a voice that rang out throughout the buildings. I thought that he had perhaps come to the *Kuchery* on some business of his own and was making this cry through sheer force of habit. But when it was well after 5.00 in the afternoon and I found he was not gone I felt somewhat surprised and asked my *Peshkar* to find out what he wanted. On this return my *Peshkar* told me that the man wanted to see me. This was odd. Still I said to my *Peshkar,* "Call him in."

As soon as that man had my permission to come in, he promptly entered my room. He had a small bundle with him which he had laid open on my table and took out its contents one by one before arranging them neatly on. I noticed that they comprised a variety of articles, such as flowers, bananas, handful of rice, a coconut, etc. that are offered in the worship of a deity. He then dropped on his knees by the side of my table with folded hands and a penitent look written large on his face. I kept on watching his activities, as if spell bound. Then it occurred to me that he was probably demented and saw in me reincarnation of his favourite deity. I felt sorry for him and asked him what he wanted of me. In reply he meekly said, "Nothing," and continued gazing at me with supreme satisfaction. Being anxious to get rid of him, I said to him, "You may go now." Upon this he replied to me. *"Bhagwan,* I have a request to make. I pray that you may give me your *darshan* whenever, I may wish to have it." By now I had already wasted 15 to 20 minutes of my time. So I promptly said, "Your prayer is granted." He then walked away tamely, with his son.

After this, hardly a day or two had passed, when one morning I heard shouts of *Bam Mahadeo* outside my residence. After coming out I saw the same man locked in a combat with my two orderlies. He was arguing with them that I had given him my word for my *Darshan* to him, whenever he desired it. Thereafter, the moment I came up to see him, he became a changed man and fell down on his knees to strike the same old prayerful attitude. I then said to him, "You may go now", which he did, tame as lamb.

This incident gave me some cause for concern for I feared that he felt at any moment of the day or night walk straight into my house in quest of me. I was still considering what I should do in that case, when once again I heard his shout outside my residence.

I purposely avoided meeting him and decided to send for the head of his family. The next day when the latter who happened to be his elder brother came to see me, he told me that ever since the day I had met his younger brother for the first time, it was becoming increasingly difficult to keep him in check, so strong was his desire to meet me. He (the elder brother) was therefore thinking of sending him to Ranchi for treatment. I fully endorsed this idea and I am glad to say that thereafter, I had no more visitations from his younger brother.

In retrospect, I am inclined to think that this youth most likely had a screw loose even before he came to see me for the first time and his malady was unfortunately aggravated by my offer to help him whenever he felt the need for it. My readers may rest assured that I have no pretensions to divinity of any kind.

* * * *

Chapter 29

Mahatma Gandhi Causing Trouble for Me

Between the signing of the Gandhi-Irwin Pact in 1931 and the Quit India Movement of 1942, there was a comparative lull on the political front in India. This was because most of our political leaders found themselves behind the bars during this period and few were left free to carry out on the struggle for Independence, launched by the momentous Congress Resolution of Lahore. The Government of the day on their part, were determined to crush all subversive activities, at first in the name of law and order and later, of the war effort. All this while Mahatma Gandhi kept moving in and out of jail, and such was his popularity that he always attracted large crowds wherever he went necessitating elaborate police arrangements to be made to prevent any mishap.

I am reminded of an incident that relates to an occasion when he was on his way to Lucknow from Kanpur by rail. His train was due to stop at Ajgain in district Unnao of which I was then holding charge as Superintendent of Police. The news had percolated to the remotest corner of this district with the result that the men and women in their thousands turned up at Ajgain to have his *darshan*. Sub-Inspector Suraj Narain Tiwari, the then Station Officer, Ajgain, was in attendance at the Railway Station for the occasion with a number of policemen under him. When the train arrived, Mahatma Gandhi was noticed sitting with a beaming face in the corner seat of a third class compartment. He had a cloth bag in his hand which he held out to the crowd for their donations in cash and kind.

In their anxiety to have a closer view of their idol and also to hand him their gifts personally, the crowd surged forward in ever-increasing numbers towards his carriage. At this stage S.I. Suraj Narain Tiwari intervened to save him from being mobbed. He placed his two arms on the two side posts of the window in front of Mahatma Gandhi and thus created an artificial barrier between him and the crowd. The latter were then forced to remain content with just lobbing over their garlands and gifts from the point they could get to him. Inevitably some of the garlands aimed at Mahatma Gandhi fell short of the mark and even fell on Tiwari who passed them on to him.

After this all went well for sometime, till I had a letter from Mr. R.A. Horton, D.I.G., C.I.D., to say that according to a source-information in his possession, S.I. Tiwari had been seen garlanding the Mahatma and that I should hold an enquiry, preliminary to taking suitable disciplinary action against him.

I must confess, this letter gave me much cause for concern. In the first place because Tiwari was a good officer whom I liked and, in the second place, because I did not see how he could be taken to task for an act that in my judgement did not constitute an offence and ascertain the facts at first hand. I, therefore, pushed off to Railway Station at Ajgain by my car, when I questioned there with the station staff, they gave me a graphic account of all that had passed. I promptly recorded their statements and forwarded them to Mr. Horton along with my finding on the case, exonerating S.I. Tiwari of any such monstrous offence as the garlanding of Mahatma Gandhi. In return for all my pains, all that Mr. Horton had to say was that he had no doubt of the veracity of the source information received by him in this case but that he could see that the officer concerned stood well protected. I knew this was a barb directed at me. But that did not worry me and I was happy that I had been able to save a well meaning officer from coming to a harm at a time when patriotism was held to be a crime.

* * * *

Chapter 30

Two most Embarrassing Moments of Life

Way back to the year 1938, or so, when, one day, I accepted an invitation to a banquet given by the Maharani of Ayodhya in honour of Mr. Lane, President of the Court of Wards, U.P., little did I realise what I was letting myself in for. The invitation included all the Europeans of the station at Faizabad with a few Indians, like my wife and myself, thrown in. It was, on the whole, a gala affair. Everybody at the table seemed to be thoroughly pleased with himself and both conversation as well as drinks flowed freely.

I was sitting opposite an Army Major who commanded a local Artillery unit. Suddenly, he addressed me to say, "Lahiri, do you play Polo?" Not having played the game, I said, "No, I am afraid, I don't." But this made no impact on him and he retorted by saying, "Surely, you have a horse, haven't you?"

At this stage, the Major's wife, who was sitting next to me, intervened to say "My husband is trying to raise a Polo team to which you will be most welcome." I could plainly see that I was fated to be the victim of a conspiracy to rope me in. Yet, in a last bid for escape I said apologetically, "But I am sorry, my horse is not broken in the stick and ball." To this, the Major's simple reply was, "But you and your horse should be able to pick up the game soon enough. We are going to play slow *chukkars* only to start with." With this remark he looked upon the matter as settled and simply added that he would expect me to turn up at the Polo ground the next day at 4.00 P.M. sharp.

The banquet over, the party broke up and we all went home. For my part, although I tried hard during the night to forget all about my next day's engagement, I could not get my mind off the certain catastrophe that seemed to be hanging over my head. I felt disturbed for the greater part of the next day also, till I was due to go and meet my doom. Thereafter, when I reached the Polo ground at the appointed hour, I found my syce waiting there for me, along with my excellent charger. But I was not prepared for the sight that greeted my eyes.

There, stretched the polo ground before me, looking resplendent with its green grass spread out like a carpet, the goal posts and the markers all in position and a group of British Army Officers, stick in hand, some wearing red, some white slip overs, exercising their ponies on it, like mad. Obviously, the stage was set for a regular match between the two teams. As if in confirmation of my conjecture, a Subaltern of the Gunners presently walked up to me and held out a red slip over for me to wear. At this stage I wanted to mention that if I say that my heart went into my boots, would be no exaggeration. What added to my discomfiture still more, was the sight of the entire female population of the local European community, their knittings in hand, seated under a *Shamiana,* to witness the game. In my unenviable position I would have given anything to get out of the hole in which, willy-nilly, I found myself landed. But there was no line of escape now open to me and I had do accept my fate with a smile on my face.

Soon the gong sounded for the match to begin and henceforth I was led in my conduct more by intuition than by my knowledge of the game. Some one said I was to play as number three. I then noticed the two teams making an effort to draw up in two single files half way between the goalposts and at right angles to one of the side lines. This I took as a cue for me to move into position among the reds, which I did without much difficulty.

Facing us was Mr. Sheriff, the referee, seated on horseback, ball in hand, poised for a throw. The moment he threw the ball in his hand, a state of chaos set in, with everybody bent on riding off everybody else. After a while, when it somehow got detached from the jumble of men and horse, I found it lying temptingly in front of me. Instinctively, I took a swipe at it with my stick and, much to my delight, found it tearing away from me. I then gave it a chase and, as I did so, I heard the rest of the cavalcade thundering after me. Quite undeterred, I took a swipe at it for a second time and, lo and behold. I managed to hit it again, although unmindful of the direction in which I was required to send it.

By now, my horse seemed to have had enough of the game and he simply refused to cooperate with me further. He reared and bucked and then dashed across the field, this way and that, like a perfect fiend. With the polo stick in my right hand, I had only my left hand free to pull at his reins. Therefore, no matter how hard I tried to curb his spirit, I failed to do so. He continued to give an exhibition of his mettle in full view, as it were, of the gallery and quite independently of the game that was proceeding in another part of the field with which he and I had no connection any more. In an effort to keep my prancing steed under some sort of a check, I felt a void in my stomach and a lump in my throat, with my tongue gone quite dry.

I have no idea of the time that passed before the gong sounded for the close of play—All I can say is that on termination of the game, I felt as happy as any school boy does dashing for home at the close of the day's work. Thank heavens I was not invited again to play any more slow *chukkars* of the kind which I had experienced.

There is another episode of my life—Again, during the period of my posting at Faizabad—that was equally, more, embarrassing for me.

One day during this period, I had come to Lucknow for a personal work. My host for the occasion was my old friend, Mr.

R.N. De an I.C.S. a keen tennis player, much above the average in his proficiency at his game. On this very account, instead of joining the Oudh Gymkhana or the Mohammad Bagh Club, where he could at best expect to meet second class players, he had joined the Rifah-i-am Club for the sake for the high class tennis to be had there.

On the afternoon of my visit, wishing to give me a good time, Mr. De asked me if I was interested in playing serious, as opposed to what he termed social tennis. In my anxiety to show myself off as a player of no mean order, I unhesitatingly expressed my preference for the former, which made him take me to his Club, duly equipped with a spare racket of his. But when we arrived there, I had the shock of my life to find that I required to play a doubles match in partnership with my friend, against Ghaus Mohammd and Jasbir Singh. Ghaus Mohammad was in those days seeded as among the world's best eight tennis players and as India's number one, while Jasbir Singh had made a name for himself as one of the best doubles players of our country, having annexed the All India Lawn Tennis Double's title more than once.

It was quite natural for me, I felt unnerved at the very sight of these giants pitted against me and whatever little skill I had acquired over the years, through playing odd games of mixed doubles and those, too, of the social variety, at Mufassil stations of my posting, seemed to evaporate, leaving me a total wreck at the mercy of my opponents. But not it was too late in the day for me to back out. So I steeled myself as best I could to face them. For their part, they took no time to get the measure of me, with the result that the match soon degenerated into an one sided affair, in spite of the herculean efforts of my partner to make up by his dash and daring, for my poor play.

Partly from a sense of shame for the sorry figure I was cutting and partly from the exertion I was making to go all out, I found myself perspiring from every pore of my body, as also doing everything in the wrong way. This made me fervently pray for my ordeal being soon over. And when at long last, after what appeared to be ages, it did come to close, I heaved a sigh of relief, such as I had never done it before.

* * * *

Chapter 31

Shahji of Lucknow

During the course of my posting at Faizabad, one morning my Reserve Inspector Mohammad Siddiq informed me of the loss of a 303 Rifle from his Armoury. When I informed him that I would have to send a special report to my Range D.I.G. Police and at the same time institute an enquiry of my own, to fix the responsibility for the loss, he begged to me to give him some time to enable him to consult a certain *Shahji* of Lucknow who was reputed to have some occult powers. I readily granted him his request, although I felt certain that this would mean sheer waste of time.

I had actually given up the rifle as lost and therefore felt greatly surprised when a couple of days later, Mr. Siddiq turned up at my residence, accompanied by *Shahji* and placed it before me. The account he gave of the recovery was something like this. *Shahji* desired him to buy him some sweets. With these he (*Shahji*) went to the river bank at Guptar Ghat and the first thing he did was to draw a few drops of blood from a slit in his forehead made by him with the help of a penknife he had with him. These he threw into the river along with the sweets, at the same time saying, "I have done my utmost for thee. It is now thy turn to do thy best for me." These words *Shahji* addressed to an invisible spirit familiar to him, On his return from the river bank, he was busy making arrangements for his return journey, when a man rushed in to say that the missing rifle had been found abandoned, covered with mud under a culvert in front of the quarter guard. All is well that ends well. Therefore I did not consider it necessary to pursue the case any more. In fact the entire episode of the recovery struck me as a huge joke and I put it down merely to the holy fear of the old *Faqir* from Lucknow that had induced the culprit in this case to dig it out of its hiding place and then place it under the culvert in front of the quarter Guard where it was sure to be discovered.

As always happens in a case like this, its novelty soon wore out and there were no discussion about *Shahji* till some six months later, when the wife of the Dy. Commissioner, Mr. S.S.L. Dar, happened to lose her pearl necklace one afternoon in the local ladies' Club. The occurrence caused quite a stir and the local police put up their best efforts to trace it, but in vain. It was then that my Deputy, Abdul Rashid Khan, thought of requisitioning the services of *Shahji* and also arranged to have him fetched from Lucknow.

Shahji was a man of God, fairly advanced in years besides being blind. He also appeared to be very meek and submissive. On being led by hand into Mr. Dar's sitting room, he preferred to squat on the floor, instead of sitting on a chair. Thereafter, having heard the facts of the case, he placed the palm of his right hand on the ground in front of Mrs. Dar and said very meekly, "will the *Rani Saheba* be pleased to put her right foot on this palm of mine?" On her doing so he asked her name. She said "Kamla". He then asked after a pause, "does the *Rani Saheba* remember if among the ladies present in the Club on the afternoon of the occurrence, there was one wearing sari of the colour of *Phalsa*?" In answer to this question, Mrs. Dar replied in the affirmative after some reflection and the interview was over. But before *Shahji* left he asked to be given a piece out of any old garment Mrs. Dar had been wearing next to her person and also a sum of Rs. 13/-. This he said he would need to meet the expenses over a *tonga* he would have to engage in Lucknow for thirteen days to take him to the Gomti for the performance of certain rites by him. Another request he made was someone should write to him from time to time acquaint him with the substance of any dreams Mrs. Dar might have. This Mr. Khan offered to do.

After this, some weeks, even months rolled-by without developments of any kind and I lost all interest in the case. The necklace had been lost in the month of October and now we were half through April when, one afternoon it so happened that a few of us were relaxing in the open after a game of tennis at Mr. Dar's residence. I was then sitting next to Mrs. Dar. It occurred to me to ask her if lately she had any dreams. I did it only banteringly. In reply she said to me cheerfully, "Oh, yes, this very afternoon while I was resting, I had a delicious dream. I saw my maid coming towards me with my missing necklace in hand and shouting *mil gaya* which made me dance with joy."

While Mrs. Dar was thus relating her dream to me, I heard a shout of "*mil gaya, mil gaya*" coming from the far end of the ground on which we were sitting and as I looked in that direction I saw Mrs. Dar's *mali*, who had necklace in his hand approaching us with a host of others. The next thing he did was to place it on the table in front of us; He said it had been found by the *mali* of the ladies' club under a bush in the club compound. How it came to be there is a mystery to this day. But what is even more mysterious is the coincidence in point of time between Mrs. Dar's narration of her dream and the appearance of her *mali* on the scence which is borne out in this case.

Was it not Hamlet who once said "There are more things in Heaven and Earth, Horatio than dreamt of in your philosophy."

* * * *

Chapter 32

Ram Dass' Escape from Jail

There is nothing unusual about an occasional escape from jail. But sometimes it causes a sensation, either because of the importance of the escapee or the means adopted by him to effect his escape. It is said Shivaji escaped from confinement ordered by Aurangzeb on the head of a porter in a basket meant for carriage of sweets. While Chandra Shekhar Azad, a well-known freedom fighter of recent times, once smuggled himself out of prison, hidden in a drum used for the disposal of night soil. Little is, however, known to the outside world of the method adopted by Ram Dass of Tanda in district Faizabad, to contrive his escape from prison, though it was equally ingenious.

This man came to my notice, on a date in September 1939, when he was brought up before me, at Faizabad for interrogation. He was not much to look at and gave me the impression of being like any other country bumpkin without any intelligence. I had been informed that he had been arrested on a charge of vagrancy. But that he wished to confess to a case of serious burglary committed by him jointly with a number of others. When questioned by me, he not only repeated his tale, but also offered to surrender his share of the stolen property which, he said, he had kept buried in a sugarcane field at the outskirts of his village. I, therefore, promptly put him in my car, along with the Station Officer Tanda and proceeded to his village. On our arrival there after a couple of hours or so, he took us from place on the pretext of looking for the spot where the stolen property, he had promised to surrender, lay buried. After some play-acting like this, he gave up the attempt, saying that somebody must have removed it. The expression on his face on this occasion feigning both surprise and grief, was made for a perfect study. Anyway, there was nothing one could do in that circumstances. So I came away thoroughly disgusted with whole show, leaving it with the Station Officer to deal with him further. He was duly put up for trial on a charge of vagrancy and awarded rigorous imprisonment for one year.

After this, some weeks passed till one day I was informed that Ram Dass had staged a *Satyagrah* inside jail, as a protest against the jailer for his rough handling of him. The method he had adopted to express his resentment was unique. Taking advantage of a tall mango tree that stood in the inner enclosure of the jail, he had climbed up to one its topmost forks, to sit there with a noose around his neck and threaten to hang himself in case nothing was done to redress his grievance. There he sat hour after hour like a *Yogi,* impervious to the entreaties of the jail and other officials to him to come from his perch. The Jailer came first, then the Superintendent of Jail and when they failed to make any impact on him, they passed the buck in turns to the City Magistrate and the District Magistrate, but all in vain. In this way full forty eight hours passed before Ram Dass consented to come down to solid earth from his perch on the tree top. Once he was down, the Jailer to teach him a lesson for his tomfoolery ordered his confinement in a solitary cell by night. This happened in October and all went well till the month of December when an alarm was sounded announcing his escape.

I was one among the first who turned up to make an enquiry into the case. The cell in which Ram Dass had been locked up for the night was, I noticed, at an end one of six such cells in a row which stood inside a walled enclosure. It had a gaping hole in its outer wall, just big enough for a man to pass through. The material from this hole had been neatly arranged inside the cell and covered up by a piece of cloth to give the impression of a man lying there. A few of the bricks, dislodged from the wall lay on top of one another against one of the surrounding walls to make a foot hold for scaling it. A long bamboo pole made up of two smaller poles tied together, lay hidden in an outer drain of the jail.

Further investigation revealed that this was a case of escape behind which there had been much systematic planning over a long period of time, of which only a master mind was capable to do it. To begin with, Ram Dass had arranged his allotment for labour to a shed in which there were various building materials, ready at hand. From there he had quietly helped himself to picked an iron spike some six inches long, and smuggled it into his cell. Thereafter, he had been busy, several nights, dislodging one by one with the help of this spike, the bricks that made up one of the outer walls of his cell. We had to work both patiently and diligently to make a hole big enough for his purpose. In order not to give any suspicion against him he took care to put them back daily in their old place, till the digging was completed.

Once the hole was ready, Ram Dass made a neat pile of the dislodged bricks in the shape of a human being lying on the ground covered it up with his own *dhoti* before slipping out of his cell at the dead of night. His next step was to provide himself with a substitute for the *dhoti* he was leaving behind him. This he did by slipping in his hand through the iron grill of an adjoining cell and whisking away a piece of turban cloth from under the head of a man who lay fast asleep in it. Thus clad he scaled the boundary wall of his cell with the aid of the bricks he had placed against it. On the other side of the wall lay another enclosure with a work shed in it. He scaled to the top of this building to remove some of its tiles and through the opening, thus made, to let himself into it. Having done so, he helped himself to a couple of bamboo shafts and some rope to improvise a long pole with which to clear the formidable looking outer perimeter wall of the jail. For him this was easy. For he had made a close study of the topography of the entire area from his perch on the tree top, which gave him a grand stand view of it, as also of the movements of the sentries, who were required to patrol the perimeter wall. His so called *Satyagraha*, it was now clear, formed part of a scheme for his escape which Ram Dass had worked out in his mind after much deliberation.

The problem now was how to lay this master tactician by the heel. I had a hunch that he must first go to his village and hang around it for some time before clearing off in a bid for safety. The chances were that he would cross over to the other side of the Sarju which flowed past his village. On this presumption, therefore, I made arrangements for a strict watch being kept on a ferry that regularly plied from a *ghat* near the village. In addition I also arranged for a couple of constables in disguise to act as helpers to the man who was in charge of this ferry. Now began a game of waiting till one morning Ram Dass unsuspectingly came into the trap laid for him. This was a remarkable achievement for the police, even though the man thus tracked down was neither Shivaji nor Chandra Shekhar Azad, or famous Laiq Ali of Hyderabad. Given the opportunity Ram Dass might have done very well in life, but unfortunately for him it was so ordained that he should spend another term of imprisonment, this time for three years, on a charge that was much more serious than the one for which he had been previously convicted.

* * * *

Chapter 33

A Chance Encounter

One evening in the year 1941 or so at about 9.00, when I was Chief of the Crime Branch of the C.I.D., U.P. my wife and I were seated in our drawing room after dinner, having a chat. Suddenly, I noticed a man, apparently a European in a white shirt and white shorts, but without any shoes, standing against a door opening into the room. He had some scratches on his body and was seemingly out of breath. The time was during the Second World War, so I took him for a Tommy who had got drunk. Feeling slightly alarmed, I ordered him to clear out. But instead of doing so, he struck on exceedingly apologetic attitude and after some deep bowings, this is how he delivered himself, "*Ah, ah, ah,* you, you—Indian gentlemen? *I—I*—Italian prisoner of war—you gentleman?"

Who he was and what he wanted was now crystal clear obviously, he had escaped from custody and desired my protection, not knowing that he had come to the wrong man, one who was duty bound to hand him into custody. After some quick thinking and wishing not to cause him any alarm, I asked him to sit down first. Thereupon he lowered himself into the nearest chair and went on to say, "I, I, no home, no home, for years, prison, prison, sentry, sentry, all round. I—run—I come here—you, gentleman?" What he could not express by words he expressed by signs.

As the man was still in a state of excitement, I decided to offer him a drink and asked what he would like to have. He asked for whisky which I did not have. Then I fetched from our cupboard two bottles of vermouth an Italian, the other French, and held them up before him. On seeing them, he jumped up excitedly and pointing to the Italian bottle exclaimed, "This, this, my home, my home, my country." Thus, indicating his preference in no uncertain manner. After he had finished his drink, I asked him to follow me, which he did like a lamb. I then took him to my garage and asked him to sit down in the rear compartment of my car. At this he moved his arm vigorously before his person a number of times, meaning thereby that he would like to have a piece of cloth to cover himself up. I told him that he would be all right without it, then he tamely climbed in, but, poor man, instead of depositing himself in the rear seat of my car, lay down in a crouching position on its floor board to make himself invisible.

I next drove him to the nearest police station at Hazratganj, all the time feeling heavy at heart for having to play false with him. The moment we reached there and he saw the large number of policemen assembled at the spot, his face clouded over. But there was nothing he could do. So he sat down on a chair by my side, looking the very picture of misery.

Thereafter, while I informed the police station staff how the man had dropped into my house, they told me how they had been carrying on a frantic search for him. Possibly from the respectful manner in which these men were addressing me, he inferred that I must be a Policeman of some standing. Therefore, looking at me questioningly he said, "You, you, Police Chief?" On my answering him in the affirmative, his face brightened up and slapping his forehead with both hands he exclaimed, "Oh, my for-choon". This change in his expression caused no small relief to me and I expressed my regret to him for having had to give him up. This he seemingly understood and thus we parted as friends.

* * * *

Chapter 34

A Trek to Yatung

Sitting astride the Himalayas at an altitude of some 15,000 feet on the north-east border of India with Tibet, the two mountain passes, Nathula and Jelapla have for centuries past, served as important connecting links between the two countries. Unfortunately, they are not open to traffic now, but I am reminded of a walking tour I had in 1943, along with my younger brother and my elder son, when this was not the case and when we crossed the Nathula on our onward journey from Kalimpong to Yatung and the Jelapla on our way back from Yatung to Kalimpong.

That was a round trip covering some 165 miles which we did in a fortnight's time by easy marches, ranging from ten to fifteen miles a day. Before setting out we took good care to stock ourselves with enough provisions to last us the whole of our journey. We also hired a pack-mule to carry all this stuff which combined with our beddings and articles of daily wear, made quite a respectable pile. For our mule driver we had a Tibetan lad who proved to be more than his money's worth.

Our first day's march from Kalimpong, a Sub-Divisional town of Darjeeling, took us to Pedons. We found the road fairly level for most part of the way and the landscape picturesque, made up of green meadows dated with fir trees. Incidentally, it was at the dak bungalow here that we had our first experiment at cooking. As was but natural for us, we slipped up by putting too much salt in our vegetable curry. Although to deal with a situation like this, was not in our line, it occurred to us to dilute the stuff with good deal of water as a first step and, thereafter, to strain out the excess water. In this way we managed to make a vegetable soup of some sort as a bye-product and at the same time to cure the curry of its fault. When we finished our meal, we slept like a log to wake up only the next morning, quite refreshed and ready to hit the road once again.

The task of packing up of all our belongings at the commencement of our journey each day, devolved on our Tibetan mule driver. Always on his toes, he was ever ready to lend us a helping hand with a smile on his face. We also admired him for the ease with which he scaled the steepest of gradients. If there was any stream to be negotiated on the way, he would take off his clothes, put them on the mule and take a plunge to swim across to the other bank, no matter how cold the water might be. On these occasions, he struck me as another Caliban whose dash and daring left me gaping.

From Pedong we first marched to Pakyong and then to Gangtok. The road that time lay mostly through a forest country and was shady, which was a great relief after our experience of the previous day when we were much troubled by the sun. The travelling, however, was pretty stiff, alternating between an ascent uphill and a descent down-dale, all the way. On this very account a trek in the mountains can be very fatiguing. But the beauty of it is that howsoever tired one may feel at the end of the day, one is sure to find oneself fully refreshed after a night's rest. While this is largely due to the bracing mountain air which acts as a powerful antidote against fatigue, I am sure the quiet that envelops one at night has something to do with it. Even the murmur of a rivulet in the distance, seemingly helps to emphasise the quiet which has to be experience to be realised.

The forests we passed were composed of a variety of trees, some good as timber and others as having a market value of their own.

I saw some of which the bark called *bhurjapatra* was freely used for writing in the olden days. We also saw some cinnamon trees of which the leaves being scented are in common use for flavouring.

During our march, we once saw a venomous snake of dark grey colour crossing the track in front of us like a streak of lightening. This caused us no small alarm and we were careful enough afterwards to keep clear of the undergrowth, for fear of disturbing one in its sleep.

A thing that particularly attracted our notice, was a chain of grocery shops owned by Marwaris from Calcutta, at select spots all along the route. To be able to live in isolation, hundreds of miles away from home, we thought called for a rare type of courage on their part. Locally known as *Chayeces* they also acted as money-lenders at exorbitant rates of interest and this perhaps explains how this term has, in common parlance, come to stand for a usurer of the worst type.

Like Kalimpong, Gangtok is another very pretty township, but with an old world look. From there we walked to Kerpongong which stands on a ridge at a height of 9,000 feet. Far below to our right, stretching up to the horizon, stood in serried ranks, the very hills we had crossed, all clothed with the foliage of vegetation while to our left, like a gigantic wall almost touching the sky and entirely blocking the view beyond, stretched an arm of the mighty mountain we had set out to cross.

Our next halting place was Changu of which the altitude is some 12,000 feet. The dak bungalow here stands in a basin facing a lake. Along the edge of this lake, were to be seen tiny wild flowers which with their variegated colours made a carpet of a rare design. Like the road from Gangtok to Karponong, the one from Karponong, to Changu turned out to be a melange at places hewn out of the rock surface of the gigantic cliffs, hundreds of feet above the yawning gorge below. The entire landscape to our right, with the hills and hillocks, its rivers and rivulets hundreds of feet below and bathed and doubly distilled sunlight, presented a picture hard to forget. Likewise the scenery to our left, composed of numerous streams of the purest white, cascading down the mountain side and countless varieties of flora clothing it, was no less captivating. Among the latter there were orchids of delicate shades which seemed destined as the poet has said, "to blush unseen in the mountain (if not desert) air."

Curiously enough, in each of the mountain streams, we noticed a prayer wheel of varying size, inscribed with the Tibetan prayer *"Om Mani Padma Hum"* (Hail jewel of the lotus), constantly revolving with the impact of the water pounding on it. Here in India and elsewhere, the religious minded use a rosary to say their prayers. But, the Tibetans obviously thought of a labour saving device to do the same work for them.

I should add that any casual observer in Sikkim or Tibet can see how the practice of religion takes priority over all other occupations. This accounts for the presence in both these territories of numerous *gompas* or monasteries which are almost invariably situated in the most picturesque and commanding positions. In Tibet, it is said, no less than one sixth of the population are priests and practically every family in the land has at least one of its male members serving as a Lama.

A prominent feature of many of these gompas is a gigantic prayer wheel with millions of prayers on it which are believed to be wafted heavenwards with its each rotation. I saw one measuring some ten to twelve feet in diameter, being rotated slowly on its axis with the help of connecting rod by a blind woman hired to do this job by some one desirous of earning merit by proxy for himself.

Surrounding many of the monasteries are to be seen lofty poles to which are attached strips of a printed cloth. These are the famous prayer flags and every time they flutter in the wind, the prayers printed on them are believed to be wafted heavenwards for the benefit of the persons who fixed these poles. Prayer flags are also to be seen in the mountain passes to propitiate the spirits of the storms and the mountains and to ensure safe passage for all travellers.

We saw an abundance of firs, pines, larches, rhododendrons and spruce between Karponong and Changu. I had never seen such a variety of rhododendrons as I saw in northern Sikkim. Each mountain slope had its own particular shade of flowers carried on trees and shrubs ranging from some forty feet to only a few inches in height, the plant becoming smaller as the altitude increased. I saw thick clusters of them on the wayside, which with their colours of various shades, made the spot on which they stood, look like a garden of paradise. Pretty little birds constantly flitted from bush to bush, free from all fear and added to its beauty.

Enroute we passed several convoys of pack animals, mostly sheep and goats, tripping along merrily with their loads evenly balanced on their back. Tun-a-ling, ting-a-ling, ting-a-ling, rang their bells, making a music extremely soothing to the ear. As I listened to it, I said to myself who knows but that a time may come when these innocent beasts will be supplanted by huge honking motor vehicles as symbol of our progress. To come to think of it, what I apprehended has actually come to pass in regions which at one time echoed to the footsteps of only man and his domestic animals.

After we had covered some distance from Changu, we found the ground all around carpeted with a thick layer of snow and covered by a haze which made visibility so poor. On top of this, there was not a soul in sight. We were now crossing the Nathula Pass. To avoid snow-blindness we were wearing dark glasses. We trudged on and on, but the progress we were making was painfully slow. To add to our sense of loneliness, which was becoming increasingly oppressive, we noticed a number of carcasses of dead mules that had fallen by the wayside, unwept and unsung, in the service of humanity and had remained there undisturbed for months. Thanks to providence, suddenly through the surrounding mist caught a fleeting glimpse at some distance above us, of a cairn with a cluster of the inevitable prayer flags fluttering. We instantly knew it marked the summit of the Pass and this acted as a booster for our flagging spirits and made us hasten our pace. Once we reached to the top, all became easy afterwards.

On our downward journey from Nathula Pass, we derived a feeling of companionship with a snow capped mountain peak named Chumalhari, which raised its massive head in front of us. Its view was enchanting. I have no idea of how and when it came to be named so. Towering head and shoulders above all the other mountain peaks by its side, it can certainly claim the distinction of kissing the very heavens, as its name signifies. The sight this hoary headed mountain with the evening light playing on it, presented against the background of a sky of the purest blue, was, for me, one never to be forgotten.

It was almost dusk when we arrived at Champithong our next halt. I was feeling so spent up that I sat down for a while, all on a heap, in the front verandah of the dak bungalow there, to recover my breath. Thereafter, I staggered into the room facing this verandah, hastily unrolled my holdall and flung myself on it, dressed as I was, unmindful of the odds and ends of articles embedded in it. If mine was not a bed of thorns, it was something akin to it, although I was quite oblivious of it. When I felt a little better, I lifted myself from my horizontal position and got busy with the preparation of our meal. We were all anxious to turn in as soon as possible and the moment we did so we were fast asleep.

Early next morning, as we were getting ready to proceed on our journey to Yatung, we had a caller, a British Captain of the Army Medical Corps who was on his way back from distant Lhasa. He enquired if we needed any help from him, which was indeed very nice of him. A remarkable thing about this officer was his smart turn-out. He probably carried a spare kit with him in his rucksack. Even though, I thought it was surprising how he managed to keep himself so spruce on a trek that must have taken him weeks to cover.

The countryside between Champithong and Yatung which now lay through Tibet, turned out to be one of the loveliest I have seen. It is grassy and wooded. We passed many a glade full of wild strawberries. No wonder, that we could not resist the temptation of picking them to our hearts content and were thus delayed on the way.

Yatung a small township Tibet is situated in a lovely valley at a height of some 10,000 ft. Through the heart of this valley, which cannot be more than five to six hundred yards at its widest point, runs a stream with crystal clear water. On either side of this stream, there were lush fields of wheat and barley which looked golden with their ripening ears. Above these fields and on the hillside, there were plantations of apples, pears, apricots, plums and cherries, which being in their flowering season, were at their best. Their effect was heightened by numberless butterflies of all the hues of the rainbow, making merry among them. The local women folk with their pink cheeks and children with their chubby faces seemed only to accentuate the loveliness of the place.

We called on the Indian Trade Agent at Yatung who lived in solitary glory in his lovely mansion surrounded by fruit and flowering trees. Close by, there were a number of barracks for a Company of Indian troops posted there as his military escort. We were given to understand that there were similar establishments elsewhere also in Tibet, to guard our trade and other interests. Unfortunately, they have all been withdrawn now, leaving the Chinese in supreme control there.

Having spent a night at Yatung we set out on our return journey, this time via Jelapla Pass. On the way we first halted at Kupup and then successively at Gnatong, Sedonchen, Ari and Pedong. Jelapla with its massive head of snow, we thought was a sight for the gods. One inspiring thing about it was that at intervals it let lose from its height thousands of tons of snow and rubble which came crashing down its slopes with a noise that was ear splitting. We could see this from a safe distance, while lodged comfortably in the dak bungalow at Kupup, some two and a half miles away.

I had a strange experience at night here, and felt a choking sensation which made me wake up. The first thing I did was to throw open the window by my side to let in fresh air straight from the Jelapla, which gave me the desired relief. I cannot say for certain what this uneasiness was due to, but it is possible that it was caused by the rarefied atmosphere of the place which stood at a height of some 13000 feet.

Our arrival at Kupup coincided with the full moon. Therefore the Jelapla draped in the purest white, with the moon been playing on it, looked to us more like a phantom than a reality, when we cast our eyes on it.

Our trek from Kupup to Gnatong remains memorable for the taste we had of the elements in the course of it. All was clear at the commencement of our journey for the day. But after a time the sky became suddenly overcast and it started raining. Never before in my life had I experienced such a torrential rain as I did on this occasion. It poured and poured with ever increasing fury, till the road in front of us was converted into a gushing stream which brought with it in its mad onward rush, much of rubble. The frequent clapping of thunder, coupled with the shrieking noise the trees made in their life and death struggle with the prevailing tempest, created pandemonium hard to equal. In the absence of any shelter close by, there was nothing one could do beyond waiting for the rage of the elements to subside. It is written somewhere, "after winter cometh spring". We fully realised the truth of this saying, when the clouds cleared up as abruptly as they had gathered, to reveal a landscape that lit up by the benevolent sun-god above looked glorious. We were landscape that lit up by the benevolent sun-god above looked glorious. We were soaked to the skin and were shivering with the cold when we reached at Gnatong. But a hot cup of coffee put us right in no time.

Our next halting place was Sidonochen which stands at a height of some 9,500 feet from sea level. From a spot a mile or two from Gnatong one can have a wonderful view of the Kanchanjungha to the west and the plains of India spread out like a carpet to the east.

The gradient of the road from Sedonchen to Ari is very steep, particularly between Lungtan and Lingtu which are connected by a veritable staircase of cobbles set in a dilapidated causeway built ages ago. We had literally to pick our way on this stretch of the road to avoid a sprained feet.

Another march of some eight miles from Ari through tropical jungle country took us to Pedonge. In this leg of the journey and in the one between Pedong and Kalimpong the heat was oppressive. While it is true that there was no one to meet greet and garland us on our arrival at our journey's end there we were filled with a sense of achievement that made up for the toil and trouble we had undergone in the course of it.

* * * *

Chapter 35

Theft from a Regimental Armoury

We received an information from Lucknow of the theft of a batch of seven service revolvers from the armoury of the 10th/7th Rajput Regiment at Fatehgarh, it was at once put down to these hypothetical men who, it was thought, were prowling about the country, bent on mischief. Necessarily, such important investigation had to be carried out by the CID and that is how I came into the picture in my capacity as head of its Investigation Branch.

On my arrival at the spot, I was amazed to find how the theft had taken place under the very nose of three sentries, two of them mounting guard over the Armoury itself and a third over the quarter guard, only a few paces away. It was also apparent that the offender or offenders had made use of a duplicate key to gain access into the Armoury, apart from taking advantage of an *Arhar* field behind the armoury to come within close range of it without being seen.

Along with Lt. Kuldeep Singh, Adjutant of the Regiment, I

interrogated a fairly large number of men belonging to the Regiment, but unfortunately, could not succeeded. The next course open to us was to arrange for the censorship of all incoming letters, just in case any of them provided a clue. Hardly had a fortnight passed when Lt. Kuldeep Singh came across a letter that looked suspicious. It was addressed to Naik Rampal Singh by one Ram Lakhan Singh of village Barbatpur in Police Circle, Pihani in Hardoi district and stated, among other things, that the latter was awaiting Rampal Singh's return home to take charge of the stuff consigned to the writer's care.

Straightaway, we got busy interrogating Rampal Singh. But he proved to be hard nut to crack and we, therefore, decided to interrogate another man, a recruit named Ujagar Singh who belonged to the same village as Rampal Singh. He was a lad of about 18 years, who had enlisted only a couple of months earlier at the same time when Ram Lakhan Singh, had resigned and gone home.

At first this lad also pleaded his innocence. But he soon broke down not only to confess his knowledge of the theft, but also offered to take us to his village where the stolen revolvers were kept hidden. According to him, Rampal Singh and Ram Lakhan Singh, were the other two culprits in this case and their idea was to use the revolvers for the commission of dacoities, for which Hardoi was notorious in those days. Here is the rest of the story in Ujagar Singh's own words:

> "The theft was actually committed by Rampal Singh once while he was on sentry duty at the quarter guard, he managed to take an impression of the key to the armoury, hung up at the quarter guard along with other keys. He then had made a duplicate key. On the night of the occurrence, all the three of us took advantage of an *Arhar* field to move unobserved within a few feet of the armoury. Thereafter, Rampal Singh slipped into it at an opportune moment when the two sentries over it, were out of sight.
>
> Having thus got inside the Armoury, Rampal Singh helped himself to the seven revolvers which lay on a box there and tied them up in a piece of cloth before making his exit. He then

carried the bundle to a quiet spot on the bank of the Ganga, where he buried it in our presence and where it remained for some ten days. Meanwhile, Ram Lakhan Singh had tendered his resignation and as soon as he was free to go home, he left taking with him the stolen revolvers."

By the time Ujagar Singh had finished his statement, it was past midnight and the next thing to do was to take him to his village and confront him with Ram Lakhan Singh. The idea of a journey in the month of January at that time of night to an obscure place was by no means alluring. But my spirits were fully buoyed up by the prospect of a recovery that would make history in the annals of the CID. So, exactly, at 1 o'clock at night I set out on my car, a brand new Ford V8 of 30 horsepower, along with a number of others. There were altogether nine of us including Ujagar Singh seated in the car and we managed to get along without any mishap, although the road, and the Shahjahanpur, which lay on our way, was abominable and we had to cross two rivers, the Ganga and the Ramganga which were on our way. A thing that helped us was the moon which shed a refulgent light over the entire countryside and made it look like a day.

During the course of this nocturnal journey of ours it occurred to me to ask Ujagar Singh how he felt. This was primarily because I wanted to keep him in good humour and also because I thought it was perhaps for the first time that he had an occasion to travel in a motor vehicle much less a four-wheeler like mine. In answer to my question he promptly said he felt like one riding the air, which I thought was quite clever of him. I could also infer from his reply that he was thoroughly enjoying this trip, for the very novelty of it, if nothing else. Except for this minor exchange of pleasantry between the two of us, all of us kept mum the whole night, as if by a mutual understanding, so as not to disturb the spell that appeared to have been cast over us.

At about 2.30 in the morning we reached Shahjahanpur and from there took the road to Sitapur where we arrived at dawn, I filled up the petrol tank here, before proceeding on our onward journey first to Bilgram and then to village Babatpur where we arrived at about

9.00 in the morning. I might mention it here that I took turns with my driver at the steering wheel of my car all the way from Fatehgarh.

Fortunately for us, we found Ram Lakhan Singh at home. And now began another spell of interrogation lasting for some three hours before our efforts bore fruit and Ram Lakhan Singh took us to a field where he had hidden the stolen revolvers and where we found them neatly tucked away in a hole in the ground.

But my story does not end here. Being anxious to return home as soon as possible, I left Pihani at about 12 noon. As I had nothing to eat since the previous evening, I uprooted a sugarcane stick from a neighbouring field and sucked its juice for whatever little satisfaction this could give me in my famished state. I had to go for some distance over a *kucha* road, before hitting the highway to Hardoi. But, unfortunately, I got stuck in midway by an earthen ridge on the ground which had formed up in course of time between the two wheel tracks of bullock-carts passing that way. This meant a delay of another hour or so, for me, since I had to get hold of a man with a spade, to remove the obstruction in my way before I could proceed any further.

On my arrival at Hardoi at about 4.00 in the afternoon I made a beeline for the SP's Bungalow where in the absence of Mr. B.B.S. Jetly, I was received by Mrs. Jetly who treated me with a couple of *Laddoos* made of *Besan* which I relished as never before. Soon after, I again set out on my onward journey to Lucknow, being anxious not to miss a dinner, which was scheduled for the next day at the Government House there to which I had been invited.

This time I went for some distance by a regular highway to hit a canal road which went past Lucknow. But again, unfortunately for me, before I realised my mistake I took a wrong turn and went for some distance up the canal instead of the other way. This meant a delay of another hour or so for me.

Thereafter, when I reached to the village Mohan I noticed that the indicator of my petrol tank was very close to the danger mark. So, instead of proceeding further down the canal, I took the *pucca* road to Malihabad which branched off from there. In short, when I reached Malihabad, it was close to 3.00 o'clock in the morning. The next thing I did was to go to the Police Station there and wake up the officer-incharge who managed to obtain for me a bottle or two of petrol by having it siphoned off the petrol tank of a motor bus parked there for the night.

The distance from Malihabad to Lucknow is about 12 miles by road and it was close to 5.00 o'clock in the morning when I was back home, thoroughly tired by my hectic journey by car over a distance of some 200 miles. I then flung myself on my bed to sleep like a top till about mid day. It was only then that I realised for the first time, how except for the two *Laddoos* at Hardoi and the mouthful of sugarcane juice at Pihani I had been without any food or drink for the past 36 hours or so.

At the Government House the same evening, I happened to meet the Area Commander, Major-General Fitzgerald, to whom I related my tale of recovery of the stolen revolvers. But so far as I could see, his primary concern was how he should deal with the Subedar-Major of the Battalion concerned who, according to him, deserved to be sacked for lack of proper supervision over his men. He also gave me the impression that he was not at all interested in my achievement in the case, which I must confess rankled in my heart. But there you are.

* * * *

Chapter 36

Shahjanwa Railway Mail Van Dacoity

Now-a-days railway train dacoities are of such common occurrence that perhaps it will be news to many that the first one ever of this kind, which caused a sensation throughout the country and was known as the Kakori railway mail van dacoity, which took place in the year 1925 at a spot close to Lucknow. It was purely a political dacoity designed to rob the Government of the day and was worked out by Mr. R.A. Horton of the C.I.D., U.P. After an interval of several years, three other cases of the same nature occurred successively in 1940, 1941 and 1942, namely, the Bahatpur Mail Van dacoity of Varanasi, the Nandganj Mail Van dacoity of Ghazipur and the Shahjanwa Mail Van dacoity of Gorakhpur. All these three were worked out by me in my capacity as S.P. Investigation branch of the C.I.D., U.P. I will now confine myself to the last named case which has an interesting story in itself, revealing, as it does, the temper of the time.

The incident took place at about 8.30 in the evening of March

24, 1942 and the information was first received at Police Station Shahjanwa of district Gorakhpur through a village *Chaukidar* who happened to witness it. The Station Officer Shahjanwa then flashed the news to Mr. C.P. Luck, Superintendent of Police, Gorakhpur, who arrived at the scene of occurrence promptly and after having made a cursory spot enquiry had the ill-fated Mail Van detached and sent back to Gorakhpur.

According to the eye witnesses, the culprits, all young men, looked like school students and were an assortment of *hats, turbans, dhotis* and *payjamas*. Most of them had handkerchiefs tied around their faces to hide their identity. One exploded and four unexploded crackers were found at the spot, apart from a 22 bore rifle bolt. One marked feature of the case was that the culprits gave themselves out as members of the 'Hindustan Socialist Republicans Army of India'. Another, that they scrupulously avoided causing any harm to or panic among the passengers of the train, who sat huddled up as mute spectators of the whole show. The leaflets they distributed also made no secret of their aims and objects. It was therefore as plain as a pike staff that this was a case of politico-criminal dacoity, committed in furtherance of a deep rooted conspiracy to cause a severe jolt to the Government of the day, its pattern being the same as the previous two cases of 1940 and 1941.

Within a short time of the occurrence, wires started jangling to convey the news to all relevant quarters, As was inevitable, its investigation was entrusted to the C.I.D. U.P. and it was thus that I found myself speeding by car on my way from Lucknow to Gorakhpur, early next morning, along with my deputy, Rai Bahadur Tika Ram. Directly we reached there, and the first thing we did was to carry out a systematic inspection of the ill-fated mail van in this case. Among the scores of torn envelopes lying about on its floor there were some with finger impression stained in blood on them. Similar impressions were also to be seen on a broken glass window pane of the van. This clearly showed that at least one of the culprits had sustained a cut in his finger in an attempt to smash it open with his fist and that he had left behind him those tell-tale impressions lying all around, in trying to wipe off the blood oozing from it.

Our next step was to have these finger prints developed and their photographs sent to the Finger Print Bureau at Allahabad. This had been done, we turned our attention to the task of tracing out the man with the injured finger. Following the age-old method of working through a source, we soon came to know that the man in question was one Oudhraj Tiwari of Gorakhpur. We then raided his village home as well as all his other possible haunts but could not succeed. Again through a source we have been informed that he was in the habit of visiting a certain tea shop at Gorakhpur after dark. This was a game with its thrills for us. One evening I along with Rai Bahadur Tika Ram planted ourselves in a narrow lane close to the tea shop in question and at a suitable opportunity swooped upon our quarry to whisk him away to the Kotwali. There we questioned him about his complicity in this case, but in vain. One thing he could not explain away was the tell-tale scar on the tip of his right thumb. Oudhraj was not much to look at, being no more than a slim young man with a dark complexion and a pock-pitted face. One thing noticeable about him was his determination not to speak up, in spite of our best efforts to make him spill the beans. We had taken his finger impression and sent to the F.P.B. at Allahabad, and, sure enough, they were matched with those found in the mail van.

Having thus assured ourselves of the complicity of Oudhraj in this case, we proceeded to fix up the identity of the others involved in it. Days and even weeks passed without any development and we had all but abandoned our hopes of making any head-way, when we came to know that some local students of Gorakhpur, led by Hari Pratap Tewari and Indra Prasad had been experimenting at making a bomb in a house hired by them for use as a private hostel and that following an explosion they had thrown away its fragments into a refuse dump at the back of this house. We then raided the spot to find that while fragments of the bomb these boys had been making, were to be seen there, but the boys themselves were missing.

Our next link in this chain of events was supplied by a resident of Azamgarh who made a statement throwing a flood of light on the activities in general of the H.S.R.A. in the eastern districts of U.P. during the past few years, including a case of blackening of

Queen Victoria's statue in the Town Hall grounds at Gorakhpur. Following a series of arrests in this connection, some tools for the manufacture of explosives along with heaps of subversive literature were recovered from various places.

Next followed recovery from the possession of one Ramadhar Singh, a contact of Indra Prasad, of a list of names of certain youths including that of one Raja Ram Passi, a student of the Gorakhpur High School, who was found to be absconding.

We had been informed at that time that two students of the Queen's College of Varanasi were in touch with one of the important suspects of this case. Their house having been located was this time raided by Rai Bahadur Tika Ram one day when both of them were arrested by him along with three others, namely Hari Pratap Tewari of Gorakhpur, Brij Bahadur of Barabanki and Ramji Ram Vaish of Ghazipur, all of whom walked in unsuspectingly while Rai Bahadur Tika Ram was busy making a search of this house. This was indeed providential with hardly a parallel. Incidentally Hari Pratap Tewari and Brij Bahadur Singh were found to be in possession of service revolvers that were fully loaded.

One other suspect Bhagwan Prasad Shukla, was arrested along with a number of others on the night of the 3rd December at Lucknow by Khan Sahab Nasir Khan of the C.I.D. (Special Branch).

Kailashpati, still another suspect of this case was arrested at Gorakhpur in circumstances reflecting credit on a certain local resident of this place. He had come on a visit to an accomplice of his which aroused some suspicion in this man's mind. He relayed the information to a Home Guard of his acquaintance who then took Kailashpati to the *Kotwali* where he was identified and locked up. He was wanted both in this case and one of postal robbery of Varanasi in 1939.

Raja Ram Passi, whose name found mention in the list recovered from the possession of Ramadhar Singh surrendered himself on the 28th December and made a detailed statement confessing his guilt and naming at his accomplices in this case. According to his confession, there were in all fourteen persons involved in it. Balrup and he

(Raja Ram Passi) boarded the ill fated train at Gorakhpur Railway Station, four other boarded it at the next station while the rest of them awaited its arrival at the spot where by previous arrangement it was to be stopped by pulling its alarm chain. Balrup had brought with him some leaflets for distribution among the passengers of the train. Bhagwan Prasad Shukla directed the operations while Balrup and Baij Nath Singh took charge of the booty amounting to a little over ten thousand rupees in this case. Baij Nath Singh, Uma Shankar Upadhya and Balrup each had a revolver with them.

Raja Ram Passi's statement further revealed that on the 13th May Balrup and he (Raja Ram Passi) left for a village to Nepal where they met Uma Shankar Upadhya, Raghunath Singh and Bhagwan Prasad Shukla. The following day Uma Shankar Upadhya and he (Raja Ram Passi) left for Rewan with six hundred rupees for the purchase of arms. But failing in their efforts to obtain any they left for Gwalior where they rented a room. Here they were joined by Gauttan, Misra, Hari Pratap Tewari, Baij Nath Singh and Balrup.

Following the recording of this statement, Rai Bahadur Tika Ram and Inspector Faizanullah proceeded with haste to Gwalior where they managed to arrest Uma Shankar, Baij Nath and Rajnath Singh, along with two six chambered revolvers, a large number of cartridges, a quantity of gunpowder and some lead.

In this way nearly all those involved in this case were rounded up and sent up for prosecution. In the result, barring, Raja Ram Passi, who was granted pardon and examined as an approver, the rest were sentenced to six years imprisonment each, by the Court, sessions of Lucknow. Thus with the conviction of these accused, the curtain was rung down on a serious politico-criminal case of U.P. in the course of investigation of which much information was gleaned about the activities of a large number of youths belonging to the eastern districts of U.P. who were out to over throw the Government of the day. Most of them were inspired by patriotic motives is borne out by a letter written by Hari Pratap Tewari to his newly wedded wife, exhorting her to live up to the traditions set up by the women of Chitor, and, if need be, to wipe off the memory of his from her mind.

There is a sequel to this case which needed to be mentioned here. Years later, and long after my retirement from the police when I was holding the honorary office of Chief Commissioner, Bharat Scouts and Guides, U.P. I had occasion to go to Rudrapur in district Nainital, to preside over a rally of Scouts and Guides of that region. When it was over, I was accosted by two elderly men with beards who asked me if I remembered them. While I was still cogitating over it, they introduced themselves to me as two of the ex-convicts of this case of 1942. They further informed me that they were cultivating a piece of land, granted free of rent to them, in recognition of their services as political sufferers. They seemed to be well-off and I could not help reflecting how the wheel of time had turned a full circle and how those who were at one time considered to be rebels, were now acclaimed as heroes. What gave me some cause for satisfaction was that neither of them bore any ill-will against me for the part I had prayed to bring them to book at one time.

* * * *

Chapter 37

A Sad Story

In Hamirpur, a small town in Uttar Pradesh, the morning walkers had the shock of their lives when one day they discovered five corpses. Three of them of boys and two of girls, lying unattended on the bank of the Jamuna which flows past this town. News of this most unusual spread through the town like wild fire and the town folks, young and old, flocked to the scene in their hundreds. Soon enough, the bodies were identified as those of Kumari Sarda, Kumari Swatantrata (daughter of Thakur Y. Singh), Prakash Chandra Dixit, Ram Narain Gupta and Shri Prakash, all the five being residents of Hamirpur.

A remarkable thing about the bodies, was that they lay arranged more or less in the form of a Swastika, their relative positions being roughly as follows:

Kumari Sarda lay to the right of Prakash Chandra with her head resting on his shoulder. Ram Narain lay at the feet of Prakash Chandra with Kumari Swatantrata's head resting on his thigh while Shri Prakash lay with his head resting on the feet of Kumari Swatantrata.

It was noticed, that the deceased were well-dressed, the girls with their hair neatly parted and done to perfection, their sarees drawn right down to their ankles and having no creases at all. Lying near the bodies were torn pieces of a letter written in Hindi, a glass tube with some white powder in it, a cork, a tin cover, a handkerchief, some sweetmeats, three small bundles and a picture of Lord Krishna. In addition, some vomited matter lay near the bodies of Sarda, Swatantrata, Prakash Chandra and Sri Prakash. A few foot prints, apparently from the shoes of the two girls, were also to be seen there. There were, on the other hand, no marks of injury on any of the deceased, nor there were any signs of struggle on the ground.

The mystery that confronted the Police was whether it was a case of murder or a suicide. The first reaction in the minds of the local public was that the father of the girls, being anxious to save himself from disgrace arising from their amours, had the murders committed in a cold and calculated manner. Some went even to the extent of explaining that he had gone to fetch some strong poison and had returned with a phial of potassium cyanide to be administered to the deceased, who had actually died of cyanide poisoning, as was established from the chemical examiner's report.

At one time, therefore, as a result of the popular resentment against him, Thakur Y. Singh came to be the most maligned man of Hamirpur; for, apart from a regular campaign of vilification launched against him in the local yellow press, numerous petitions were addressed to Government for a thorough enquiry being instituted into this case by the C.I.D. A thing that helped to fan the fire of this agitation was bad blood against him, due to certain recent elections in which he had taken an active part on one side.

Unfortunately, the Police had no direct evidence to go upon. But, there was no denying that this case presented some features which were tell-tale. In the first place, the total absence of any signs of struggle on the spot where the bodies were found, was a strong indication of the fact that there had been no foul play. It was also revealed from enquiries that all the five used at one time to go to the same school where Sarda developed a liking for Prakash Chandra and Swatantrata for Ram Narain. As time passed, this friendship ripened into love in which they were helped by a boy named Prem, who was obliging enough to act as a go-between. The father of the girls got wind of this and set out to find a match for each of them. This would appear to have made the lovers all the more desperate and enter into a solemn agreement to put an end to their lives in case their friendship was threatened in any way. Presumably Shri Prakash who happened to be deeply attached to them joined this suicide pact, of his free will, having come to the conclusion that he would much rather die along with the rest of them, than live to mourn their loss.

About this time, while the father of the girls was away, one of his friends chanced to see them moving about freely in the *bazaar* in company with their boy friends and besides scolding them for their misconduct, threatened to report it to their father on his return, which only aggravated the situation. Consequently, when Thakur Y. Singh returned home with the tidings that he had fixed-up the marriage of both the girls, the only thing left for all of them to do was to put into effect the decision which they had already taken and it was thus that, by previous arrangement, they gathered on the bank of the Jamuna at the dead of night, when everybody was asleep, and sacrificed their lives at the altar of love.

Incidentally, a letter addressed to Sarda by Prakash Chandra (of which the contents, as translated into English, are recorded below) further clinched the issue in this case, insofar as it went to show that the latter had been trying to obtain some poison, presumably potassium cyanide.

"Bannoji,

This morning I met the Punjabi photographer on my way back from Kanyakubj College. He informed me in detail that I should first obtain permission from the Deputy Commissioner. But I proposed to go to his house again in the evening and try to bring him round. This may do the trick and he may give me the stuff.

Prakash Chandra."

It further came to be known that the photographer, mentioned above, was one Hira Lal Talwar of Kanpur; who gave the statement mentioning that he had known Prakash Chandra, who had been his regular customer and had got several photographs of the girls enlarged at his studio. For some time past, Prakash Chandra had been asking for some potassium cyanide which he had refused to supply. (It will perhaps be readily understood that the last part of this statement is not to be relied on.)

Thus there was no room left for doubt that this was a case of suicide, pure and simple and, consequently, no need for further investigation into it that is why it was closed, but, all said and done, the fact remains that its sad memory still haunts the minds of the people residing in the little, out-of-the way, town of Hamirpur.

* * * *

Chapter 38

A Murder Story Retold

Here are the details of a case of gruesome murder of a lady in Lucknow, which was worked out from clues left on the scene by the culprit. Preparations had been going on for some time for the wedding of the deceased's daughter. In that connection, the deceased had been collecting valuables to be given away in dowry. Some jewellers had also been making frequent visits to her house. One day during this period, a man turned up to say that he was in search of employment as a domestic servant. The deceased being in need of one engaged him straightaway. He told his name Tulsi Kahar and said he resided in Mohalla Daliganj. He was always neatly turned out and it was his practice to come early in the morning and leave late at night.

The house in which the deceased lived had two portions. At night she used to sleep all by herself in a room facing a court yard which was practically cut off from the rest of the house. On the night of the occurrence the deceased's husband heard a piercing cry emanating from the courtyard side. He took no notice of it. But later on, hearing an incessant groan, when he opened an intervening door, he was shocked to see his wife all in a heap leaning against it, with numerous stab wounds on her person. He immediately look her and rushed to the hospital, but she failed to survived and died on the way, without being able to tell who her assailant had been.

Two stumps of smoked *biries,* a few burnt match sticks, one match box, two bunches of keys, a small cup like receptacle for sweets made up of Sal leave stuck together, lay abandoned on the open terrace above the deceased's room. A rope was also seen dangling in it from one of its ventilators. Immediately below an outer drain pipe leading to the roof, lay an old pair of shoes, while some distinct finger impressions were visible on the drain pipe itself. What was more, a *Kukri* which lay an open shelf inside the house, was found missing.

The next morning Tulsi failed to turn up. Enquiries made at Daliganj proved futile. For a time there was no clue to Tulsi's location and whereabouts and the prospect of running him to earth appeared to be gloomy when information was received of a case of burglary in another part of the town of which the circumstances were somewhat similar. This occurrence also took place on the eve of a wedding when a number of relatives had come with their valuables to join it. One day during this period a man who gave his name as Ram Bharose, turned up in search of employment as a domestic servant and was engaged straightaway. He worked for a few days before clearing out with much booty. His description tallied with that of Tulsi, while a pair of shoes left behind by him was found to be of the same size as the one left behind by Tulsi.

From an examination of the C.I.D. records, it was discovered that the *modus operandi* of these cases was similar to that employed by a gang of domestic servants led by one Ram Samujh of Barabanki who had been convicted in the case of Lucknow in 1938. But it was found that Ram Samujh had been untraced ever since his release from jail on 11th December 1942.

Then followed, two other cases of a similar type, one in Kanpur and another in Lucknow. The suspect had given his name as Ram Bharose Kahar in one case and as Debi Kahar in the other.

The photograph of Ram Samujh as contained in his release notice in the Intelligence Gazette was shown to the complainants of all the four cases and they instantly recognised it as that of the man engaged by them. The finger impression left on the drain pipe in the murder case were also found tallying with those on record of Ram Samujh of Barabanki.

The identity of the culprit in all these cases having thus been established, it now merely remained to lay him by the heels. In this task one Chutku Kahar who knew him well, was of great assistance. After some hard work on his part he managed to trace Ram Samujh to a boat on the Gomti which lay anchored at some distance down the river from the town. He had chosen this as an ideal hideout from where to go occasionally into the city for his nocturnal forays. After this discovery, it was not much of a problem to round him up which was actually done, under the leadership of Inspector Indra Kumar of the C.I.D. in dramatic circumstances.

After his arrest Ram Samujh confessed his guilt in all the four cases and surrendered his share of the stolen property in all of them, apart from the *Kukri* used by him in the case of murder which was committed by him. He also named six others as his accomplices, all of them were arrested one after another. When put up for trial, however, Ram Samujh resiled from his confession and spun out a cock and bull story in his defence. But the cup of his sins being full, there was no escape for him and he was ultimately sent to the gallows on a charge of murder, while his accomplices were sentenced to varying terms of imprisonment for the possession of stolen property relating to one or other of the four cases in which they were involved.

Inspector Indra Kumar of the C.I.D. investigated this case under my supervision. The result achieved was a triumph for the C.I.D. which goes to show how perseverance always pays.

* * * *

Chapter 39

All about an Orgy of Bloodshed at Kanpur

On the night of the 2nd January, 1942, three persons, named Ram Das, Badloo and Raja Ram were battered to death in cold blooded manner at a spot named Kataria Bagh in Kanpur Cantonment while another man, named Avadh Bihari was likewise done to death outside a shop in the Civil Lines of Kanpur, in almost identical circumstances.

A report of the incidents at Kataria Bagh was lodged at the same night at P.S. Cantonment of Kanpur district, by one Muneshar, according to whom some *Gora log* had suddenly swooped upon this place, when everybody was fast asleep, and caused red ruin, including the murder of several of his companions.

This was followed up by another report soon after at the same Police Station to the effect that some men sleeping outside Lala Ratan Lal's shop in the Civil Lines of Kanpur had likewise been beaten up by a group of British soldiers.

S.I. Ram Swaroop Sharma of P.S. Cantonment Kanpur, on his arrival at Kataria Bagh found the whole place reduced to a shamble. Lying in front of him were the dead bodies of Badloo, Ram Das and Raja Ram which bore a silent testimony of the orgy of blood-shed that had taken place there. He also noticed one green forage cap, two bicycles marked CUP 1435 and HV 3161, an *ekka* without its pony or driver and four paper festoons lying abandoned on the spot, all of which he took into his possession. He also taken into his custody a soldier named Lynch, who had been seized during the scuffle that had ensured there.

In the other case also, S.I. Ram Swaroop saw distinct signs of vandalism on the spot, including a number of broken flower pots and some broken pieces of a beer bottle. There also lay before him, three persons Avadh Bihari, Maya Ram and Sheeraj with numerous injuries on them in which Avadh Bihari's injuries were of a serious nature.

On his part, Mr. E.F.G. Chapman, Senior Supdt. of Police Kanpur, had Lance Corporal Church, Lance Corporal Green and Pt. Rogers of the South Wales Borders arrested on the ground that they had been seen sitting in Bristol Café at the same table with Pte Lynch and also leaving the Café in company with him, immediately before these tragic happenings.

News of these brutal and senseless murders having reached the Governor of U.P. Sir Maurice Hallett at Lucknow, he desired the investigation of these cases being taken over by the C.I.D. U.P. It was thus that I had to rush to Kanpur along with my Deputy, Rai Bahadur Tika Ram.

So far, this case hinged only on the apprehension of Pte Lynch at Kataria Bagh, apart from recovery of the green forage cap, the two bicycles and the four festoons at Kataria Bagh.

But Lynch had a very plausible explanation to offer. His plea was that when he got close to Kataria Bagh he saw a scuffle going on there and a man covered with blood. Thereafter in trying to lift him he got some bloodstains on his own clothes. At this stage the police arrived and took him into custody under the mistaken notion that he had been involved in the rioting.

Lance Corporals Church and Green also pleaded not guilty. From our enquiries it was revealed that the bicycle marked CUP 1435 belonged to Corporal Price of the SWB and that it had been quietly picked up by Lynch and Rogers from the verandah of Barrack Number 3 where it had been left standing.

The other bicycle marked HV 3161, it was discovered, had been allotted to L/C Church for Garrison Police Duty. His explanation in his defence was that he had found it missing on coming out of Bristol Café.

All the four festoons recovered at Kataria Bagh were found to have been removed from Bristol Café.

As a result of our enquires into this case of quadruple murder, it was established that Lynch and Rogers were seen breaking barrack by their room mates at about 10.00 on the night of 2nd January. That they quietly picked up L/C. Prices bicycle and proceeded to James Restaurant where they had an altercation with its proprietor Trilok Singh. The latter threatening to call up the garrison Police, they made a hurried retreat to Bristol Café where they jointed L/C Church and L/C Green and sat at the same table with them. Thereafter, all the four of them regaled themselves with generous quantities of drinks of all kinds and at the same time hatched a plot to have it out with Trilok Singh, the proprietor of James Restaurant. Green and Rogers took down in a playful spirit four of the festoons hanging overhead.

After coming out of Bristol Café the quartet raided James Restaurant where out of a sheer spirit of mischief they started pounding with some flower pots on the heads of a number of labourers lying fast in sleep outside the restaurant. They also made free use of a beer bottle in the assault made by them.

Having done their worst there, they proceeded towards their barracks and when they came to Kataria Bagh, they had another go at the labourers lying fast asleep there, resulting in a scuffle during the course of which Lynch came to be seized by the opposite party.

In brief, the four culprits involved in these two cases were found to have planned and later executed a raid first on the premises of

James Restaurant, where by a quirk of fate a number of persons got beaten up, of whom on died. Once they had drawn blood, they became thoroughly brutalised and engaged in the second assault at Kataria Bagh, the liquor they had imbibed having given an edge to their vicious spirit and heightened their lust for blood.

All the four were tried by Mr. Justice Hamilton of the Allahabad High Court under Section 304 of the Indian Penal Code and while Church Green and Lynch were sentenced to penal servitude for life, Rogers was sentenced to rigorous imprisonment for 5 years.

From our enquiries it was further revealed that there had been frequent clashes previously between some of the SWB men and members of the public so that the incidents in question were only of the nature of a sequel to these clashes. They were also illustrative of the depths to which these men of the SWB had fallen and, for the matter or that, British Tommies generally on all counts. This was without any doubt, largely because of the highly preferential treatment to which they had been accustomed under British rule and which had made them look upon all Indians as petty things.

Incidentally, the successful ending of this and the Shahjanwa Mail Van dacoity case added yet another feather to the cap of the C.I.D. U.P.

* * * *

Chapter 40

Ballia Reconquered

Concurrently with the Quit-India Movement launched by Mahatma Gandhi in 1942, a number of districts of eastern U.P. went up in flames. In those days, the worst affected was Ballia which ceased to have the rule of law for quite some time when it got isolated from the rest of the country. This was simply because all the telegraph lines in and around it had been cut, off, its railway tracks uprooted and its railway stations burnt down to the ground by the insurgents. Still another feature of the mass uprising in this area was derailment and looting of the goods trains carrying supplies to our troops on the Eastern front.

During this period, one man Chittu Pande, a Congress worker became the virtual ruler of the district and earned for himself the pseudonym of "The Lion of Ballia". His word became Law. An idea of the lawlessness that prevailed at the time can be had from an occurrence that took place one day when the insurgents raided the residences of some half a dozen deputy-collectors living in the city as opposed to the Civil Lines side of this station, and carried off in broad daylight most of their moveable property, down to their chairs and tables, without any let of hindrance. This also shows how the ire of the insurgents was directed purely against the Government of the day and against all Government servants.

It was also during same period that the District Magistrate, Mr. J. Nigam ordered the destruction of all the currency notes in the Government Treasury there, to prevent them from falling into the hands of insurgents. It may however be stated in his favour that he had no choice in the matter in the absence of any hope for reinforcement. Actually currency notes to the tune of Rs. 4,44,000 were reduced to ashes on the occasion.

In some cases the insurgents are reported to have shown rare courage. At one time they surrounded a Police Station named Baria in the interior of the district, in order to take possession of it. The Station staff then threatened to fire at them. Upon this some of them bared their chests and were actually shot down. The incident in this case can be clarified to have been the reverse of those at Chauri Chaura, where 22 policemen were beaten to death by the insurgents.

It was inevitable, in course of time all this lawlessness was put down with a heavy hand. The Governor of U.P. in those days was Sir Maurice Hallett. He had termed this insurgence as Congress rebellion and had announced that he was prepared to accept the challenge. In pursuance of this declaration, he had chosen to send to Ballia, Mr. Nethersole, an I.C.S., who was reputed to be a strong man, in overall charge of the operation to be carried out and Mr. Marsh Smith as second in command. Both of them are said to have taken pot-shots at many a straggler from among the insurgents.

I will now refer to an incident of this period with some overtones of its own. As was to be expected, a number of picked officers of blue blood had been rushed by the Government of the day to the eastern districts for posting as District Magistrates or as Superintendents the Police, in replacement of others. One of them happening to be officer named Madge of the Indian Police posted to Ghazipur. One day he took it into his head to scour the countryside for odd insurgents. Mounted on an elephant, commandeered for the occasion he carried out his operations with the help of some 200 armed Policemen, during the course of which he spotted a solidly built double storied house which seemed to proclaim the opulence of its owner. Wishing to give his men a good time he let them loose on it and they ransacked it of all its valuables, including some silver ware of the nature of *tea sets, thalis, tumblers,* etc. Then when they came across a sword with some inscription on it showing that it had been presented to its recipient by His Excellency the Viceroy and Governor General of India, they had a rude shock and made a precipitate retreat. But the mischief had been one and there was no way of undoing it.

The owner of this house happened to be a retired Subedar Major-cum-Hony. Captain with a brilliant record of his village which had also supplied numerous J.C.O.'s and men to the Army during the two World wars. Therefore, out of a sense of indignation he wrote a personal letter to the Viceroy and at the same time returned the sword of honour presented to him. The Viceroy wrote to the Governor of U.P. who in his turn wrote to the I.G. Police about the incident. Thereafter, following a spot enquiry by the Range D.I.G., Mr. Madge was ordered to pay a sum of Rs. 3,000 as compensation to the aggrieved party which brought this episode to a close. Mr. Madge, on this part, is said to have taken this punishment much to his heart and drunk himself to death soon after.

I must not forget to add that Mr. Hunt of the Police had been sent to Ballia along with Mr. Nethersole and Mr. Marsh-Smith to function as officer in charge of communications. Wireless had been his hobby ever since he joined service. It also goes to his credit that he was the first to establish contact between Ballia and the Government Headquarters at Lucknow when he flashed a wireless message, which read "Ballia reconquered". Needless to say it caused much jubilation combined with some amusement over the text of it.

* * * *

Chapter 41

Two Notable British Characters

I have two notable British characters in my mind, one was Sir Maurice Hallett and the other Lady Sloan. Sir Maurice was Governor of U.P. during the Second world war and came into same prominence, during the disturbances in eastern U.P. in 1942, which he termed as the Congress rebellion and which he suppressed with an iron hand. But my anecdote has nothing to do with his conduct vis-à-vis these disturbances. In fact, it relates to an incident in which he was personally involved. He had a son aged 18 years or so, who, while studying in the Cambridge University, had got himself enlisted in the British Air Force and was killed in action on the Burma Front. News of this occurrence was duly conveyed to Sir Maurice by the Ministry of Defence and spread all over Lucknow. It so happened that the Annual Police Parade at which the Governor was due to take the Salute and give away the Medals, was fixed for the very next day. Sir Hugh Inglis who was then I.G. Police, U.P., felt that at a time like this when Sir Hallett had lost his young son, it would be hard on him to have to face the ordeal of the parade. So he called on him to express his condolences and at the same time to suggest that Sir Tenant Sloan, Advisor to the Governor, might profitably be called upon to deputise for him.

According to Sir Hugh, on hearing this suggestion, Sir Maurice kept mum for a while and then said in no uncertain terms, "Am I the only person who has lost his son in this war?" This clinched the matter and Sir Maurice presided over the parade, as was customary and went through the entire proceedings which lasted for some two hours, without showing the least signs of distress over the loss of his young son. Sir Hugh himself narrated this incident to me and I could not help marvelling at the strength of character that Sir Maurice showed on this occasion.

The other person I have in mind in this connection, was Lady Sloan, wife of Sir Tennant Sloan, Adviser to the Governor U.P. She had organised a work party in which some of the senior Ladies of the station together ran a canteen at the Railway Station to serve tea and coffee to the soldiers passing Lucknow by road on their way to the eastern front. In order to save the consumption of petrol, they had arranged that each of them by rotation reminded of a day when it was Lady Tennant's turn to do so.

She wanted to pick up my wife and leaving her car at our outer gate, trotted up to our doorsteps over a distance of barely a few yards and then said to my wife by way of an apology, "Mrs. Lahiri, I am sorry, I have left my car by the roadside, if only to save a few drops of petrol."

This incident goes to show what a fine sense of patriotism Lady Sloan had. It is also of some relevance today when we see that most of our countrymen have no conscience at all, over the consumption of petrol by them and that, too, at a time when the very economy of our country depends upon a judicious use of it.

* * * *

Chapter 42

A Rare Experience

On a day early in June 1943, when I was on holidays at Darjeeling, I had booked a pony to take me at the dead of night to Tiger Hill, which was said to command the best view of Mt. Everest at sun rise—but the man who had promised to bring me pony, having failed to turn up in time, I decided to set out on foot, to get to Tiger Hill before dawn.

I chose a short cut to do this, via Jalapahar 'a military station of some importance'. For me the risks involved were two fold. I might either be mistaken for a suspicious character and locked up for the night at Jalapahar or I might encounter some nasty meddlesome watch dogs who should take a dislike for me. My ordeal actually began with my arrival at the outskirts of this place. I discovered that in crossing it I would have to run the gauntlet of more than one armed picket posted on either side of the road. My first reaction was to retrace my steps. But on second thoughts I decided to go ahead, whatever the consequences. To avoid the attention of these pickets, I took the precaution of walking on tiptoe. With a throbbing heart, I alternately took a few steps and stopped for a while to see the lie of the land, thus behaving like any footpad on the prowl. In the process I started sweating so profusely that I was soon wet through. Luckily, while I could clearly see the men on picket duty with the lights showing them up, I remained invisible to them. I cannot say how long I took to clear this military area—but it certainly it was felt like ages and I heaved a sigh of relief the moment I did so.

My road hereafter lay through a forest belt for some two miles. Fortunately for me, I had a bright moon overhead to light me on my way. Even though, in the prevailing stillness, I soon began to be assailed by figments of my imagination. My footsteps, which I had no reason to muffle any longer, rang out, sharp and clear, which caused me a feeling that I was being followed by some one close at my heels. Without a living soul within miles of me, I felt scared—I pricked up my ears and looked furtively this way and that. I also increased my pace at times felt like taking to my heels. I hollered and hullered to keep up my spirits till I heard the faint sound of a car going in the direction of Ghoom by another road which lay only a few feet below mine. This put new life into me and before long, when I reached Ghoom, I felt like walking on thin air.

From Ghoom one had to go another three miles uphill on foot to Tiger Hill. As I trudged on, I overtook some groups of men going in the same direction with me—when they came to know that I had been coming singly on foot, all the way from Darjeeling via Jalapahar, they were lost in admiration of me and took pride in introducing me to others whom we passed on our way. Thus by the time I got to Tiger Hill, I had become a celebrity whom every one was anxious to meet.

The time was now close on 4.00 in the morning. Perched on the roof of a circular building on top of this Hill, sat several groups of men, waiting expectantly for the moment when the Sun-god would smile upon the snow peak in front of us. This was no time for loose talk. The prevailing atmosphere was one of reverent silence heralding a great event.

With the advance of dawn, the sky became brighter and brighter and the stars faded away one by one in quick succession, leaving the moon for a time sole mistress of it—"But she too, presently looked like a poor imitation of herself and there came a point of time when one could hardly see, but only feel that she was there". All eyes were now riveted on the snow-peak in front of us at a distance of some fifty miles as the crow flies. Hitherto, in the light of the moon it had looked like a great mass of molten lead. But with the break of day, it took an increasingly brighter hue till it looked like burnished silver. Then when the first streak of sunlight fell on it, its colouring changed to light rose, thus transforming it into a thing of rare beauty which it was a delight to behold. Concurrently with this transformation, a lusty shout went up from the throats of the crowd assembled there as if in acclamation of the Master Craftsman behind this glorious vision.

As time passed, the colouring of the peak changed from light rose to pink and from pink to beaten gold. In common with others, I was lost in admiration of it till it was time for me, slowly and reluctantly, to wend my way home, for which this time I chose the slightly longer but safer route.

My experience on this occasion was of a mixed kind. Even though, I am glad I was able to witness a sight fit for the gods.

* * * *

Chapter 43

An Object Lesson for All Budding Policemen

I remembered a visitor who came to see me one morning at Saharanpur, around 1944 or so, when I was posted there as Superintendent of Police.

As we all know, the indigenous word for visitors is *Mulaqatis.* A point of interest is that in the early part of my service, when most of my colleagues were Englishmen, they found it difficult to pronounce this word correctly. So they were accustomed to call them *"Mollycats"*.

Let me now relate what my *"Mollycats"* had to say to me. Judging from his looks, he appeared to be an ordinary villager, who was in some trouble. So, the first thing I asked him was who he was and what had brought him to me. Then when he told me that he was so and so and belonged to a village in Meerut district, I felt surprised and asked him why he had come to me instead of going to S.P. Meerut? I will now relate all that he had to tell me in reply to my query. "Sir, I have made several attempts to see S.P. Meerut. But it is my misfortune, I have to date failed in my efforts to see him, because of his orderlies who keep a sharp look out all the time, to make sure that no visitor who may have any grievance against the Police, is able to see him. I beg of you to give me a patient hearing and, thereafter, decide what you can do to help me. I own a cow which yields me some ten seers of milk daily. Having come to know this, the local Station Officer of Police, named so and so, under the threat of dire consequences to me, has forcibly made me part with her, in exchange for his own cow which has gone dry and is not good. I have been moving from pillar to post for the redress of my grievance, but in vain. I am thankful to you for having given me a patient hearing which has afforded me at least some mental satisfaction, if nothing more.

I felt pained to hear this sad story of high handedness on the part of a policeman. But all I could do for my visitor was to give him the name and address of the Range D.I.G. concerned, that he might petition him. It occurs to me now that I could perhaps have sent a copy of his statement which he has given to me to S.P. Meerut in a closed cover and I feel sorry that I failed to do so.

I mention this case in order that it may serve as an object lesson for all budding Policemen, whose look out should constantly be to see that the Police, instead of being a sources of pride to the community, do not make a menace of themselves.

As is common knowledge, corruption is rampant now-a-days all over the country and in all branches of the administration. The need of the hour, therefore, is a crusade against it on the part of all right thinking persons, high and low, who have anything to do with the administration of our country.

* * * *

Chapter 44

Some Odd Characters of the Police in the Past

In old days there were to be some characters in the Police who were famed for their oddities. One such character was Mr. Mac Dowell who joined service in the nineties of the last century and was posted at Ghazipur towards the end of his career. His one and only interest in life was carpentry. Instead, therefore, of wasting his time and energy on crime and criminals of his district, he used to devote most of it to cabinet making in which he excelled and which he carried out at his residence, morning, evening and night. He hardly visited his office or Reserve Lines and consequently had only a vague idea of their location. If there were any papers to be signed by him, his office assistant sent them to his residence.

Mr. Mac Dowell was, in fact, his own master and the only person to dispute his sovereignty was his Range D.I.G. But since the latter came only twice a year, Mr. Mac Dowell was not much bothered about him. Here is an account of one such visit of this dignitary, during the course of which he proposed to inspect the Reserve

Lines. For his part, Mr. Mac Dowell offered to take him there in his car and true to programme the two of them left for this place at the appointed hour, the next morning.

Here it is necessary to explain that the Reserve Lines at Ghazipur stood at a distance of less than a mile from the S.P.'s residence. To get there, all one had to do was to go due west for about half a mile and then take a turn to the right. But somehow Mr. Mac Dowell missed this turning and went for some distance to hit the provincial highway to Varanasi. But still rather vague about his bearings, he next proceeded in that direction to cover another two to there miles when his D.I.G. asked him, "Are you sure you are taking me to your Reserve Lines?" This was because he had noticed that the mile posts on the roadside successively gave the distance from Varanasi as Varanasi 32, Varanasi 31, Varanasi 30. It was only then that Mr. Mac Dowell realised his mistake and turned round to get to his destination which he had left far behind.

A happening of this kind which cannot be conceived today, is of interest to us as showing how life in the Police in the past, was not half as bad or irksome as it is today.

The other character whom I have in mind was one Mr. Crawford. Made of a powerful build, if somewhat stocky and having a massive head, a thick moustache, bushy eyebrows and eyes of which the whites were unusually large, he looked forbidding. He was also high and mighty in his bearing. But one thing was good about him that, unlike Mr. Mac Dowell it was his practice to attend his office daily, if only for a hour or so in the afternoon. But since it was impossible for him to go through all his official work within that period, he had evolved a system whereby his *Peshkar* used to dispose of a large mass of his papers and put up for his order only such of them as he (the *Peshkar*) thought to be urgent or important enough.

It so happened that one day, as Mr. Crawford sat in his office, his *Peshkar* read out to him an application written in Urdu and seeking permission to let off some *Atasbazi* (fire works) and to release into the air some *Gubbaras* (balloons). Having heard the application Mr. Crawford asked, *"Atrasbazi sala kya hota hai?"* The *Peshkar* in his turn duly explained to him what is meant. Then he asked, *"Aur Gubbarah sala kya hota hai?"* The *Peshkar* again told him what it was. Thereupon he thundered, *"Hukam Likho, Atasbazi Sala Manzoor, Gubbarah Sala Namanzoor"*. In this way, after he had summarily disposed of a few more papers, Mr. Crawford drove off to his residence in his smart little horse drawn trap which he had in attendance.

By virtue of his strong armed methods, Mr. Crawford had established his reputation in Government circles as a very efficient officer. He was therefore chosen at one time for posting to Raebareli which was reported to have gone out of hand, its figure for dacoities having touched an all time high of some 25 to 30 cases. His method to put a stop to them was unique. The day he received the very first report of one, he called for the station officer concerned and stormed at him for his inefficiency in the choicest indigenous words he could think of. This served as a cue for this as well as all other station officers of the district, not to register any further case of dacoity. In the sequel, at the end of the year, Raebareli with its solitary case of dacoity on record, was declared to be the best run district in the State thus earning further distinction for Mr. Crawford.

Another anecdote current about him during my tenure was that while he was posted at Shahjahanpur, he contracted close friendship with the wife of the Commandant of the Clothing Factory there. When this came to the notice of the latter, he locked up his wife one day before leaving for his office. His wife then somehow managed to send a note to Mr. Crawford for his help. Mr. Crawford, in his turn, had an F.I.R. lodged in the *Kotwali* for her wrongful confinement and got his *Kotwal* to rescue her by breaking open the room in which she had been confined. Thereafter he sent off a telegram to the I.G. Police to say, "So and so's wife has taken refuge in my house after her release from wrongful confinement by her husband. Wire instructions." The I.G. Police, in return replied through wire back, "You must apply for six months leave, failing which you will be transferred to Ghazipur." In the sequel, Mr. Crawford having prepared to go on leave, the matter ended there.

A confirmed bachelor by choice, Mr. Crawford took life quite easy. He sat up till late in the night and plied himself with drinks from four bottles of whiskey, one at each corner of his sitting room. His time for dinner was around midnight. Consequently he was a late riser. He also dawdled over his morning routine till it was time for lunch. After this he had his afternoon siesta till 3 in the afternoon when he went to his office.

All this may sound like a story today. But such was life in the services in the past and such was the prestige their officers enjoyed that they could be sure of a plain sailing no matter how indifferent they were to their work, which seemed to take care of itself and run of its own well oiled castors. To come to think of it, half the trouble with the administration today is lack of this prestige all along the line.

* * *

If Mr. Mac Dowell and Mr. Crawford of the Police marked themselves for their oddities, Mr. Darling, an I.C.S. was no less queer in his ways. He carried himself in a manner designed to convey the impression that the entire weight of the British Empire, the white man's burden, as it was, called in those days, rested on his shoulders. He was extremely bumptious and fussy, to say the least. His tour programme as Commissioner, Lucknow Division, was drawn up by himself, with all the meticulousness characteristic of the state Governor's tour programme. Here is a specimen of it. "The Commissioner, Lucknow Division, will arrive at the Unnao Railway Station by the Bombay Mail on the morning of such and such date at 10.05 hours. He will be met by the District Magistrate and the Superintendent of Police, among others. The Tahsildar Sadar will arrange for the transport of his personal effects to the local canal inspection house, etc., etc."

Once a while he was out on tour in Unnao, he wanted to go to Safipur Tahsil for inspection. The District Magistrate, Mr. Sucha Singh (later known as Mr. Khera), accordingly reserved for him a Canal Inspection house close to Safipur which happened to be of C class, as opposed to A or B class in its classification in the records of the Irrigation Department.

Mr. Darling felt scandalised when he came to know of it and ordered the District Magistrate to have the booking cancelled at once in favour of another inspection house of B class, a little further away.

May it be known that the masterpiece about Mr. Darlings's flamboyance relates to a talk he gave to a crowd assembled to greet him on the occasion of his visit to Purwa Tahsil. It went some what like this: "Listen, you folk, You should know that at the very apex of this Government is the Lat Sahib. Immediately below him comes the Commissioner Sahab. Next in order of seniority come in succession the District Magistrate, the Sub-Divisional Magistrate and the Tahsildar. If therefore you have a grievance of any kind, you should approach the Tahsildar Sahab in the first instance and failing him, the persons up the ladder in the sequence mentioned by me. There is, of course, finally the Lat Sahab, the god head, the fountain of all authority who like a presiding deity keeps an eye on the rest of us and guards everyone's interests without fear of favour."

The beauty of this harangue of his lay not so much in its words as in the manner in which he delivered it.

With the palm of his right hand crooked and turned outwards, he made a few jab slightly lowered down followed by a tap on his chest, to indicate where he, in his position as a Commissioner came, in the hierarchy. He followed this up by a succession of jabs in the air in a descending order to indicate where came the District Magistrate, the Sub-Divisional Magistrate and the Tahsildar. Whether or not his audience felt impressed by this performance of him one cannot say. But there can be no doubt that Mr. Darling, on his part, felt satisfied that he had done his duty by his King and country.

In passing it may be stated that Mr. Darling's one and only aim in the demonstration he gave, was to impress upon his audience the fact that the Indian Ministers, who had lately come into the picture, were of no consequence.

There were various stories about Mr. Darling's predilections. One was that he felt pleased if his visitors alluded to his wife as Lady Darling. It is said that some people therefore in the course of their conversation with him, went out of their way to enquire of him how this mythical Lady Darling was doing.

In all fairness to the British affairs of the pre-independence days one might however say that while Mr. Darling was high and mighty in his ways, there were others like Percy Marsh of Meerut, Hobart of Gorakhpur, Percy Wyndham of Mirzapur and Ramsay Mac Donald of Kumaun, who were known for their solicitude for the poor and the downtrodden. When I was posted at Faizabad, I had a District Magistrate named Hugh Stephenson, who was equally interested in the welfare of the masses.

Likewise, in the Police there were men like Freddie Young, Marsh Smith, Hugh Inglis and Nott-Bower, who have left a name behind them as administrators of the first order, very sympathetic and fair in their dealings with the masses.

* * * *

Chapter 45

Immersion of Mahatma Gandhi's Ashes

I remembered the day when Mahatma Gandhi's ashes came to Allahabad for their immersion in the Sangam. They were contained in an urn made of burnished copper which was carried in a motorcade from the Railway Station to the Sangam, on top of the leading vehicle. A number of dignitaries of all-India status, including the Prime Minster, Pt. Jawaharlal Nehru, were present on the occasion.

All arrangements at the Sangam were under the over-all charge of Mr. J. Superintendent of Police who was on special duty, while I was present there in my capacity as I.G. Police, U.P.

A number of amphibian vehicles called ducks had been requisitioned from the Army for the immersion ceremony and the drill laid down for them was that with the urn displayed on a pedestal in the leading vessel and with all the dignitaries aboard, they were to ply a number of times up and down the river for a mile or so, upstream from the Sangam, before it was laid to rest.

The ceremony lasted for an hour or so, while thousands upon

thousands of men, women and children dressed in their variegated colours, lined the river bank on the city side and kept chanting Mahatma Gandhi's favourite hymn, "*Raghupati Raghab Raja Ram, Patita Pawan Sita Ram*", with a deep resonant voice that filled the skies. Needless to say, the atmosphere became emotionally charged to an extent not known before within living memory.

As was to be expected, the day's proceedings ended with some orations from a seven foot high rostrum, specially erected for the purpose on a site close the Sangam.

Here are some sidelights on the day's events which I remembered as an interesting moments.

As I have stated above, the ducks were required to ply up and down the river a number of times with all the dignitaries aboard. Now, the problem facing Mr. T. was how to collect them with the minimum of delay, considering that most of them stood on the riverbank, mixed up with the crowd. He had to make a number of sorties in his duck for the purpose, but the unfortunate thing was that each time it touched land, the entire crowd assembled there, swarmed in to gain a forcible entry into it, which naturally led to some rough handling by him. It so happened that at one time he had to deal with hefty looking army officer of the rank of Captain, who, by virtue of his position as such, claimed preferential treatment for himself. Mr. T. in his effort to stop him from boarding his vessel, gave him a push which greatly enraged him and eventually led to an exchange between the two of a string of cockney swear words in which both of them appeared to be adept. Hot blooded as they were, they might have come to blows, but for my intervention at the crucial moment.

To proceed, I can perhaps flatter myself over my role as a mediator in the case of another young man, who turned out to be close to Mahatma Gandhi himself, being the husband of one of his grand-daughters. He, too, being mixed up with the crowd pushed about by Mr. T. which gave him some cause for offence. In this case, therefore, I had to bring into play all my tactics in an attempt to make him forget and forgive and board the duck, which he ultimately did, under protest.

There is a saying, "Those also serve, who stand and wait". The truth of it was fully borne out in the case of two men, who stood on one side looking unconcerned and watching the fun. One of them turned out to be a veteran Congressman-cum-Governor of a state, while the other turned out to be a lifelong companion of Pt. Nehru, both of whom had to be ferried across at his special request.

Another incident which I wish to mention because of for its piquancy only. What happened was something like this. In his preoccupation, Mr. T. had somehow missed to notice the urn being consigned to its final resting place. So, when he found that it was no longer to be seen where it had been, he felt confused and exclaimed repeatedly, "Where is that thing gone?" Where is that thing gone?" This being within the hearing of Pt. Nehru, gave him some cause or irritation. He was perhaps in a pensive mood at the time and did not particularly appreciate the somewhat off hand and irreverent manner in which Mr. T. had thought fit to refer to the urn which had an importance of its own. So, by way of his answer, with the thumb of his right hand turned down and pointing to the bed of the river in front of him, he gave it a jerk or two, before saying somewhat acidly, "That thing is gone there", "That thing is gone there." His words, sharp and clear as they were, spoke volumes.

And this brings out the close of my tale of the incidents of that memorable day.

* * * *

Chapter 46

Inside Story of Upgrading of Badges of Rank for Police

It will perhaps be news to many that there was a time when the badge or rank of the Chief of Police in a State was one corresponding to that of a full Colonel in the Army, while that of a Superintendent of Police was one corresponding to that of a Captain in the Army. At least this was the case when I joined service in 1922. Later on, I cannot say when exactly, the rank of an I.G. Police was upgraded to one corresponding to that of a Brigadier in the Army. In fact this was the position in 1947 when I took over as I.G. Police, U.P., which I did not like in the least. So far as the ranking of a Superintendent of Police was concerned, I issued orders, off my own bat, upgrading it to one corresponding to that of a Major in the Army, in the case of all those with less than 15 years service and to one corresponding to that of a Lt. Colonel in the Army, in the case of all those, with service for 15 years or more.

As for the ranking of an I.G. Police, I took up this matter with the Chief Minister, U.P., Pt. Govind Ballabh Pant who, in his turn, took it up with the Government of India and recommended that it should correspond to that of a Major General of the Army. The Ministry for Home Affairs in their turn, asked for comments of the Ministry of Defence on this proposal. As was customary in a matter like this, the latter referred the case to the Chief of the Army Staff, General Cariappa, for his comments, if any. But it so happened that General Cariappa was strongly opposed to the very idea of the Police aping the Army, as he put it, in the matter of their badges of rank. So he wrote out a lengthy note to express his views on the subject. His suggestion was that the Police should evolve for themselves an entirely different pattern of badges, more or less in line with the London Metropolitan Police. Mr. Sanjivi, Director of the Intelligence Bureau in his capacity of Adviser to the Home Minister in Police matters, concurred with this view and detailed his Deputy, Mr. G.K. Handoo to avail from the Metropolitan Police, London, sketches of their badges of rank.

Soon after the return of Mr. Handoo from London, I met him in Delhi and on my enquiry at to what was the position in regard to upgrading of the badge of rank of an I.G. Police, he showed me the sketches he had obtained. I noticed that they were replicas of the oak leaf. I then had an informal meeting with Mr. H.V.R. Iyengar, Secretary to the Government of India in the Ministry of Home, along with Mr. S.R. Chaudhuri, I.G. Police, Delhi and explained to him, in the first instance, how we were opposed to the idea of having to switch over to a fresh pattern of badges when we had those in vogue, for more than a century. Thereafter, I explained to him at some length how there was strong case for upgrading of the badge of rank of an I.G. Police.

As a result of this meeting, Mr. Iyengar offered to take up the matter personally with the Home Minister, Sardar Vallabhbhai Patel and told me to explain him 28 points of discussion from my list, which I had prepared in support of our case before my meeting with him.

According to Mr. Iyengar, following his meeting with Sardar Baldeo Singh, Minister for Defence in the Government which more or less ran like this:

Sardar Patel: "Baldeo"

Sardar Baldeo Singh: "Yes Sir."

Sardar Patel: "I have before me a case for upgrading of the badge of rank of an I.G. Police. I consider that the Police in India have lately given a very good account of themselves and that they amply deserve it. What do you say to it?"

Sardar Baldeo Singh: "I fully agree with you Sir."

After this brief talk with Sardar Baldeo Singh, Sardar Patel turned to Mr. Iyengar and said to him, "Go ahead." It was then that a notification which was issued in the Government of India Gazette, upgrading the badge of the rank of an I.G. Police to correspond to that of a Major General.

The manner in which Sardar Patel dealt with this case, cutting across all red tape, was only his characteristic and speaks volumes for the regard he had for the Police in India. This episode is of some historical interest also, because it goes to show how, but for the intervention of Sardar Patel at a crucial moment, we would have been flaunting us our badges of rank today various permutations and combinations of oak leaves or leaves of some other variety.

* * * *

Chapter 47

Story of a Perfect Policeman

About the year 1950, or so, when I was working as I.G., Police, U.P., I received through the post a letter purporting to be one from a person who professed to be lecturer of a College at Jalandhar. It was written something like this:

"Sir, sometime ago, while I was on my way by rail to Patna, I de-trained at Allahabad to have a dip in the Sangam. I then hired a rickshaw and on arrival there, took off my clothes to deposit them on a wooden platform close-by, before having my bath. Later on, when I proceeded, to don them again, I found, much to my horror, that my wallet, which contained in it some two hundred rupees, besides my railway ticket, was missing—I then started a frantic search for it, all around the place. This attracted the notice of a Policeman standing there who asked me politely, 'Sir, what are you searching for? Can I help you?' Then I told him of my misfortune, he expressed his sympathy for me and said, 'I will be glad if you will accept as a loan these twenty rupees which I have in my pocket and proceed on your journey—I will give my name and address to enable you to return my money to me at your convenience. You may also leave your name and address with me so that if I am at all able to recover your purse, of which the chances seem to me to be remote, I may be able to inform you of it.' I then left for the Railway Station. After a couple of hours, or so, when my train for Patna was about to leave, the same Policeman came running to me and held out my missing wallet to enquire if it was mine. My joy knew no bounds at it, and I came to know from him that he had been able after some strenuous efforts to trace it. I found all its contents intact and offered to pay him Rs. 50/- as a small token of my appreciation of his services. But he refused to accept this money mentioning that he had merely done his duty for which he was being paid by the Government."

The writer of this letter ended it up by saying, "Sir, when there are such good men in your force, you need not to have a worry about its future. You have my highest regards."

Needless to say I lost no time to ascertain the identity of the officer concerned in this case. He turned out to be a Head Constable of Kanpur who had been deputed to Allahabad on Mela duty as an officiating Sub-Inspector. I then had a wireless message sent to S.S.P. Kanpur, desiring him to give immediate out-of-turn promotion to this officer as a confirmed Sub-Inspector of Police, which I thought was the least that I could do for him.

Incidentally, this story has a moral of its own, fit for all serving Policemen to emulate.

* * * *

Chapter 48

Story Behind the Creation of our Check Posts on the Tibetan Border

Around the middle of 1950, news trickled down to the Government of U.P. of considerable military activity in the form of construction of strategic roads and air strips by the Chinese across our Tibetan border. This gave cause for particular concern to the Bhotias, a hill tribe of Indian nationality who lived on our side of the border and had been carrying on a trade with Tibet in sundry goods for centuries. Hitherto the Treaty of 1904, resulting from the Younghusband Mission to Lhasa in Tibet, had provided for joint administration of the trade route between the two countries. But concurrently with the transfer of power to us by the British Government in 1947, this arrangement lapsed and all the Outposts on this route, which used to be manned by our troops, were abandoned. Tibet not only thus got cut off from us, but also provided a source of threat to the integrity of our country.

In view of the necessity for safeguarding the interests of our countrymen on the side of our border, Pt. Govind Ballabh Pant,

Chief Minister, U.P. sought the intervention of the Prime Minister, Pt. Jawaharlal Nehru, in dealing with the situation. In the Prime Minister's view, all that was indicated the establishment of a few Check Posts on this border, manned by the Police, to prevent the infiltration of undesirable elements from across it. When Pt. Pant told me about it, I explained to him, how this was "possible to follow the order and it was practically impossible for the police with their limited resources to function at heights ranging from ten to eighteen thousand feet, which were moreover snow bound for more than half the year.

On Pt. Pant carrying my point of view to the Prime Minister, he said that I should discuss the matter with General Thimayya. But when I saw the latter at Delhi, he told me that I should see the Chief of General Staff, Lt. Gen. Thorat who was the proper person to deal with and the matter is in his hand. Accordingly, I met Gen. Thorat the next morning in company with Mr. D.P. Kohli, D.I.G., C.I.D., U.P. and explained to him about my point of view. General Thorat, in his turn, explained to me at some length how the Army was not meant for static duties and how the police were best suited for the type of job I had in mind. He also assured me that the Defence Ministry would be prepared to bear the cost whatsoever is involved. Then I understood that it would perhaps not be a bad idea to have our men at these Border Posts for that would mean an extension of our domain over a territory which had hitherto remained as no man's land. Then I prepared the estimated cost of the project which was Rs. 1 crore 20 lakh and provided three additional companies of the PAC (fully equipped for service in the region). Later on, the project was duly approved by the Ministry of Defence.

Thereafter, while I proceeded to select the sites for the Base Camps of these three Companies, Mr. Kohli proceeded to select those for the forward Posts. Incidentally, the stand taken by me initially was fully vindicated during the Chinese aggression of 1962 when we were caught on the wrong foot so for as our military preparations were concerned.

In my assessment of the suitability of spots for my purpose, I had to take into account various considerations namely whether or not water in sufficient quantity was available at the site, Secondly whether or not it was sufficiently level and wooded and finally, whether or not it was exposed to the wind. Mine was a wonderful experience, trudging about uphill and downdale in country of extreme scenic beauty from where I could catch occasional glimpses of some of the Himalayan snow peaks of rare splendour. In fact, I felt like an explorer with the world at my feet. One of the sites selected by me was at Dharchula, some 80 miles north of Almorah, which was strategically well suited (being close to Garbyang an important Trading centre on the Tibetan border), if not of much scenic beauty.

Of the other two, one was at Uttarkashi on the route to Gangotri and the other at Joshimath on the route to Badrinath. Both had much to commend them from the scenic point of view. Joshimath had a special attraction, with its orchards of apple and other fruit trees all around. Situated at a height of some seven thousand feet, it commands a pictorial view of Alakanada flowing several hundred feet below through a gorge by its side. Another attraction of it is that for almost half the year when the shrine of Badrinath is snow bound, the worship of its presiding deity is carried on here. Incidentally, it was here that the Adi Sankaracharya had his enlightenment in a cave which goes by his name and is the centre of attraction for many a pilgrim.

To revert to my story it was thus that the P.A.C. U.P. was the first to enter the field for the protection of our Tibetan border. The I.T.B.P. which now shares this honour with the P.A.C. U.P. came into the picture at a later date. As such it may perhaps be claimed with some justification that it was the P.A.C. U.P that blazed the trail for the I.T.B.P. Through the courtesy of Mr. Sheopuri, D.G., I.T.B.P. I had the rare good fortune to go to Gangotri some years ago, when I had occasion to come across several detachments of this force at various points of this route and when I was much impressed by their smartness and efficiency. Mine being a round trip I had also occasion to visit its Training Centre close to Mussoorie and see how under the supervision of one of its commandants, Mr. Man Singh, training in rock climbing and other exercises was being carried out vigorously here.

While I was on my way to Gangotri I to passed by the site which I had selected years ago for the base camp at Uttarkashi and I could not resist the temptation of stopping there to have a look round. With the Bhagirathi flowing past its very door steps, it looked like a dream come true and I could not take my eyes off this stream, Which judging from the break neck speed with which it was flowing past this camp, seemed to be in a desperate hurry to go and water the vast plains down below, stretching from one end of the country to the other, which were crying for it. I had a cup of coffee with the Company Commander who took me an a round to the building complex that had come up there since my last visit.

I must say I felt nostalgic to see the place because of my association with it years ago, at one time, and in quite another capacity, when it was bare of any habitation and when it looked like a virgin place of land, unsullied by the hand of men. I had then been captivated by the sight of the river and I noticed it was still the same. This reminded me of Tennyson's famous lines "Man may come and man may go, but I go on for ever."

* * * *

Chapter 49

A True Story

Never before in the history of Varanasi, had there been such a furore among the press and the public of that place as there was, following discovery of as many as seven dead bodies—tied together with a rope floating in the Ganga opposite Tulsipur, on the morning of the 20th March 1951, at about 8.00 AM.

The sight of a solitary dead body drifting with the current in the Ganga, it is true, is nothing very unusual, but of seven of them tied together, took the incident out of the realm of the ordinary. Was it an instance of family vendetta? or of a diabolical crime committed in the dark alleys of Varanasi? or of some obscure ritual hitherto unknown?

The police were soon on the scene and had the bodies taken out of water. When this done, they had them laid in a row on the river bank, when it was found that the dead included one grown-up man, three grown-up women, two boys and one girl.

From their looks and dress, the deceased appeared to be *Yatris* (pilgrims) who had come on a pilgrimage from some distant place and had been fairly well-to-do. A tin box, a tiffin carrier, an aluminium jug, a brass jug, a brass pot and a brass bucket—some of them filled with sand—were found tied to the bodies to serve as weights. But there were no marks of injury to be seen on any of them.

It was now left to the police to determine, who these unfortunate people could possibly be and where they had come from. If only it could be known where they had been staying, then, it was felt, much of the mystery surrounding their death would be solved.

Obviously, the best thing to do was to make enquiries among the *pandas* of the place. Accordingly, a number of them were interrogated and, soon enough, it came to be known that the deceased had been staying at House No. D-3/100 Mirghat with one, Uma Shankar *Panda.*

But Uma Shankar, unfortunately, was nowhere to be seen. In his absence, therefore, recourse had to be taken to break his house, in order to open it, which was actually done in the presence of a Magistrate, Mr. B.D. Jayal, on the 21st March. And now followed a search of the house, resulting in the recovery, among other things, of a number of hand-written notes, allegedly written by one Bhalchand.

Two of the notes, translated into English, which were as follows:

1. Our regards to all. Let no one harass any one on our account. This is to inform you that we have left for an unknown destination in quest of my daughter Pushpa who is no more.

   Sd/- Bhalchand Babu Rao Patel

   17.3.51

2. Saturday 17.3.51 Kashi, dated 17.3.51. This is to inform all and sundry of Kashi, this Saturday, the 17th March 1951, that having decided to go on pilgrimage to an unknown land for the good of the soul of my beloved daughter Pushpa who departed this life on 15.3.51 here in holy Kashi, we have today actually set out on our journey. Let no one interfere with our project. This is our own affair. No one else has anything to do with it. Our revered priest Uma Shankar ji Upadhya has no hand in it. He is not aware of our decision. Do not harass him. All the stuff in our room here is hereby presented to Pandit Barkhandi Maharaj.

   17/3

The letters, it will be seen, were quite simple in their purport. But there was no guarantee that they were not faked and had not been planted? By this time, popular feeling had been whipped up to such an extent, that no one was prepared to take them at their face value. On the contrary, the stories that gained currency, did credit to the imagination. One such story was that Bhalchand had brought Rs. 7 lakh with him from home, wishing to build a temple at Varanasi, but that Uma Shankar *Panda* and the local police had got him murdered with the rest of his family and had shared the money between them.

Luckily, Bhalchand's papers recovered from his lodging at Varanasi, gave a clue to his home address, which was Nursery Garden, P.O. Ubali, Nagpur. They also gave a clue to the identity of all the seven persons found dead, namely (1) Bhalchand Babu Rao Patel aged 45 (head of the family), (2) Sita Bai aged 34 (wife), (3) Ganga Bai aged 20, (4) Suman Bai aged 18 (daughter), (5) Uda Ram aged 13 (son), (6) Reoti aged 11 (daughter), (7) Sripal aged 7 (son).

Enquiries at Varanasi disclosed that the youngest child of the family, Pushpa, a girl age 2 years, had died on the 15th of March. Following this event, Bhalchand had bought four sarees for Rs. 300 and four blouses for Rs. 80 for his wife and three surviving daughters. Subsequently on the 17th, clad in their new clothes, they had left the house of Uma Shankar, saying that they were off to Vindhyachal for three or four days. Then they hired the boat of Baddu *Mallah* at Mirghat.

What Bhalchand and his family did after this must, unfortunately, for ever remain mostly a matter of conjecture. But fact is that they had taken with them their Puja accessories, which were later found scattered on the boat, would go to show that they presumably spent a considerable part of their time over it.

Here is the statement of Baddu *Mallah* in his own words: "At about 3 in the afternoon of the 17th March, the seven *Yatris* boarded my *bajra* (big boat) at Mirghat. They had with them one small tin box, one bucket, one tiffin carrier and one *lota*, among other things. When the *bajra* reached Tulsighat, the leader of the party asked me to anchor it in midstream. Then they built an image of Mahadeo in sand, intending to do its puja. But before launching on it, they asked me to go back to Tulsighat and wait there till I was called. I left in a *dinghy* and at 7.30 or 8 p.m. when no one called me from the *bajra*, I went over to it to see what the matter was. Great indeed was my surprise to find all the Yatris lying dead. I precipitately left the *bajra* where it was and returned with haste to my house in Mirghat. I then went to Uma Shankar *Panda* to consult with him. Thereafter, under his advice, I took his servant, Bhola, and another man, Moti Ahir, and returned back to the *bajra*. We then rowed it towards Ramnagar, on the opposite side of the river. When we reached near Ramnagar Fort, where it was quite lonely, we took out the bodies of all the seven pilgrims from inside the *bajra* and placed them on the wooden platform in front. We then tied their waists, each to each, with a rope and having done this, we filled the tin box and the utensils with sand, before tying them to the bodies, to serve as weights. Finally, we threw all of them overhead into the river, along with their clothes and other belongings. I did this, for fear I might otherwise be in for trouble and possibly be charged with murder."

The big question now was, whether Baddu was telling the truth or not.

Let us switch over to Nagpur, the hometown of Bhalchand where some interesting documents left behind by him were seized by the police. These, coupled with the result of enquiries made into his early life, throw a flood of light on the working of his mind and explain much of what would otherwise have still remained a mystery.

Bhalchand, it transpired, was left an orphan at a tender age. He was brought up by a grand aunt and after her death inherited her property. He spent a year at Ujjain and another at Varanasi in an endeavour to get through the School Final Examination, but could not succeeded. One of the subjects he offered for this examination was French and model drawing. While at Ujjain, and again, at Varanasi he developed a keen interest in religion. This allegedly took an increasingly strong hold on him as he grew older for he was known to devote most of his time, lately, to the study of religious books. He was even heard talking of higher regions and the world beyond. By and by, he lost all interest in life and in the people around him, excepting his wife and children, to whom he was much devoted. In the year 1945, he married off his two elder daughters, Ganga Bai and Suman Bai.

Being a firm believer in *Ahimsa,* Bhalchand had a profound regard for Mahatma Gandhi, As a result, therefore, of the Mahatma's assassination in January 1948, he was said to have lost his mental balance for some time and behaved like a mad man. As for instance, on the occasion to mark the cremation ceremony of Mahatma Gandhi organised by his village people on the bank of Chandra Bhadra, he insisted on burning a photograph of the Mahatma and was prevented from doing so with much difficulty. At this time, his brother-in law, finding something wrong with his mental condition, took him to a medical man, Dr. Patwardhan, who besides prescribing a medicine for him, advised a change to an airy and cool place. But after this, even though he became apparently all right, a wall of misunderstanding grew up between him and the rest of his village folk, compelling him completely to withdraw into himself.

Towards the end of 1950 he developed a strong desire to go on pilgrimage along with his entire family. He gave an indication of this to his brothers-in-law, Narain Rao and Dhanna Lal, but kept the exact date of departure, a secret from them. Not having sufficient money with him to defray the expenses of his projected journey, he let out some of his land on lease and thus managed somehow to scrape together a sum of Rs. 2,015 before his departure.

Another thing he did before setting out was to fetch his two married daughters, Ganga Bai and Suman Bai, from their houses.

The party, that was Bhalchand, his wife and children, left Nagpur on the 4th March and arrived at Allahabad the next day where they spent from 5 to 6 hundred rupees on puja and on feeding some 50 to 60 Brahmins. Next, they moved to Varanasi where the condition of Pushpa, the youngest daughter of the family, who had been ailing for some time, became more and more critical, finally ending in her death on the 15th. Whatever transpired after this, is already known to us from the result of enquiries made at Varanasi as also from the statement of Baddu *Mallah*.

The post-mortem report in this case proved death by drowning, while the chemical Examiner's report on the viscera of the deceased, testified to the presence of some irritant poison in it. Therefore, the only inference possible which, incidentally, confirms the statement of Baddu *Mallah*, is that while the deceased were still under the influence of some poison, their bodies were thrown into the river, in the belief that they were dead. But one would ask, "How did these persons come to be under the influence of some poison? Did they took it, with free will, or was it administered to them?"

That it was not a case of murder for gain is established, from the fact that all the belongings of the deceased, including the trinkets worn by the female members of the family, were found intact. Likewise, there was nothing to show that they had been put to death on account of some other motive. Obviously, therefore, one of two things happened: Namely, either that all the deceased took the poison of their own accord, or that it was administered by one of them. But it is inconceivable that either of the two married daughters of Bhalchand, one of whom, besides, happened to be in the family way, or any of the three minor children or, for that matter; his wife, Sita Bai, would give up their lives for nothing or be party to an act which was nothing short of murder. Inevitably, therefore, one is driven to the conclusion that it was Bhalchand, and Bhalchand alone, who was responsible for the grim tragedy enacted in this case. One thing that leads further support to this conclusion is the fact that from a search of Bhalchand house at Nagpur, several phials containing poison were recovered; another, that he was generally known to dabble in Ayurvedic medicine.

And now, we come to certain documents, belonging to Bhalchand, which were recovered from a tin box left behind by him at Nagpur in the charge of his brother-in-law Ramanand and which clinch the issues in this case, beyond the shadow of a doubt.

Among the contents of the box, there was a coloured drawing by Bhalchand on a big sheet of paper in which he had shown all the seven members of his family standing in the Ganga at the bottom, with a cord in the form of a circle, linking them with the supreme being, at the top. A number of jottings over his signature, recording his decision are to be seen all around this picture.

The trend of Bhalchand's mind is also apparent from several other sketches, depicting himself as a restless soul in quest of peace. In one of them, there is a picture of a man on the run who is supposed to be saying *"Prabhu keon daurate ho? Prabhu milne me keon der? Ye kya apka nyaya hai?"* (O Lord, why do you make me run? O Lord, why this delay in our meeting. Is this your justice?)

In another, the entire family is shown standing by Manikarnikaghat in Varanasi, while in a third, which is dated 30-1-51, there is a marginal note saying in English "Most Urgent require to act in Ganga, if 'God' agree, within Holi."

Similarly Bhalchand's diary, of which he had developed several pages to the record of his "Will" bequeathing his entire property to Ram Mandir and expressing his decision to quit the world along with his wife and children, provide further proof, the proof which were needed by us of the working of his mind.

In short, Bhalchand's past history, the letters left behind by him in his lodging at Varanasi (which were verified by his brother-in-law, Dhanna Lal, as being in Bhalchand's handwriting) the numerous entries recorded in his diary, specially the one purporting to be his last testament and, above all, the tell-tale sketches drawn by him, leave no room for doubt that the tragedy enacted at Varanasi, was really the consummation of an idea he had been working out in a cold, calculated manner over a long period of time, in the innermost recesses of his mind.

But all things considered, the most remarkable feature of the whole affair is how Baddu *Mallah* and his two companions, by throwing into the river the seven seemingly dead bodies, unwittingly carried out, to the last letter, the very idea that had become an obsession with Bhalchand.

So far, therefore, as the police was concerned, the mystery of the seven corpses of Varanasi had been fully cleared. But human prejudice, once it is embedded in the mind, in hard to dislodge.

Consequently, the man-in-the street there continued to entertain a strong belief that a third party—most likely the *Panda* who had played the host to the deceased had a hand in this ugly affair. He even wrongly accused the police of being hand-in-glove with the latter, and it was on this account that I had to go over to Varanasi to try and remove this false notion from the public mind. With this end in view, I also held a press conference which was attended by most of the local press representatives. Even though, I regret to say, the common man there still discuss this case with much mental reservation.

* * * *

Chapter 50

A Lady with a Mission

> "Dear Inspector General—Welcome to Dharchula. I am sending you a small home-made cake and a bottle of cherries in syrup which, I hope, you will do me the honour to accept. With kind regards. Yours faithfully—Sd/-."

Such was the note that was delivered to me, along with the cake and the cherries in syrup one afternoon in the month of April, 1952, soon after my arrival at this place.

A present of this kind, received from a total stranger, and that too, at a place which appeared to be beyond the pale of civilization was something I could never have anticipated. But great as was my surprise at its receipt, it became greater still when I learnt that the person who had sent it, was a lady belonging to a foreign Mission, who stayed, all by herself, in a hut in the local *bazaar.* Anyway, I accepted the present and sent her a letter of thanks. At the same time, I decided to pay her a courtesy visit, the next morning, by way of my appreciation of her kind gesture towards me.

For me a visit to Dharchula, was like going to the other end of the world. Lying some eighty miles north of Almorah, it was accessible, in those days, by a foot track which at places having been literally carved out of the rocks, was extremely narrow. As I passed along one of these mountain ledges, I remember how I was told of a certain individual who had been deceived by his enemy into going there, before being pushed down into the *khud*, several hundred feet below, to be there for ever.

Distances in the mountains, as I found much to my vexation, can be very deceptive, so that there is nothing one can do but go tramp, tramp, tramp, on and on, with only the echoes from one's footfalls to keep one's company; except, of course, for the occasions where one comes across a string of goats or sheep carrying their small loads of merchandise, beautifully balanced on their small backs, and tripping along merrily, with their bells sounding ting-a-ling, ting-a-ling, ting-a-ling.

Strangely enough, I have noticed that the note from these bells, hung round the neck of all such pack animals, is always the same. I have heard it in the early hours of the morning, from inside my tent, cosily tucked up in my bed, while out camping in the jungles of Mirzapur in Uttar Pradesh and, again, while out on a trek through Sikkim. And it has always brought me a feeling of peace. What a pity we do not fully realise our debt to these dumb animals which have for countless centuries, provided our one and only means of transport between certain places, not connected by rail or by road? Most of them even seem destined to lay down their lives by the roadside in the service of humanity, as is borne out by the numerous carcasses that may be seen strewn at almost every twist and turn or the track across the Himalayas. But who knows that, with the onward march of civilization, a time may soon come when these innocent animals may be altogether supplanted, on the old routes which seemed reserved for them, by great big honking motor vehicles, trundling along at break neck speed and when we shall hear their jingling bells no more.

Return to my story of Dharchula, soon after I had refreshed myself, I decided to go around and see what it was like. Flanked on either side by high mountain walls, for the most part bare of vegetation, and traversed in the middle by a hill stream, of which the water had gone down very low, it had all the appearance of a valley, if somewhat uninteresting. Such of the fields as were there, had been shorn of their crops, leaving only their stubbles behind, while quadrupeds of all varieties, were to be seen dotted all over the place and grazing the bare fields with the avidity of starved animals. Add to this, varieties of poultry, strutting about to pick up their fare and the picture is complete.

The entire population of the place, young and old, appeared to have turned out in a body to see what was on. For them my camp was a novelty and so was I, for this was the first time in recorded history that an Inspector General of Police had cared to visit the place. Understandably enough, they watched the proceedings with a curiosity which was at times embarrassing. But they were all very friendly, with an openness of good characteristic of all men living in the mountain regions, away from the corroding influence of the plains.

Whatever little time I had before the sun went down, I spent on wandering about the place in an effort to make a study of it. But the thing that struck me most was the squalor and the filth evidently a consequence of the prevailing poverty and ignorance—noticeable almost everywhere. In marked contract to this, the American Mission, only a few furlongs away, presented a pretty picture with an orchard, a vegetable garden, a dairy and a poultry of its own. In fact, it was refreshing to see how the American couple living there, and made a beautiful home for themselves, for which one wondered why our Indian Missionaries could not likewise set up their establishments in these remote regions, where there was a good deal of work for them to do.

My business at Dharchula was connected with the establishment of Police Check Posts on our border with Tibet. I made certain enquiries in this connection, but I had been at this place for hardly a few hours when I had a message conveyed to me over my mobile wireless set, calling me back to my headquarters, with the minimum of delay. This was rather annoying, for after my long and arduous march, I had thought of making a halt here for at least a couple of days, before trudging all the way back to Almorah. But now I had got to set out on the return journey, the very next morning and, much as I abhorred the idea of having to do so, I had to reconcile myself to it.

Early next morning, I woke up quite refreshed. These Himalayan regions, I discovered, had a tonic effect hard to beat, for howsoever tired one might feel after a long day's march, one was sure to regain one's strength after a night's rest. They have also a soothing effect on the nerves and helps to bring one a sense of oneness with the Universe.

My first task in the morning, after I had got ready for my journey, was to pay a visit to the lady of the foreign mission, who had been so kind to me. I found she lived in a small wooden hut in the nature of a log cabin, built specially to suit her requirements. It was supported on beams and stood several feet above the ground level. One had, therefore, to climb a wooden ladder to enter it. A couple of book cases neatly arranged against the walls, a few coloured prints of Jesus Christ and of scenes from the Bible, hung on pegs in them, a writing table at one corner, two or three chairs disposed carelessly about, a few knick knacks placed here and there, and a rug spread on the floor, made up the entire composition of her cabin. But though simple and unostentatious, it had all the appearance of taste and provided a fit setting for its owner who, to my utter surprise, turned out to be a mere girl, fresh as a lily, and looked not more than 25 years of age.

Not being able to suppress my curiosity about her history, I asked her where she had come from and what had brought her to Dharchula of all places. From what she told me, I gathered that she belonged to Montreal in Canada. Early in her life she had felt a call and had, therefore, joined the Canadian Mission. One day she was examining a map of the world showing all the centres of this Mission, when she discovered that the area around Dharchula had no such centre. At this she at once made up her mind to come and work here. Her family, she said, consisted of her parents, who were still living and a brother, all of whom had concurred in this idea of hers.

Simple as the statement was, it caused me a surprise beyond measure, for I thought that for a young woman to come from quite another part of the world and work in surroundings quite foreign to her and that too, all by herself, required a rare kind of courage, for which it would be hard to find a parallel. The fact that she knew little Hindi, did not seem to discourage her in the least. Nor did she mind the distance that separated her, not only from her home, several thousand miles away, but also from nearest rail head situated at a distance of something like 300 miles from Dharchula. But much as I admired her for her courage, the thing that raised her still more in my estimation was the type of service she was engaged in. Her main occupation, she told me, was to render first aid to the numerous pilgrims to Kailash who stood in need of it. For such of them as were found to suffer from sore feet, she did the washing and the bandaging with her own hands.

It is a long time since I visited Dharchula. But whenever I think of the place, I remembered that lone young woman from Canada, dedicating herself in the name of Christ—to the service of humanity, and my head bows to her in salute.

* * * *

Chapter 51

A Gripping Episode of Bareilly

Here are details of an episode of Bareilly which made headline news for one time. The trouble began one fine morning in the month of January, 1952, with a case of pillion riding on a push-bike by two students of the Bareilly College. This being an offence under the law, at least in those days, they were stopped by a keen and conscientious policeman, fresh from the Police Training College, Moradabad. The incident attracted a number of other boys of the same college, resulting in a scuffle in which the policeman was badly manhandled. A posse of policemen from the *Kotwali* close by, then rushed to the spot to rescue their comrade in arms. Upon this, while a majority of the boys took to their heels, a dozen of them came to be rounded up and were marched to the *Kotwali* for taking a suitable action against them. This proved to be a signal for the student community of Bareilly, as a whole, to flock to the *Kotwali* and forcibly secure the release of their fellow students. For his part, Thakur Saudagar Singh, Dy. S.P. City, Bareilly, thought fit, by way of a precautionary measure, he closed the gate of *Kotwali* in order to take his stand outside this building along with a handful of policemen.

As always happens in such cases, one thing led to another, so that it was not long before the crowd, which had by now swelled to a couple of thousand and included the hooligans of the station, started pelting stones on the policemen standing there, one of which of a fairly large size happened to hit a junior Sub-Inspector of police causing a big gash in his forehead. Being unable to hold himself in check, he then fired his revolver point blank, thus hitting one of the crowd, unfortunately a student, and thus causing his death on the spot, while the others melted away.

But this only added fuel to fire. The entire population of Bareilly took the side of the students and all business of the town came to a grinding halt. They passed resolutions against the Police and demanded the head of Saudagar Singh on a platter. The conflagration soon spread all over the town culminating in stray assaults of the hit-and-run type against solitary policeman on traffic or patrol duty. They were mostly committed by bands of hooligans who never miss an opportunity to settle old scores against the Police. They even went to the extent of carrying out a couple of raids against outlying police out-posts, thus setting them on fire.

In view of this progressive deterioration in the situation, I made arrangement to rush in reinforcement from elsewhere which brought about a partial lull in it. Beside this, the presence on the spot of two seasoned officers in the person of Mr. R.T. Shivadasani, Commissioner, Bareilly Division and of Mr. S.C. Misra, D.I.G. Police Range, gave me some cause for satisfaction.

About this time, one morning, while I was discussing the situation with Sri Lal Bahadur Shastri, Home Minster in the Government of U.P. and informing him how I expected the storm to blow over soon, I chanced to learn that the Chief Minister Pt. Pant was on the point of leaving for Bareilly at the request of a local M.L.A., Sri Ram Murti. This was indeed news to me and I rushed to see him, only to tell him that he must on no account agree to see the student community there. When he had given me an assurance to this effect, I came away fully satisfied.

But as the luck would have it, the moment Pt. Pant arrived at the Circuit House in Bareilly, the news spread all over the town like lightening, which made hundreds of students to *gherao* him there and extract a promise from him to suspend the *Kotwal*, Saudagar Singh.

Meanwhile, the city police personnel had assembled in the *Kotwali* in a body in the expectation that Pt. Pant before his return to Lucknow, would care to meet them and listen to their tale of woe. But somehow it did not occur to him to drop in at the *Kotwali*. This commission on his part, coupled with the news that he had given his consent ex-parte to the suspension of Saudagar Singh without any fault was like adding insult to injury and they decided to resign en mass, to token of which they surrendered their articles of uniform at the *Kotwali*.

Mr. Misra, D.I.G. Range, tried his level best to pacify them. Then they insisted upon an interview with me before deciding their future course of action. It was about 8.00 in the evening when this news was conveyed by Mr. Misra to me by wireless, while Mr. Shivadasani carried the same news to Mr. Bhagwan Sahay, Chief Secretary to the Government of U.P. Mr. Bhagwan Sahay at once got into touch with me and deplored the manner in which Pt. Pant had acted in this case. At the same time he told me that since the mischief had been done, it was up to me to pull the chestnuts out of the fire.

The two of us then went over to the Chief Minister's residence where we were joined by Sri Lal Bahadur Shastri, Home Minister, Sri Govind Narain, Home Secretary and Sri Shanti Prasad, D.I.G., P.A.C.

In the deliberations that ensued, I found Pt. Pant dog-tired and, for once, somewhat apologetic. But he said to me by way of encouragement what he was confident I would be able to deal with the situation suitably. In the result, I left the same night by car for Bareilly at about 11.00, accompanied by Sri Shanti Prasad and a gun-man.

The distance to be covered was some 150 miles. As there was nothing for me to do, I kept gazing at the countryside with unblinking eyes and an alert mind. Bathed, as it was, with a brilliant moonlight, it looked enchanting, even if somewhat dreamlike and insubstantial.

My mind being thoroughly worked up, I did not have a wink of sleep till we arrived at Bareilly. It was by then around 3.00 in the morning, when we found Mr. Misra, D.I.G. Range, Mr. T.P. Srivastava, S.P. Bareilly and Saudagar Singh. Dy. S.P. City, waiting there to receive us. We at once went into a huddle at which all gathered that the situation was well under control. This was a good news and put all of us in excellent humour. After informing Saudagar Singh that it was my painful duty to order his suspension, if only as a face saving measure, he went to the extent of explaining me that he owed such loyalty to Pt. Pant and to me that he would not even hesitate to lay down his head to be chopped off if called upon to do so. He also assured me that it would be his look out to see that all his force to a man, gave of their best. For my part, I gave an assurance to him that I would see to it that he came to no harm. I then told him that I would address his men at a parade in the *Kotwali* later in the morning at 9.00. This brought our confabulations to a close and I lay down to rest for a while after my night's vigil.

Later at 8.45 in the morning, when I was poised for a visit to the *Kotwali*, I had a message from Mr. Shivadasani Divisional Commissioner, requesting me to drop in at his place for a few minutes on my way there. I felt this message to be most ill-timed, yet courtesy demanded that I should comply with it. This slight hitch in my programme, it will be seen, had far reaching consequences.

While I was discussing with Mr. Shivadasani his telephone bell rang with an insistence that sounded ominous. It conveyed a message for me from the *Kotwali* that the men assembled there had broken loose and were on the war path. I then drove off at-once to the *Kotwali* and on my arrival there, the first thing I noticed was that a number of Policemen, who appeared to have gone berserk, were tearing off, *lathis* in hand, in small batches in different directions. What made them behave in this extraordinary manner was more than I could tell. The best thing I could do was to give a chase to some of them on foot. This, I reflected, was a fantastic situation in which no policeman of my rank had perhaps ever found himself. I soon managed to overtake a few of them and catching them by the scruff of their neck commanded them to go back to the *Kotwali* at once which they did, perhaps through a force of habit, since they had no reason to know at the time who I was. In this way, I had hardly gone some distance when I noticed a large crowd of rioters brandishing their *lathis*, heading in my direction. In a situation like this, I was unarmed and unaided so I thought to make a right about turn at once and take refuge in the *Kotwali.* Close on my heels, Mr. Misra came in dripping blood from a deep gash in his forehead. This infuriated the *Kotwali* personnel still more and made them shout for the blood of the rioters.

On their part, the rioters, feeling greatly emboldened by the precipitate retreat of the policemen, took the offensive and raided the *Kotwali* to bombard it from outside with whatever missiles came to hand. The din thus caused was ear-splitting. My one concern then was to prevent a head on collision between them and the *Kotwali* police, for I knew and certain in that event dozens of rioters would kiss the dust and my name would be mud. I had, therefore, got all my men bottled up inside the *Kotwali* and its iron gate barred. At his stage, I must confess, my men were behaving like mad men and were entreating me with a voice choked with emotion to let them loose. "*Hazoor*, let us out, *Hazoor*, let us out" was what they were repeatedly saying to me, therefore, to devote every ounce of my energy to the task of keeping them from breaking away. To gain time I ordered them to sit down and help themselves to a *Lota* full of water each, which made them clam down to a certain extent.

Then only they informed me that what had made them loose there temperament in the morning. They told me what they had been waiting for my arrival, two of them felt an urge to go into the bye-lane behind the *Kotwali* to relieve themselves. There they were assaulted by a couple of ruffians which made them rush back with blood coursing down their cheeks. This proved to be the proverbial last straw on the camel's back and sent them careering in all directions determined to have their own back after the harassment they had been suffering for days.

While I was still addressing my men inside the *Kotwali*, I heard the sound of a gun from one corner of the *Kotwali* building. This struck me as odd, but I could see that it had the magical effect of putting all the rioters to flight.

My enquiries revealed that an armed guard of one and four, had been stationed there as a precautionary measure, what had happened was that one of them, being unable to tolerate any longer thc bchaviour of thc rioters had taken aim at one of them and fired, thus killing him on the spot and causing the rest of them to ran away. In view of the prevailing situation curfew was clamped on the town for three days and all was well thereafter.

Following a magisterial enquiry held by Mr. Shivadasani into the entire episode, Saudagar Singh was exonerated of all guilt and thereafter reinstated in service.

I have cause to remember this case particularly because of the extraordinary nature of it.

* * * *

Chapter 52

Role of the Police

Many years ago, while out on tour during my tenure as Inspector General of Police, U.P., I visited Gupt Kashi, a lovely little hill station a few miles short of the famous shrine of Kedarnath. Its importance lies in the fact that in winter season, when this shrine is snowbound, the daily worship of the aforesaid deity is carried on here. Perched at a hight of some 7,500 feet, with a magnificent and panoramic view of some of the giant snow peaks of the Himalayas, like Nanda Devi, Chowkhambha and Pancha Chuli, among others, it is fit to be an abode of the gods. As such, I should have thought, any one with the least sense of scenic beauty, would love his posting to this spot. But to my utter surprise, the officer in charge of the local Police Station, came up to me with a request for transfer his posting to any of the police stations in plains. His argument was that at Gupt Kashi, where there was hardly any crime, there was no scope of work for him. My answer to him was that for a police officer, if he only understood his role properly, there was enough scope for work, wherever there was any human habitation.

This is exactly where most of our police personnel go wrong. They seem to think that they are meant purely for the prevention and detection of crime and that the general welfare of the people residing within their beat, is not concern with them. The police are employed, and rightly so, for relief and re-habitation work on various occasions. Flood or fire, they are expected to turn out in large numbers for rescue of the victims thereof. But a thing that is generally lost sight of is that their help even in trifling matters, may not only gain them popularity, but at times also help to ward off crime of a serious nature, like murder or riot.

In defining happiness, Aristotle, one of the greatest philosophers the world has ever produced, is believed to have said that it consists in making others happy. What a great difference it would make to the world, if only all of us realised the import of this definition.

Our Policemen have a particular need to commit this aphorism to memory, for the simple reason that, ordinarily, they are apt to be very callous or indifferent in their dealings with the public, in marked contrast with their counterparts in some of the developed countries of the world. I once read an account of a London Bobby, for instance, who, during the course of his night round, assisted in the delivery of a baby in an emergency. In this context, I am reminded of a recent occurrence within my knowledge, which being a typical one, but is worthy to mention here. One day an ordinary villager named Jag Lal, whom I knew, came to see me. He said that he had lost his buffalo and went to the local Police Station to lodge a report, but that the Head Constable writer (Jag Lal) there asked him a hundred rupees or so, for the issue of notices all round, the cost of paper being as high as it is today. The object of Jag Lal's visit to me was to seek my help in the case. For my part, I thought fit to advise him to send in his report by registered post, as this would serve the purpose he had in mind. He did so and, fortunately for him, his buffalo was traced by him a few days later.

This episode makes it abundantly clear how indifferent our policemen generally are to their duty, apart from showing how they are out to fleece the common citizen on the least pretext. No wonder therefore that they are very unpopular today. Prima facie, they are themselves largely to blame for the apathy that characterises the public in their relations with them and if they wish to establish themselves firmly in the hearts of the masses, infinite patience coupled with a missionary zeal for their work is the only answer. In other words, if they are to improve their image, they must understand squarely that while they are required primarily to deal with crime and criminals they are expected at the same time to render service to the public in various other ways.

"A good turn a day", is the motto of Scouts and Guides all over the world. It should likewise be the motto of all policemen, on the clear understanding that the service rendered must be selfless. Placed as he is, a Policeman has tremendous opportunities for selfless service to his fellow citizens and it is indeed a great pity that most policemen fail to take advantage of these opportunities.

This reminds me that as S.P. Saharanpur, I had plenty of opportunity to render service of this kind, which paid me enormously in dividends, whether I wanted them or not. Let me cite one instance. One day a village woman came to see me along with her minor son-in-law. She said that following her husband's death recently, his younger brother had appropriated to himself all the agricultural land they had and thus left her destitute. I fixed a date for both the parties to appear before me and when they did so, I dictated an order to the station officer concerned that unless the accused in this case entered into a compromise with his sister-in-law, he should be sent up for proceedings under section 107 of the Criminal Procedure Code against him. This had the desired effect and the parties, aided by their respective counsels, signed a compromise deed in my presence. I am aware that I perhaps went out of my way in interfering in this family dispute which was of a purely civil nature. But my conscience is clear on this score.

Here is another case of the same district, which is not without its humour. A middle-aged man who lived there came to see me one day with a complaint that his young wife whom he had only recently wedded, had run away—Could I do something to restore her to him? I said to him light heartedly, "Why worry? She is a vile woman. Let her go wherever she chooses. You had better take another wife to yourself." In answer, pulling a long face, he said to me, "But, Sir, this will mean much pecuniary loss to me; for, I had to pay a lot of money to her parents in exchange for her." I am afraid, I could do nothing to wipe off this man's tears. But I must own, the mere fact that he at all came to me to seek my intervention in his dire distress, tickled my vanity to some extent.

I wanted to mention here still another case of Saharanpur which constitutes for me the best compliment I have ever had from persons quite unknown to me. During the period of my posting there, one morning I had a visitor who told his name as Gulam Rasool. He was well-dressed and distinctly cut well above the average. He said to me that although he was a resident of Saharanpur, he lived mostly at Mussoorie. I understood from him that he owned some house and landed property at Saharanpur which fetched him a fairly good income annually. He further confessed to me that, it was for the first time, that he had ever come to call on the S.P. of his district. On my enquiry as to what had brought him to me this is what he told me "I came here a couple of days ago to collect some funds. My house which is also my ancestral home, is situated in the heart of the city. Last evening while I was sitting in the outer verandah. I heard two of my neighbours, both old women in their sixties, having a free exchange of hot words, which went on for some time without a break. Ultimately I heard one of them saying to the other, 'If you go on prattling like this, I will go to Lahiri Sahab.' It was then that I made up my mind to call on you if only to satisfy my curiosity about you."

Naturally, all this sounded like heavenly music to me and I have cause to remember it to this day with a sense of pride, a charge to which I feel guilty.

One thing that grieves me is to find how, the Civil Police all over the country appear to have downed their tools today with disastrous results. If there is a vicious spurt in both heinous and non-heinous crimes all over the country, it is simply because as an instrument for the prevention and detection of crime, they have lost their hold, in spite of the facilities in the shape of housing, transport and communications they enjoy as compared with the past. There can be no denying that their efficiency instead of going up, has gone down alarmingly and that they are far from full value for the money spent on them.

All this is undoubtedly a sequel to lack of a proper sense of devotion to duty or of discipline among them, resulting from outside interference in purely internal matters of administration, such as postings and transfers. That was the time when a Policeman going over the head of his immediate superior without permission to seek any favour for himself or redress of any grievance of his, was liable to be taken to task for it. But this being no longer the case, it is no wonder that discipline in all ranks of the force has gone to pieces.

The Government have a responsibility to discharge in this respect by avoiding all false steps that may adversely affect the discipline for the force. They must steel themselves particularly against all recommendations from third parties relating to postings and transfers among other things. By doing no, they will be safeguarding their own interests, for, if the Police as an agency for the enforcement of law and order or for the eradication of crime, prove to be a failure, then Military rule has to step in.

If the Civil Police appear to have downed their tools, the Armed Police cut an equally sorry figure for want of a proper understanding about their appropriate utilisation—We shout from the house-tops that we stand for a socialistic pattern of society. But judging from the number of armed guards that are deployed for the protection of top ranking officers, we are actually feudal at heart.

Most of these guards being superfluous can easily be replaced at best by one or two armed shadows. In London, incidentally, only a couple of unarmed Policeman are to be seen on duty outside 10, Downing Street, the official residence of the Prime Minister there. Alas, an armed guard has come to stand for a symbol of office with us, which is all wrong, worse still, these guards are sometimes drawn from the P.A.C., which is a blunder of the highest order. This force was originally designed for use in aid of the regular Police to meet emergent demands, or, as a striking force in conditions of grave emergency. In other words it was meant to be held mostly in leash and used only sparingly. To ensure its efficiency, one of the conditions laid down for its administration was that its personnel must be given intensive training in drill and discipline, both initially and at regular intervals thereafter. This was actually done in the past, resulting in a holy fear of it. But today, if my information is correct, there is ordinarily less then even a company strength left at the headquarters of each Battalion and that too, for the performance of mere garrison duties.

Excessive and prolonged use of the P.A.C. for static duties, which should be the concern of the regular Police, has helped largely to knock the teeth off this force and leave it as a poor imitation of itself.

As is the case with Army Units, P.A.C. Units also (which are essentially of paramilitary character), are, in their best interest, required to be kept, if not strictly in purdah, yet in partial seclusion, as they may otherwise prove to be a menace, instead of a boon. But then, who cares for this wise precept today? What a pity, the lesson learnt from the revolt of the P.A.C., some years ago, stands completely lost today on those who have the administration of it in their hands. Let us hope, they would wake up same day to a sense of their responsibility in this regard, before it is too late once again.

* * * *

Chapter 53

When the Prime Minister Lost Temper

There are persons whose very oddities are lovable. This remark can be said to hold good in case of Pt. Jawaharlal Nehru. His one oddity was that he was accustomed to flare up occasionally. But he was no less lovable on this account. He had probably inherited this trait of his from his illustrious father, Pt. Motilal Nehru. By way of an explanation for it, it may also be stated that being a perfectionist, he was put out by anything that failed to come up to his expectations or square up with his sense of propriety. He did not also suffer fools.

I happened to be present on a number of occasions when he lost his temper. Those were the days of post independence era of our country when Pt. Nehru found it necessary to visit Lucknow time to time and again and again. Although most of these visits were of a non-official character, yet, every time he came I was served with a routine order from the Secretariat, desiring me to arrange for a Guard of Honour for him at the Amausi airport. I was the I.G. Police, U.P. and felt that the thing was not quite correct. But even though, I said to myself an order is an order—why worry about it? As such, I refrained from raising any objection from my side.

Pt. Nehru also felt like I did about the fatuity of a Guard being mounted for him in season and out of season. So, on one of these occasions, the moment he alighted from his plane, he remarked to Pt. Govind Ballabh Pant who, as Chief Minister, U.P. stood there to receive him along with a number of other dignitaries, "Pantji, why should you arrange for a Guard of Honour for me every time I come here? I do not consider it at all necessary. After all, I am not a puppet *(Kath-Putli)* that I must walk like one." As he said all this within my hearing, I made a special note of it in my mind for my future guidance.

It so happened that Pt. Nehru had a chance to visit Lucknow again within a few weeks of his previous visit. True to pattern, however, I was served with a routine order from the Secretariat to arrange for a Guard of Honour for him at the airport, I then made it a point to discuss the thing with the Chief Secretary to U.P. Government, Mr. B.N. Jha, who assured me that he would consult the Prime Minister's Secretariat about it and then let me know of the upshot. Thereafter when only a couple of days were left for the P.M.'s arrival and, yet, I had heard nothing further from Mr. Jha, I thought fit to speak to Sri Lal Bahadur Shastri, Home Minister in the Government of U.P., He then promised to have a discussion with the Chief Secretary on the subject. But, unfortunately, he too, forgot all about it. As a result, the order I had received about the guard held good, and, on the appointed day, it stood facing the plane, resplendent in its best uniform and with its bayonets glittering in the sun.

Thereafter, following his arrival, as Pt. Nehru stood on the landing platform of his plane surveying the landscape, the moment he caught sight of the Guard, he went red in the face and bellowed at Pt. Pant to say, "Panditji, I told you explicitly the last time I came that I do not care for a Guard of Honour being put up for me, every time I come—I see no sense in it. Am I an automaton that I must behave like one?" In short, he appeared to be in a towering rage which non-plussed Pt. Pant who, after all, had nothing to do with the routine order issued to me. So in his utter confusion, all he could think of explaining this. "What can I do? The I.G. Police wants to have it this way." This made the P.M. still more furious and he resorted by saying, "The I.G. or no I.G., I will not have it so." Being on the spot, I was listening to all this conversation. But I thought it best not to open my mouth. In fact, I felt vindicated and inwardly chuckled over what had come to pass. Thereafter, when the Guard Commander, sword in hand, came up with measured steps to the saluting base to say, "The Guard is ready for your inspection, Sir," he brusquely said. "I do not think it necessary for me to do so," and then walked off in a huff to his waiting car with this came to an end that day's show.

To the eternal glory of Sri Lal Bahadur Shastri I must say that he lost no time to clear my position with the Prime Minister and explain to him how he himself was to blame for having failed to take suitable action on my representation to him a couple of days ago.

There is another incident of a similar nature which I feel tempted to mention. This time, the occasion of Pt. Nehru's visit was a public meeting in the premises of the Allahabad Junction Railway Station which he was slated to address. A rostrum some ten foot high had been erected for the purpose on the city side of the Railway Station and the gathering, numbering several thousands waited for him to arrive, which he did right on time. As he mounted the rostrum and stood on it facing the crowd, he appeared to be in a cheerful mood. To the best of my recollection it was then 6.00 in the evening.

As was his practice, before commencement of his speech, Pt. Nehru wanted to satisfy himself that the transmission system was working satisfactorily. So he gave a few taps to the mike in front of him and asked in a loud voice to know if he was fully audible in all corners of the ground around him. Upon this one sector of the crowd raised their hands to signify that he was not audible. This made him very angry and he began to fret and fume. Thereafter, when Mr. Kaul, General Manager of the Northern Railway, came up to him to apologise for the inconvenience caused to him, he bellowed "I call it the height of incompetence on your part," which caused Mr. Kaul to make a hurried retreat head over heels. Mr. Mushran, Member, Railway Board, was the next to approach the P.M. to express his regret for what had come to pass. The P.M. was then in no mood to listen to him and shouted at him to say, "Who are you?" In short, pandemonium prevailed for half an hour or so before the fault in the transmission system was put right and the P.M. was in a position to deliver his speech.

Incidentally, I had then retired from my office of I.G. Police, U.P. and sat there merely as an invitee and so did Mr. Panna Lal, I.C.S., who happened to be miles senior to me—I remember how he felt prompted at one stage to whisper to me with a touch of complacence, "Lahiri, this sort of a thing did not happen in our time."

The meeting lasted for an hour or so, after which we dispersed, thoroughly worked up by all that we had seen or heard.

* * * *

Chapter 54

A Cherished Memory

I went to the Railway Station to see off my wife, who had to leave for Delhi by the Kalka Mail. There was still an hour or so for the train to arrive. This was because my wife was very particular that she should allow for sufficient marginal time if she is to catch a train. Naturally, like all good husbands, I have to toe the line with her.

As we were cooling our heels in the passenger hall, a beautiful young woman, apparently in her early twenties, accosted me to ask if I had small change for a rupee. She said she needed thirty paise to buy a platform ticket. On examining my wallet, I found that while I had some small change with me, it did not add up to a rupee. Intending to help her out in any case, I took out thirty paise and gave them to her as a small gift from me—at least, that was what I meant.

After a while, she came back to me and said sweetly, "Uncle, here is your money." This took me by surprise, as I did not expect her to return my money to me, nor did I expect her to call me uncle. Somewhat absent-mindedly, I accepted the coin she held out. But when I noticed that it was a fifty paise piece, I walked up to her to return it. Although she was reluctant to accept it, yet I somehow managed to force it on her in my privileged position of an uncle now. She expressed her gratitude to me by her looks and that was good enough for us.

The next time we met was when I was crossing the over-bridge to get to the station platform and she was returning from there with someone she had come to receive. She nodded to me in recognition, as if I was an old friend of hers and then trotting up to me said complainingly, "Uncle, why did you not accept your money back?" By way of my answer, I simply slapped her on the back and moved on without uttering a word.

I cherish a sweet memory of this chance encounter—illustrative, as it is, of the kinship a small good turn helps to establish at time, between two persons poles apart and quite unknown to each other.

* * * *

Chapter 55

Departed Glories

With its towers and turrets, its spires and its pinnacles, the little old-world township of Datia is of marked tourist interest. I, therefore, felt happy to receive an invitation to lunch from His Highness the Maharajah of the place one day towards the end of February 1949, while as Inspector General of Police, U.P., I was on my way from Jhansi to Agra by road. Typed on a crackling handmade note paper with the Maharajah's personal crest at the top of it and placed inside a large sized cover to match, it seemed to proclaim the very distinguished position held by its sender.

Like many a city of ancient India, Datia has a massive stone wall encircling it, with stupendous gateways at all points of entry into it; gateways that are reminiscent of the Middle ages when they had to be made sufficiently strong to withstand and attack from an enemy. Like all others, the one by which I entered the city had its large-sized panels fitted with huge iron studs, designed to provide an effective foil against battering elephants of the older days. On the other side of this gateway stood a batch of local policemen, drawn up by the side of the road to give me a salute. Dressed in their indifferent raiment's and carrying arms that were pre-historic, they looked archaic. Nevertheless, I played my part as best as I could and then proceeded in the direction of the Maharajah's garden house where he resided in solitary glory, separately from his two Maharanis, the senior one and the Junior one, each of whom flourished in exclusive possession of a castle on a hill-top.

As my car sped on its way, it seemed to me as if I had been transplanted to quite another part of the world with hills on both sides of the road, some big, some small, some far, some near. But one thing that was common to them all was that they were, almost without exception, crowned by some edifice or other—whether in the shape of a temple or a fortress that looked like a diadem and heightened their beauty. In between lay open country, for the most part rocky and stretching as far as the eye could see. A tree here a tree there, stood like a lonely sentinel, thus giving, a pictorial effect to the entire landscape. I must add that to this effect, herds of cattle were to be seen dotted all over and browsing lazily on whatever little vegetation grew there. Even the population looked picturesque, the men in their large turbans of variegated colours tied in the Rajasthani style and the women in their gay skirts with bits of glass stuck in them by way of decoration. Above all, the whole place seemed to have a carefree air hard to find elsewhere in these days of hurry and bustle.

My arrival at the Maharajah's garden house was heralded by a bugle call. Then came the command, "Guard turn out" upon which His Highness' personal guard turned out to "Present Arms" to me. This, I thought, was a rare compliment paid to a visiting Policeman from across the border. But I could see that not only there were the local officers anxious to accord me a right royal welcome but that the entire population felt likewise. This was evidenced by the men, women and the children in their colourful dresses, lining the street leading to the Maharajah's garden house. Having inspected the Guard I went over to the spot where His Highness the Maharajah with a few of his top Sardars, stood to receive me. Attired in their formal dress, they looked very impressive indeed, if somewhat stiff. But the most impressive figure among them was that of the Maharajah himself, who, in spite of his old age and infirmity looked every inch a Prince.

When introductions over, the Maharajah conducted me to his parlour—a room of enormous proportions—and made me sit by his side on a Settee, facing the rest of the party. My notice was at once attracted by the numerous paintings that adorned the walls all around, a majority of them depicting various scenes with His Highness as the central figure. Among them there was one of a Dussehra procession that struck me as the most colourful of all, with the Maharajah seated on a gaily caparisoned elephant at the head of the procession and looking resplendent in his *durbar* dress.

My conversation with the Maharajah was a purely an informal affair, neither of us having anything particular to discuss. But from certain remarks addressed to his courtiers by him, I could discover that his somewhat exaggerated notion of and high regard for me stemmed from the fact that I was a senior officer hailing from a territory that he insisted on calling 'British', although its governance had long since passed over to the 'natives' of the country. This only went to show that the Maharajah still lived in the past, which was indeed pathetic. Of the buildings I visited, one was the old Fort astride a hilltop that looked magnificent from a distance. It was here that the senior Maharani lived in solitary glory with her retinue of maid servants. Inside the Fort there was an armoury, stacked with an impressive collections of weapons of attack and defence, mostly obsolete. Among them were to be seen broad swords, cutlasses, scimitars, battle axes, match stocks, blunderbusses, muzzle-loaders, as well as steel helmets, shields, gauntlets, halberds, vizars, breastplates, etc.

Another place which had been shown to me was the *Durbar* hall. On its walls there were heads of bisons and other big game shot by the Maharajah in his younger days, while hung on stand immediately behind the throne, there was a yellow silk scroll nine to ten feet long, betokening award of the title of G.C.S.I., to His Highness by Her Imperial Majesty Queen Victoria of hallowed memory.

I was much impressed by all the things that I saw in that hall. But one and all—the silk scroll with its letters of gold, the empty throne with a canopy over it, the massive cutglass chandelier hanging from the ceiling, the trophies on the walls, even the costly furniture, covered as they were with a thin layer of dust seemed to proclaim the glory that was now gone.

By the time I returned to Maharajah's garden house after my sight-seeing, it was time for lunch. This was served in the Indian style, the vessels used being of shining silver. When lunch was over, we adjourned to the parlour, where the Maharajah ceremoniously offered me pan. I accepted it with a bow and then as I was preparing to take leave, a man came and said something to him

In a whisper, what he meant to convey was that all was now set for a group photograph being taken. This, again, appeared to form part of a ritual that had to be gone through every time the Maharajah had a guest. As was customary on occasions like this, the Maharajah sat on in the centre of this group, while I sat on his right. In front of us, there was a lotus pond looking its best. Thereafter, when everybody else had been seated properly, each according to his status, click went the shutter of the camera and this brought the proceedings to a close.

From Datia I drove to Dholpur, another princely state where I had arranged to make a halt on my way to Agra. My meeting with the Maharajah was fixed for the next morning at 11.00. So I spent the intervening night in the state guest house. The Maharajah, I learnt, did not live in the old palace in the city, but in another one built some ten miles away in the heart of a forest. This, I was told, was because he was fond of watching wild game in their natural habitat.

Early next morning, I decided to go for a drive though the state forest, having nothing better to do till 11.00. This was most enjoyable with lovely trees of different hues lining the road on both sides of me and a gentle breeze that carried with it all the aroma of the forest, blowing in my face. Indeed, there are few delights to equal a jaunt through a forest in spring time when it is at its best.

Interested as the Maharajah was in jungle lore, he had every few miles inside the jungle a rest house that served as a grand stand to watch wild game from. Each of them had outside its high fencing a water hole and a salt lick by way of a standing invitation to the fauna of the forest to come and have a drink or a lick.

Deep in the forest I came across a magnificent edifice, known as *Khas Talab,* built of red sandstone and dating from the time of Emperor Jahangir. This was where the Emperor went for a rest whenever he felt inclined to do so. Being situated within close range of Agra, it suited him admirably. On my way to this place, I passed a Buick car, driven by the Maharajah himself who, I had been informed, made it a practice every morning to drive singly to some select spot in the jungle, to say his prayers in seclusion. After that, he would sound the hooter of his car, which acted as a signal for the wild game all around, tigers and leopards excepted, to come together to feed off the palm of his hand. What a lovely thing to contemplate. A staunch believer in non-violence, the Maharajah had prohibited shooting in his jungles and this was why they felt encouraged to come up to him unhesitatingly.

The *Khas Talab* looked like a dream come true. Flanked by forests on all sides and with an artificial lake of enormous proportions in front of it, it was, on the face of it, the product of a master mind. Its very size, its architectural style, its proportions and its workmanship spoke of an opulence of which the Mughal Emperors were famous the world over. With only a solitary caretaker to look after this palatial building situated in the wilderness, it looked haunted and brought to one's mind a vivid picture of the days when it had been at the height of its glory when its halls and its passages had echoed to the strains of music, the peals of laughter and the sound of human footsteps

Coming to our own times, it was in one of the rooms of this building that His Royal highness Prince Edward had stayed during the course of a *shikar* trip in 1922, while out on a visit to India at the invitation of His Excellency the Viceroy and Governor-General of India, Lord Reading. The room is still there, kept intact for anyone to see.

In an another room are to be seen markings from gun shot fired at close range. The story goes that once upon a time a tigress had taken shelter under a staircase in this room to drop her cubs there. The caretaker had unwittingly come across her, whereupon she had given vent to her feeling by a loud growl. He had then fetched his gun to fire at her. But instead of hitting the tigress, he had hit the wall. Fortunately for him, this had made the tigress to take to her heels.

My appointment with the Maharajah being fixed at 11.00 in the morning, I hurried to his Palace, left the forest to see him on time. In its sylvan surroundings with a high iron palisade encircling it, by way of a protection against the intrusion of wild animals, it struck me as unique in its conception. Imagine waking up in the morning to the chirping of birds and going to sleep at night to the sound of other denizens of the forest calling to one another. This is what the Maharajah loved to do and one may be sure he was able to indulge his fancy to the full.

On my arrival, the Maharajah's private secretary ushered me into the room where he was seated. At the entrance to this room, a dwarf, barely three feet in height, stood guarding it. In his turnout of green dotted with yellow, he looked like a clown. I could not make out what he was there for, unless it was his highness's idea to excite the mirth of his visitors.

The room in which I found myself was a spacious one with a marble floor and very well appointed. In front of the Maharajah lay an occasional table on which there was a chess-board with pieces made of solid gold. Dressed simply in a *dhoti* and *kurta*, he had a quiet dignity about him that distinguished him from others of his fraternity. I had been told that the Maharajah was an erudite scholar of Sanskrit, one who had a special study of the Bhagwat Geeta and I could see that he was not only a master of Sanskrit but also of English, which he spoke fluently.

Our conversation turned on Freddie Young of the Indian Police whom the Maharajah knew very well and treated as his friend. From Freddie he passed on to Bramley, another officer of the Indian Police, who used to be Superintendent of Police, Varanasi, at one time. The Maharajah related how Bramley had been specially selected to act as equerry to King George when he visited India in 1911. It was in fact interesting to listen to the Maharajah's account of what had passed at Varanasi when the King had gone there. According to the

Maharajah, Bramley had told the King to come with him quietly at night, if he wished to see real India. So, one evening King George went out on the quiet with Bramley who took him to where Swami Bhaskaranand, a renowned Yogi of the time, was to be found. The Yogi, a wizened looking old man who sat there without a shred of cloth on his person, looking on the two, he asked Bramley whom he knew very well, *"Beta, Yah Tu Kisko Laya Hai?"* (Son, whom have you bought with you?) Bramley replied, *"Baba, yeh Shahanshah Badshah hai"* (Father, this is the King Emperor). Upon this, the Yogi recited a *sloka* (verse) in Sanskrit in praise of God Almighty and laid himself flat at the feet of King George. Whereby he meant to convey that he saw the Supreme Being in the person before him. King George, it is believed, was much impressed by the piety of this Yogi and went away quietly after a while.

I had an hour's very interesting discussion with the Maharajah and before I left he extended an invitation to me to come again and stay with him when, he said he would show me round his jungles and give me an ocular demonstration of how some of the wild game living therein, such as *Sambhar* and *Cheeta* were accustomed to respond to his call and feed off the palm of his hand.

I regret very much that I was not able to avail myself of the invitation extended by the Maharajah, in spite of a keen desire to do so. And now that he is no more and his State has been merged in Rajasthan, I have lost my chance for ever. Like the Maharajah of Dholpur, the Maharajah of Datia also has passed away. Each in his own way represented a type and the pity of it is that one is not likely to come across the like of them any more.

* * * *

Chapter 56

Red Tapism and Me

In the year 1934 or so, if I am not mistaken, the Government of U.P. bought off the Ministry of Defence in the Government of India, the entire area covered by the A.T.C. at Sitapur along with the building standing thereon, for a paltry sum of Rupees two and a half lacs. The only snag about this transaction was that the sale deed that was prepared at the time, left with the Ministry of Defence the option to retain in their possession one of the barracks till such time as alternative arrangements were made by them for the storage of their grass-cutting tools, for which it was hitherto being used. After a year or so, when the Government of U.P. moved the Defence Ministry for surrender of the barrack in question, they took cover under the above clause and said they had been unable to make any alternative arrangement. The stalemate continued for years and every time Government of U.P. moved for surrender of this barrack, they got the same old stock reply.

I came to know of this stalemate on my visit to the A.T.C. Sitapur, after I had assumed my office as I.G.P. I then decided to settle this matter across the table with the Area Commander, Lucknow, Major-General Misri Chand and, with this end in view, invited him to the Passing Out Parade of the A.T.C. in 1948 or so. General Misri Chand offered to arrange surrender of this barrack off his own bat and to send one of his officers to liaise with the Commandant A.T.C. I then thought I had won the battle. But a few days later when Gen. Misri Chand told me that he found himself helpless in this matter in face of the stand taken by the Ministry of Defence, I felt crestfallen.

Soon after this during the time, I met one Col. Mohite at a get-together of the Air Force at Kanpur. Somehow our conversation turned on the subject of the barrack at Sitapur and I told him how Gen. Misri Chand had disappointed me. Upon this he (Col. Mohite) told me that in his capacity as Assistant to G.O.C. in Chief Eastern Command, he and not Gen. Misri Chand was the man who could settle the matter. A few days later he also sent me an officer from Ranchi desiring me to put him in touch with the Commandant A.T.C., Sitapur for the needful. I felt greatly bucked up by this turn of events and was waiting to hear from Commandant A.T.C. about the take over of the barrack in question by his when I had a letter from Colonel Mohite expressing his deep regret for his inability to do anything in the matter, in face of the stand taken by the Ministry of Defence. This certainly gave me a jolt, but there was nothing I could do.

After a lapse of six months or so, when I had an opportunity to go to Delhi on some business I thought of contacting the Secretary to this Ministry of Defence, one Mr. B.B. Ghose in this connection and on my doing so he put me in touch with one of his Joint Secretaries who was dealing with the case. The latter in his turn called up the office Superintendent concerned, who after some scratching of his head, stated that he had a vague recollection of the correspondence that had passed between the Government of U.P. and the Ministry of Defence in this connection, but that it would take him some time to trace the relevant file. I then came away feeling thoroughly disgusted.

After some time when I again went to Delhi I thought of meeting General Thimayya, Quarter Master General and when I did so I found him extremely accommodating besides being very affable. When I explained my case to him in a few words, he pressed the button to call up an officer, one Brigadier Rikhe and said to him, "Look here, Mr. Lahiri, I.G. Police U.P. tells me that we are in wrongful possession of one of his barracks at Sitapur. Isn't that scandalous?" He then turned to me and asked, "Mr. Lahiri, will 48 hours do?" I said, "By all means." Then he said to Brig. Rikhe, "Go ahead."

I came away mightly pleased with the upshot of my meeting with General Thimayya. At the same time I had a lurking suspicion in my mind that the thing would fizzle out again, as it had gone before. On my return to Lucknow I felt a great surprise when my Personal Assistant, Mr. Devendra Sen told me that one of the officers of the Lucknow Area had been badgering him for an extension of time for surrender of the Barrack at Sitapur. I was then in a generous mood and said to him, "All right. Tell him they can take a week's time over the surrender."

It was time, that a matter which had been hanging fire for years and years, was settled in no time across the table, as it were. In the sequel, whenever Gen. Thimayya comes to my mind I am filled with a sense of gratitude to him coupled with a sense of admiration for his style of working.

* * * *

Chapter 57

The Crowning Event of the Career

When the Prime Minister Pt. Jawaharlal Nehru visited Lucknow, on a date in November, 1952, for the presentation of colours to the U.P. Police and the P.A.C. U.P., was undoubtedly a red letter day in the annals of the U.P. Police. Arrangement had been made for the Prime Minister for the inspection of the Parade on horse back and all as he rode up to the saluting base on his white charger, he looked the very image of Prince Charming. He also went through the entire ceremonial—which was universally acclaimed to be the best ever witnessed in Lucknow—like one born to it. His very presence also lent distinction to the show.

The Parade was a composite one, made up of mounted and foot police. A contingent of fire fighters another of the paramilitary force raised to man the check-posts on the Indo-Tibetan border—each fully decked out in its own regalia, inclusive, in the case of the latter, of a novelty in the form of a snow cap and a snow stick—lent some colour to the Parade. It was commanded by Sri A.K. Dass of the Indian Police and as, mounted on his charge, sword in his hand and resplendent at the head of it, he looked statuesque.

One special feature of the parade was that consecration of the two flags was done in turns by a Brahman (Pandit Gaya Prasad Trivedi), a Muslim (Maulvi Haji Abdul Sikander), a Christian (Rev. P.K. Sarkar) and a Sikh (Gyani Uttam Singh) priests. Another memorable thing was that each of them spelt out his litany through a loudspeaker, it reverberated to the farthest corner of the ground to cause a thrill to all the listeners. In fact, every detail of the programme laid down for the occasion was carried out with the utmost precision. So much so, that one of the dignitaries who attended the Parade went to the extent of saying that for him it was like a dream come true. It was indeed remarkable how the huge crowd of spectators assembled at the site, numbering from some 49,000-50,000, viewed the entire Ceremonial Parade in pin-drop silence.

The Prime Minister was gracious enough in his concluding speech to pay a glowing tribute to the U.P. Police for the achievements and to the P.A.C. U.P. for lending helping hand to many a State of India in time when needed, besides complimenting me personally for my part in the game.

After the Parade in the evening, we had a banquet at the Police Mess in honour of the P.M. It was a full-dress affair attended by the Governor of U.P. Sri K.M. Munshi, the Chief Minister Pt. G.B. Pant, the Home Minister Sri Sampurnanand, the Chief Secretary Sri B.N. Jha and the Home Secretary Sri G.P. Mukerji, apart from a host of senior policemen in uniform. On this occasion also, the Prime Minister was like a shining star shedding light all around him. Being in a cheerful mood, he even felt inclined to exchange pleasantries with some of those present there.

In my capacity as host, it was my privilege to make an after-dinner speech. This I began by paying a compliment to the P.M. and expressing that his indomitable courage, his inborn optimism and his childlike simplicity had endeared him to us and we felt proud to serve under his leadership. I also took an advantage of the occasion to boost the role of the Police and emphasise how, with the partition of our country, the necessity had arisen for reorganising it as a second line force, fit to relieve the Army of static duties, such as the protection of our vital installations and of the Railways.

The P.M.'s speech in reply was characteristic of him in that he discounted the very idea of making the Police into a semi-military organisation. In fact, he said something like this "Mr. Chairman, it is all very well for you to say the Police in India have a new role to play. But if you come to think of it, where is this mad race for armaments going to end up? Take the case of the U.S.A., the U.S.S.R., England, France, Germany or Japan, Materially they are in an infinitely superior position as compared to us. Yet can it be said that they are happy? Happiness comes from inner greatness." In this way, he went on speaking for some three quarters of an hour, making a survey of present day conditions of the entire world and, like an apostle of peace and non-violance as he was, preaching love for our neighbours, for the weak and the down-trodden.

Subsequent events have proved that Pt. Jawaharlal was not clairvoyant. Yet, who can deny on that account his greatness as a man. A born democrat as he was, he disliked any show of force at the time of his arrival or departure from any station or when he was due to address a public gathering. In fact, armed policemen on security duty on such occasions were like a red-rag to him. On this very account, many a time they had to be smuggled away from his view so as not to offend his susceptibility.

In retrospect, I make bid to say that the P.M. Pt. Jawaharlal's aforesaid visit to Lucknow in November 22, 1952, which happened more or less to synchronise with the completion of my service as a Policeman, stretching over a period of some 31 years, was not only a memorable event for the U.P. Police but also marked the crowning event of my career too.

* * * *

Chapter 58

Then and Now

The ensuing accounts will give the readers an idea that how conditions have been changed. I cannot say whether for the better or worse—since the olden days when officers of Government carried more authority and at the same time enjoyed more prestige. Let me, relate a case by way of an illustration of my point, in the first instance, which took place on a date way back in 1914 or so during a Moharram procession which in the course of its progress along the prescribed route, came up against an overhanging branch of a roadside Peepal tree. Now, since this branch happened to obstruct its passage, the processionists laid down their *taboots* on the ground and refused to budge till the offending branch was cut down. This led to a communal tension resulting in congregation on the spot of a large number of Hindus and Muslims. The Hindus being strongly opposed to any such sacrilegious act on the ground that they were accustomed to worship a Peepal tree. The local Police Officer having found it beyond his competence to tackle the situation, sent word of it to the local S.P. and D.M. The S.P. being out of the station, the D.M., one Mr. W.B. Cotton took it upon himself to do the needful. He happened to be a tough man with walrus like moustache and a forbidding look. He had his horse saddled up at once and proceeded to the spot in hot haste. On his arrival there, it did not take him long to size up the situation, and the thing he did was to get hold of an axe and climbed up the tree in question dexterously. Thereafter, he started lopping off the offending branch with his own hands, while the Hindus kept gazing at the proceedings with them. Thereafter, just when the latter were on the point of resuming the procession, Mr. Cotton shouted at them and asked to know what prevented them from skirting the tree. In this process he also hurled at them many an indigenous abusive word which he had committed to memory for occasional use. It was thus that a communal riot was averted and Mr. Cotton was able to ride back home fully satisfied with the part played by him in this episode.

The other incident which comes to my mind in this connection was one that took place in 1941 or so and in which I was personally involved. I was then S.P. in-charge of the Investigation Branch of the C.I.D. and was on my way to Faizabad from Lucknow by car on an official business. The road connecting the two happened to be dead straight and fairly wide for almost the entire length and, what was more, I was driving my own 30 horse power V8 car. When I was within 15-20 miles of Faizabad, I noticed at some distance ahead of me two pairs of bullocks, each hitched to an yoke, being driven along the road. I repeatedly sounded the horn of my car by way of a warning to the driver of these bullocks. The mistake I made was not to slow down sufficiently to be prepared against all contingencies. Unfortunately, when I was within a few yards of these bullocks they fanned out in such a way as to block the road for me. I then pressed hard on the brakes of my car, but this was too late and my car rolled on to hit one of the bullocks, thus causing a fracture of his hind leg.

I felt sorry for the incident, although the fault was not entirely mine. Anyway, I offered to pay some compensation to the driver of these bullocks, but in the meantime some others people came up and started creating a scene. Upon this I thought it best to push off and make a report at the nearest Police Station. There I met Sub-Inspector Yadunandan Pande and desired him to go to the spot and see what he could do to settle the matter amicably. I also desired him to meet me there on my way back. What passed between him and the other party concerned in this case, I do not know. For my part I felt ill at ease throughout the day.

Later on, when I got out of the sight of the fateful spot, I saw in the light of my car two long rows of men lining the street on either side of it. By now I had prepared myself for an unpleasant experience. I was greatly surprised, therefore, the moment I stopped the car those men bowed low in salutation with two of their leaders, garlands in hand, stepped forward to greet me. This was certainly an anti-climax for me. But the best part of it was that when I expressed my regret to them for the incident that had taken place, they insisted that the fault lay entirely with the driver of those bullocks. Thereafter each of the two leaders garlanded me with a flourish. One of them even said "Sir, it was our great good fortune that for an incident, petty as it was, we had the rare honour of your *darshan*." After this it was with some difficulty that I was able to force into their hands a sum of Rs. 20/- as compensation.

Incidentally, all this while I could see S.I. Yadunandan Pande standing unobtrusively at the back of the crowd with a grin on his face which was quite suggestive for me.

I cannot help thinking that if the thing had happened today, I would not have been able to get away with it so easily. I will go further and say that this was possible simply because the masses had a fear of all officers who had anything to do with the administration which is surely lacking today, While I am at this topic of "Then and Now" I might mention that in public administration a fact popularly known as 'equal' meaning 'prestige' counts for a lot. This reminds me how, years ago when I was officiating as Superintendent of Police Farrukhabad, the city *Kotwal*, Md. Ayub used to greet me every morning by saying *"Hazoor ke ekbal se, Shahar me khairiat hai"* (all is well in the city by your grace).

Now an important thing to remember is that this *ekbal* flows from good governance which was a distinguishing feature of the administration in the past. Good governance again, is possible only if all those who have the implementation of it in their hands, are fully awake to a sense of their responsibilities, besides being scrupulously honest and above reproach in all respects.

As I have stated elsewhere, another thing that has queered the pitch today is undue interference on the part of most of our legislators in the internal administration of all the departments of Government, which has a very harmful effect all round. Unless therefore they realise their limitations and confine themselves to the welfare of the people in their respective constituencies, instead of dabbling in affairs which should be concern with them the prospects of a good governance can be said to be bleak.

For their part, all those who have anything to do with the administration, whether in big or a small way, must not allow themselves to be influenced by any extraneous consideration, if they are at all keen to rehabilitate themselves in the eyes of the masses.

* * * *

Chapter 59

Corruption as Genesis and Cure

The root cause of corruption is partly historical. There was a time when corruption was practically unknown. That was the golden age of Hindu Rule. With the advent of successive hordes of free looters, things took a turn for the worst. The rule of law was supplanted by law of the jungle. Might became right. The one and only thought or the average citizen centred round his self-protection. He cast his morals to the winds and turned into a time server. Corruption persisted in the days of the British Raj, when a majority of the Indian officials, particularly of the subordinate ranks, indulged in this evil and it continued to flourish through a system of graft that assumed the character of a fine art. The credit goes to a majority of top ranking Indian officers of that time, it can be stated that, by and large, however, they remained free from it. Our British rulers cared little if their henchmen made a little money by foul means, so long as the interest of the Raj or its stability was assured.

Here is a case of extortion within my knowledge, typical of the high handedness that characterised the police of the subordinate ranks in the pre-independence days. The victim of this was a village youth who earned his living as a labourer in a tea estate of Assam. He had come home on leave with his accumulated savings amounting to a little over Rs. 300/-, to spend some time with his old mother, for whom his home coming was a great event. It so happened that in his village there lived a girl slightly younger than himself who had been his playmate in his childhood, when the two suffered from no inhibitions of any kind. But now the same girl had grown into a woman who was not free to do as she pleased. One day, unfortunately for them, they took in into their head to go to a neighbouring village where a fair was being held. They had not consulted and took the permission of their parents and, left to themselves they made day to it. Later when they returned home, they discovered that they had fallen from grace. But the storm soon blew over and they settled down to their normal life.

All went well till a beat constable arrived in the village in course of his rounds. He came to know of this affair from the village *Chaukidar.* A fact the latter stressed was that the lad had brought home with him a substantial sum as his savings. "Here", said the constable to himself, "is an opportunity for me to make some money." He sent for the lad and said to him threateningly "Well, what do I hear about you? Is it a fact that you ran away with so and so's daughter?" In answer the lad could only mumble. "No *Malik,* I did nothing of the kind, I merely went with her to the mela next door." "But", said his stern interlocutor, "you should have known that this was highly improper. What you did amounts to an offence against the law. It is a case of abduction, pure and simple." In brief the youth was hauled up to the Police Station concerned and his old mother had to cough-up a tidy amount for his release.

This case of high-handedness which took place in a remote village of Mirzapur would never have come to light, but for the fact that I happened to be camping close to this village and the victim of it took courage in both hands to lodge a complaint with me.

Here is another case of Police high-handedness which came to my notice when I was S.P. Saharanpur. The victim of this case was a Muslim who had come to Saharanpur to make some purchases on the eve of *Id.* Having nothing better to do on the evening of his arrival, he went to a night show in a local cinema hall. Thereafter, when he was on his way back to his lodging, he was accosted by a number of Police Constables, out on night patrol, who robbed him of his money amounting to two hundred rupees, under a threat of his prosecution for vagrancy. Poor man! he spent the night under a roadside tree bemoaning his lot and next morning came to me on the advice of a passer-by. I made a spot enquiry almost immediately into the case, and, as a result thereof, dismissed the same day the four constables involved in it.

A monthly levy, not infrequently running into four figures, on gaming houses allow to ply their trade on the quiet, made a fruitful source of income for the police in the past. It led to other forms of crime besides setting in train an unhealthy competition among the district Police. Certain towns—Kanpur, Lucknow, Allahabad and Agra were notorious for this kind of thing.

Apropos public gambling, I will relate my own experience as S.P., Saharanpur from 1943 to 1945. On my arrival there I learnt through various sources of the extent to which *Satta* (a special type of gambling) was currently played there. I then had a man-to-man talk with the city *Kotwal* who came out with a long story and told me that his daily income from it amounted to rupees four hundred which he had to share with numerous officials to keep them on the right side. I was shocked to hear it and desired him to stop these irregular payments forthwith. At the same time I gave him an assurance that if he did so, it would be my job to see to it that he came to no harm from these men. I am glad to say that he kept his word to put an end to this type of gambling within seven days, about which I had abundant proof.

While a case of barefaced extortion like the ones I have mentioned or of open defiance of the law of gambling on a mass scale, may not take place now, there can be no hesitation of expressing that corruption in one from or another is now rampant in all the services—on a scale hitherto unknown, worse still, the malady would now appears to have spread even among an appreciable number of senior officers. It is so, because there is a marked falling off in public morals all round and also because of laxity of discipline in the services. Now a man supposed to be in authority has no authority left in him.

He can not punish any defaulter for fear of bringing the hornet's nest on him.

Corruption even if it cannot be rooted out, lock stock and barrel, can be greatly reduced, if only the person in authority is free from any blemish and is allowed a free hand. It is always open to Government to relieve him of his charge, if he fails to come up to the mark. Very often the wrong doer is able to get away with it by bringing pressure to bear on his superior. This acts as an encouragement to him to continue in his evil ways. One reason why the administrative machinery in fast deteriorating today is because of divided responsibility. What is sorely needed today, is more speed in the transaction of business and greater trust being reposed in the man on the spot, unless he is a dud, in which case he should be made to go.

The eradication of corruption has two aspects, punitive and preventive. For lasting results, it is the preventive aspect that calls for greater emphasis. Often a straight man-to-man discussion to get the best out of those who have to come into contact with the masses, will be found to be fruitful. Much will depend upon the personality of the man who has given the opportunity to speak. He will be able to make an impact on the men under his charge, only if he bears an exemplary character himself. His endeavour should be to make an appeal to the better sense of these men. If he does so, then at least some, if not all of them, will react favourably. This is the only method that is likely to yield dividends, any amount of punitive action will not do the trick. Nor with the best of intentions is it possible to track down all the offenders.

What is, in fact, needed is a crusade against the evil of corruption. If arrangement is made for a discussion being given by select public men, then it should pay. Members of the police should also be made to realise that so long as they continue to indulge in corruption in one form or another, their image in the public eye is bound to suffer.

Enquiries into complaints of corruption, if they are to yield any positive result, must be taken up on a high priority basis. As far as possible, they should be made by the S.P. himself, in case they are against an officer of the rank of Sub-Inspector or above. He will do well to visit the scene of occurrence by surprise. In this way, once it is known that he means business, half the battle will have been won.

Sufficient weightage should also be given, in the assessment for integrity. It should also find mention in one's character roll. Those with doubtful integrity should be passed over for promotion. All said and done, while there can be no panacea against corruption, it stands to reason that where there is a will, there is a way.

* * * *

Chapter 60

Some Food for Thought

In one of his essays, Sir Arthur Helps, an eminent literary figure of his time, says "The qualities of a man of business are of a moral nature." It would seem to me that the qualities of a true policeman, on the other hand to be of a dubious nature. Let me take up, for instance, the quality of honesty. There is a slogan, "Honesty is the best policy". It has the sanction of ages behind it. But the point is, if it has the same practical application in the everyday life of a police officer as it has in that of another individual. Has it not occurred to us that Honesty, understood in the ordinary sense of the term, is meaningless in the transaction of our business?

Let me cite one instance in my own case when I was posted as Superintendent of Police, Farrukhabad, in the early years of my service. One day the City *Kotwal* came to me and said, he was going to raid a gambling den and that I should sign a search warrant for it. I noticed that the warrant he wanted me to sign did not specify the house he proposed to search. When I questioned him, he said that the man who ran the show took the precaution of varying its site almost every day. So it was difficult for him to specify the site in advance, but that he would fill in the gap in good time and I was not to worry on that account. In course of time the raid came off and a number of persons were arrested. When later the case, came up in court, I was surprised to find that I had been cited as a witness for the defence by one of the accused who happened to be a man of substance.

Even though, I felt unperturbed as I was sure of my ground. Imagine my continuation therefore, when the counsel for the defence asked me point blank if, when I signed the warrant, I took care to specify the house to be searched. Directly, I found myself on the horns of a dilemma. If I said no, that case would end in discharge, the warrant being ultra-vires. If, on the other hand I said, yes, I would render myself liable to a charge of perjury. This was because of my own words, which I had said so deliberately, still rang in my ears, that "I would tell the truth, the whole truth and nothing but the truth." So, naturally, I chose the lesser of the two evils and confessed the truth. I still remember vividly the painful expression, the look of amazement, of doubt and despair in the face of the Prosecuting Inspector, whose very eyes seemed to bulge out of their sockets. I heard a later in the court, the presiding magistrate felt amused while there was a distinct look of triumph in the face of the counsel for the defence. Indeed at that moment, I felt like being an utter fool. But then, there was no remedy for it and all I could do was to make a hurried exit from the inquisitional chamber which had been the scene of my embarrassment. My point is that in the interests of the prosecution in this case I was expected to say "Yes" in answer to the question put to me by the Counsel for the defence.

To this day I am not sure how the Defence came to know about the secret of the warrant, although I have a shrewd suspicion that the City *Kotwal* himself might have given it away. Such double-faced januses, such human incongruities, who would hunt with the hound and run with the hare, are not unknown to us all. Any way, the incident was closed, but I had learnt my lesson.

To some extent I should say it is the prevailing law that causes all this conflict between the dictates of one's conscience on the one hand and one's wisdom on the other. To cite another instance, which of us has not felt the utter impracticality of the ruling issued by our own High Court that whenever one goes to make a raid on either a cocaine dealer or a distiller of illicit liquor, one must take with him two respectable men of the same locality to bear witness? Frankly speaking, can one possibly work on that principle? You have to conduct your raid first and procure your respectable witnesses of the locality afterwards. I allow one cannot defend one's conduct on strictly moral grounds, but one has to consider the practical side of the affair, rather than worry one's head over legal fastidiousness at a juncture when delay may spell disaster.

To proceed, one is continually beset with such problems even in the course of one's routine duties. This reminds me of the countless number of certificates, one is required to sign everyday. Let me cite a most familiar one. It mentioned like this: "I certify that I have satisfied myself with the amount drawn represents the actual cost of transport of luggage, not exceeding the limit of weight prescribed etc., calculated at the rates prevalent in the district and that the cost is not less than the amount claimed." Now, fancy a Superintendent of Police sitting as a presiding deity at his Headquarters being able to satisfy himself about the small details in respect of a journey performed by a constable from one police station to another. The whole thing is ridiculous in the extreme. Yet, you are compelled to shut off your conscicncc and sign away till you are blue in the face, if only to forestall an objection by the audit.

This whittling down of your conscience, I mean the finer feeling on which you prided yourself goes on little by little, till you are completely rid of the impediment. The rule of your life finally resolves itself into a simple expedient, namely, that so long as you can evade being caught out, it does not matter what devices you employ to gain your objective. Let eye not see what your hand may be doing. For, otherwise, how can you work? A fact that stares you in the face is that is case you do not want the success of your case at the cost of honesty, your percentage of convictions is bound to drop to zero.

While discussing of honesty, I am led to view this term in its finer aspect and discuss its practical application in the case of a Sub-Inspector of Police. Even assuming, that he intends being scrupulously honest, can be continue to be so? There is thing so fundamentally wrong in the existing scheme of things that it is well nigh impossible for him to follow that path of virtue. He may be a perfectly honest person, but his immediate superior the Circle Inspector may not be. In that case he has to give up his scruples unless he wants to fall foul of him.

Once I had a discussion with a Station Officer in this connection. He said, "We are helpless. Many an Inspector would, perhaps, not ask for monthly tribute, but he may be as bad as another who would. He has nasty habit of ordering supplies on particular occasions. He will say, look here, my daughter's marriage comes off next month when I shall have to entertain large number of guests. I am told grain can be had very cheap in your area. Will you be so good to send me fifty rupees worth of stuff? I will pay you for it conveniently. But the money never comes. One is afraid to remind him for it, for fear of incurring his displeasure."

Then there is the item of *Bakshish* which causes a heavy drain on a Sub-Inspector's purse. I once asked a Sub-Inspector, why they at all gave any *Bakshish.* He said, "Because we must, I go to see you I find a good many men waiting to see you, all seated in a row. They are accustomed to treat me with respect, as a superior being. So I am anxious not to lose my prestige in their eyes. Your orderly is shrewd enough to know my feeling. So unless I oblige him, I may have to keep standing for ever so long. In other words, if only I keep on the right side of him he will be good enough to fetch me a chair even from your drawing room." What is more your *Peshkar* also must have his *Nazrana.* One must keep on the right side of him, too, because otherwise he can do infinite harm. He will make it a point to put one's papers before you, when you may be in particularly bad mood. In fact, the more *Sakht* a Saheb is, the greater is the demand of his *Peshkar.*

There is indeed much point in all this. The other day a friend of mine said to me that honesty was very much at discount among the subordinate ranks of the Police. And, why not? Let us first remove the conditions which give rise to the existing evil, and then discuss about honesty. I feel under the present conditions, the discussion of honestly is mere cant. Which of us, for instance, does not know that every prosecution under the bad livelihood sections costs money and, yet, what can one do about it?

In fact, almost every single case, if you want it do end successfully, must cost some money, yet there is not nor can be, any provision in the budget for it. The odds against the successful prosecution of case are great. Every one knows it. Yet there is no help for it. Can there be any position more anomalous than this?

Talking of the bad livelihood sections, I feel that their application is becoming more and more difficult every day. If the man you wish to prosecute happens to be in ill odour with the local *Zamindar*, well and good. Because in that case, there will be no trouble whatsoever. But, if, on the other hand, he happens to be a pal of his, then it is an altogether different matter and unless the Station Officer can manage to play of an equally strong *Zamindar* against the other or unless he is prepared to spend a quite a large sum himself, the prospects are gloomy indeed. Prosecution under section 110 Cr. P.C. has now come to be regular battle of wits. You must employ every strategy and counter strategy. The merits of the case are no question at all. In the result, much abuse creeps in. I think a whole volume could be written on the use and abuses of the bad livelihood sections. And, yet, there is no denying the fact that they make a wonderful weapon in the hands of the police and that without them we could be nowhere. What I feel, however, is that insistence of the proportion of such cases as compared with those of the previous year. Results in undue enthusiasm and consequent incarceration of a number of harmless people. It is impossible for one to be able to weigh very accurately the merits of each case. On paper it may look alright and, yet, it may be pure concoction from beginning to end.

Once I had a discussion with a Sub-Inspector on this subject and asked to know if any case sent up under section 109 was true. I had cause for suspicion on this score because I had noticed that very report of arrest indicates section, was so stereotyped to nature, wonderfully alike even to the smallest details. Let me reconstruct a scene. The faithful constabulary true to his salt is making his round at the dead of night. Suddenly he is aware of presence a mere shadow in the distance which moves, then stops and then again moves. Over valiant constable forges ahead, and then shouts a challenge for all he is worth. The shadow suddenly emerges from the dark. There is no mistaking it now. It is a human being anxious to take to his heels. But, our hero of many an adventure, is as quick as lightening. There is sharp, but brief struggle and the man is pinioned. He is asked his name. At first he says it is Ram Charan. Then when he is asked a second time, he says it is Ghar Baran. Finally when he is brought out in the light, he turns out to be Prithi Passi of Turkapur. A couple of witnesses appear on the scene and when in their presence, his person is searched, to, out drops a jenny, a candlestick and a box of matches.

Surely, providence must be socially kind to some people and not so kind to others. Because you or I seldom seem to have such luck.

To revert to the question, I asked of my Sub-Inspector, he said "Sir, to be frank with you, most of our cases are stage-managed. We simply mark down our men and the rest is easy enough. What else can I do? We are in receipt of repeated reminders from you and unless we respond to them, there is to be no peace for us."

I believe that in most places, the rule underlying application of the preventive sections is simply one of demand and supply. Once I was presented at a crime conference held by my friend in a neighbouring district and was amused to notice how each Station Officer was just told of by him, to send up 2, 3, 4 or 5 cases according to the size or importance of his *thana* varied!

I have so far presented only one side of the picture and represented to you how the lot of a Sub-Inspector is a hard one. What I mean to suggest is that it is a hard one only in case he intends being honest, but not otherwise. Far from it. Further, that the conditions under which he has to work are such that it becomes almost impossible for him to keep straight, Hence the average type with which we are familiar.

In the course of my travels, I mean various postings from one place to another, I have met with some exceedingly interesting specimen whose exploits might very well supply the material for a quick seller.

This current practice of extortion has, in my opinion developed into a fine art. I shall now cite another instance of it. A boy while plucking mangoes from a tree fell from it and died. The Station Officer came to know of the incident and immediately proceeded to the spot to prepare an inquest report. What he did on his arrival at the spot, he first of all gets busy in trying to make himself comfortable. He gets a *charpoy* and stretches his tired legs on it under the tree in question. He then sends for the owner of this tree. The man comes and stands with folded hand before the great *Thanedar*, penitent like a lamb. The *Thanedar* asked him, "Are you the owner of this tree?" He says, "Yes, my lord." The *Thanedar* says, "Do you see, the tree is laden with ripe mangoes?" The man says, "It is verily so, Oh, my master and lord of the universe." The *Thanedar* says, "Do you realise that if you had been keeping watch over it yourself, or had engaged some to do so, the death of the boy would not have come to pass?" The man says, "Yes, my master." The *Thanedar* says, "Does it not therefore followed that you are indirectly responsible for the death of the boy. Now go and ponder".

Thereafter, the defender of the peace, disposes himself to sleep under the tree, formed by its murmuring leaves. In the meanwhile the ubiquitous *Dalal* (middleman) is at work. He has a quiet discussion with the owner of the tree and advises him to make some payment. Finally, in the evening the *Thanedar* wends his way home, having earned his full wages for the labour of the day.

The point arises, where is the remedy? My view is that the evil is there, first, because we would not face facts and, secondly, because of the present system of recruitment. Let us raise the status and increase the pay of the Sub-Inspector of Police. A hundred quids should do to start with. It is not very much, considering the importance of his job. Let us also recruit from an entirely different source. I have had a sad experience lately. That is why I suggest departure from the current practice. I had nominated for admission to the P.T.C., a very smart lad who was the son-in-law of Head Constable, nephew of another head Constable, cousin of a Sub-Inspector of Police, great-great grandson of a hero of the Mutiny of 1857 and third or fourth cousin of retired Deputy Collector. Apart from his family connections, he had excellent testimonials for his prowess on the play ground. I said to myself, this is my man. It pains me to have to tell you that he promptly fell a prey to temptation and got sacked. My surprise knew no bounds when I learnt all this on writing to enquire about him.

I have now told my tale and apologies for this infliction, hoping at the same time that what have said will provide some food for thought.

* * * *

Chapter 61

A Word about the Mandir-Masjid Tangle at Ayodhya

One of the most intricate problems facing the Government till date happens to be the Mandir-Masjid tangle at Ayodhya which has so far defied any solution. It is a common knowledge that ever since the Babri mosque was built some '450' years ago, the site has been the bone of contention for Hindus, on the ground that it marks the site where Sri Ram was born. They further contend that there was a temple dedicated to Lord Rama on this spot which was later demolished by Muslims to build a mosque. Incidentally, the fact that some of the stone slabs of the Babri mosque had etched on them the figures of Hindu gods and goddesses went to show that it was built with the very material of the temple that had stood there previously.

A number of Muslim graves (some of them covered in plaster with the insignia of Army Officers of them) scattered all over the place close to where the mosque stood, seem to testify to the allegation, commonly made that these Muslim officers fell in the course of a bloody battle with belligerent Hindus, that took place from time to time, over the disputed site. It will perhaps will not be out of place to mention in this connection that as late as '1939' or so, when I was Superintendent of Police Faizabad, the Pujari of the

Ram Lala Chabutra there made an abortive attempt to blow up one of the domes of the mosque with the help of a home made bomb, in the course of which he himself got blinded.

What is more, late in December 1949, when I was I.G. Police, U.P., some mischief mongers surreptitiously planted by night, the earthen idols of Ram, Lakshman and Sita, inside the mosque, which led to much agitation among the Muslims all over the country. Recent events culminating in demolition of the mosque, have only helped to aggravate the situation, resulting in much blood-shed, looting and arson, which has kept us on tenterhooks. .

For all enlightened Hindus there is no difference between a mandir and a mosque or between Ram and Rahim, Ishwar or Allah. Viewed in this light, therefore, demolition of the mosque on the 6th December, 1992, was an act of vandalism, pure and simple. On the other hand, for a predominating majority of Hindus, the spot where Sri Ram is believed to have been born had immunity of its own and that they have a proprietary right on it.

Such being the case Government have apparently done well to refer the matter to the High Court for adjudication with the idea that if it is held by them that there was a temple on this site, then permission may be given for construction of another temple on it, if only to placate Hindu sentiment of an overwhelming nature.

So for as Muslims are concerned, the site in question can have no special sanctity, as it does not mark either the birth place or the abode of any other saints. They should therefore be satisfied if another mosque is built in close proximity of the old mosque, in the interest of communal harmony.

A fact worthy of mention here in this connection is that it was during the rule of one of the Nawab Wazirs of Oudh, some 200 years ago, that the courtyard of the Babri mosque was so parcelled of as to allow adequate space for setting up of the Ram Lala Chabutra and some of the other show places, the Sita Rasoi being one of them. Who can deny that the aforesaid Nawab Wazir was thus a shining example of communal harmony for all times to come.

* * * *

Chapter 62

Lal Bahadur Shastri—A Tribute

I had the rare good fortune to work under the wings of the Late Sri Lal Bahadur Shastri for a total period of seven years. In the first instance, as Inspector-General of Police, U.P., for four years from 1947 onwards and thereafter, when he was a Union Minister for Railways. I had thus an excellent opportunity to observe him at close quarters and form a rough idea of his numerous qualities of head and heart. Diminutive of size and slight of built, he was not much to look at. Yet, in spite of this initial handicap, he made an eminent success, not only in these two high offices, but also as Prime Minister of India.

Sri Lal Bahadur Shastri's tenure of office as Home Minister, U.P., is popularly know as the golden age of the U.P. Police and rightly so. For, it was during his regime as such that the U.P. Police took long strides, such as it had never taken before nor has taken since then.

.Judging from a casual remark once passed by Lord Mountbatten in an unguarded moment, shortly before quitting office as Governor General of India, it may be inferred that, in common like most other Englishmen, he felt sure at heart that after their departure from the shores of India, there would be a total breakdown of the administrative machinery. He was at the time on his way to Kanpur from Lucknow by car, when he noticed that the policemen lining the road on the occasion were sufficiently alert at their posts. This made him say to his Military Secretary, "See what has come to pass already." Although his observation was not meant for my ear, it was conveyed to me by the Secretary to the Governor, U.P. who happened to overhear it, I had then only just assumed charge as Inspector-General of Police and took it as a challenge. The Police, as a whole, during those days, were in state of flux all over India. They had not only to be reorganised but also reoriented. For me, as well as the entire Force under me, those were stirring times, when every one of us had to work hard with his shoulder to the wheel.

Simultaneously with this process of reorganisation, the Police had to grapple with an increasingly deteriorating situation on the law and order front, necessitating large scale operations against notorious outlaws, such as Man Singh of Agra, Girand Singh of Etah, Amrit Lal of Etawah, Ram Bharose and Rishi Pal of Budaun, Bire Ahir of Farrukhabad and Bashir Pathan of Shahjahanpur to name only a few. The situation was further complicated by the influx from both the western and eastern wings of Pakistan, which thousands of refugees, some of whom indulged in mass killings, being in no mood to settle down peacefully after the ordeal of fire they had recently gone through in their old abode.

One signal achievement of those days was the formation of as many as 11 Battalions of the Provincial Armed Constabulary. Time was when for the management of important fairs and festivals or for the suppression of communal disturbances of a major character, Police reinforcements had to be requisitioned in small batches from all over the State, sometimes an at a short notice. This resulted in a chronic shortage in most districts of the man power needed for the performance of routine police duties. In view, therefore, of the unsuitability of this kind of arrangement, which had its obvious drawbacks, Government thought it fit to sanction the creation of an additional number of companies of what was then called Military Police, to meet emergent demands of man power. Later on, with the partition of the country, the law and order problem in the State became so acute, that the only way to meet it, was to add to the number of these Companies and reorganise them on Battalion basis. This is how the PAC came into force being with a total strength of 11 battalions divided into 86 Companies, of which 50 were required not only to be raised, but also trained, equipped and deployed in record time. Thanks to the zeal, displayed by a select band of officers, the impossible was made possible and these battalions were seen doing active service within three months of their formation. Not only this, such was the prestige they built up in a short time, that their services were in constant demand even outside U.P. from Jammu and Kashmir in the north to Hyderabad, Madhya Pradesh and Maharashtra in the south, from Assam, NEFA, Nagaland, Mizoram, Bihar and West Bengal in the east, to Delhi, Punjab and Rajasthan in the west.

Yet another sphere, in which the U.P. can claim to have taken the lead during those days, was the establishment of Border Check-Posts all along the Border with Tibet. Initially, three companies of Armed Police of a para-military character were raised in this connection and they continue to be the fore runners, if not the nucleus, of the Border Security Force which was later raised centrally.

No account of the U.P. Police can be completed without a special mention of its Wireless Section, which constitutes one of its show pieces and came into full play on the occasion of a mass uprising in the eastern districts of U.P. when telegraph and telephone wires were cut off and Railway lines uprooted, to isolate them from the rest of the world.

As a specialised unit of U.P. Police, its Wireless Section has provided numerous Radio Stations which continue to prove a boon to it.

A technique of locating outlaws by throwing a ring of mobile radio sets around them has resulted in the liquidation of some of the most notorious among them, like Girand Singh, Bire Ahir, Rishi Pal, Ram Bharose, Bashir, Charana and Jahan Singh and others. In the joint operations against Man Singh, over 40 mobile stations of U.P., Madhya Pradesh and Rajasthan were hooked up to form one joint grid, which were controlled from Agra.

One of the outstanding contributions of this organisation was the way it stepped into the breach when employees of the Post and

Telegraphs struck work on a mass scale.

For crowd control in the Kumbh and Ardh-Kumbh Melas of Allahabad and Haridwar, full use is made of the Police Radio. In the past, 48 mobile and manpack Radio sets have been used on these occasions with marked success.

Much of the credit for these achievements at a critical juncture in the life of U.P. Police, goes to late Sri Lal Bahadur Shastri, who as Home Minister of U.P. soon after the grant of Independence to India, took upon himself the role of its foster-father. The great thing about him when he assumed charge as Home Minister of U.P. was that he was keen to learn the ins and outs of work in the Police. Within a few days of his assumption of office, he held an informal meeting with a select number of Senior Police officers at this house, to discuss various police problems with them. Apparently he had given a deep thought to them as was evident from the numerous constructive suggestions he had to make towards their solution.

Sri Lal Bahadur Shastri did not have a closed mind and was open to conviction would be seen from the ensuing episode. At my request Government had sanctioned the direct recruitment on an ad hoc basis of a certain number of candidates of a higher age group for appointment and Deputy Superintendents of Police. Following an interview by duly constituted Board, a list of 43 suitable candidates, arranged in order of merit, was forwarded to Government for orders. Government, in their turn, selected, in the first instance, about a dozen candidates out of this list regardless of their ranking in it and mostly on the ground of their being political sufferers. When I brought this irregularity to the notice of Sri Lal Bahadur Shastri, he sought to defend his action by explaining that, in the first place, the list was supposed to be confidential one and that secondly, Government were free to exercise their discretion in the selections made by them. But the moment I pointed out to him that such action would be morally wrong, he acknowledged his mistake and agreed to amend his order. In the result all the 43 on the approved list came to be appointed.

Here is another incident that speaks volumes for his sense of propriety. One day, he was due to address some policemen at Aligarh, but being held up somewhere, he failed to arrive in time for that meeting. Therefore, as the man on the spot, I decided to address them in his place and to let them disperse. He seemed to be a peeved at this on his arrival, but after I explained him that in situation like this, it had been customary to go ahead with the proceedings. He apologised for his fault, besides being careful ever afterwards to guard against it.

A skilled administrator that he was, he never interfered in the postings and transfers of the Police, knowing full well that if he did so, he would be cutting across all discipline in the force. Once, it so happened that a number of M.L.As. came to me with a request for cancellation of the transfer order of a certain Dy. S.P. I explained to them how this could not be done for administrative reasons. Still they went on pressing their point for so long that out of sheer exasperation, I had to tell them to go and move Government in the matter, if they were so keen on it. Upon this, they disclosed to me that they had come to fresh from a meeting with Sri Lal Bahadur Shastri, who had advised them that he would have on objection to the cancellation, in case I was agreeable. I then told them plainly that I would be failing in my duty, if I gave him an advice that I knew to be wrong. In this way, I finally won the day, which gave me a sense of victory I had seldom felt before. Likewise, I hcld my ground successfully in another case of a more prestigious type in which the transfer of a Senior Superintendent of Police was involved and in which political pressure had been brought to bear on both the Chief Minister and the Home Minister.

Here is a fine example of Sri Lal Bahadur's consideration for others. He was then a Cabinet Minister in the Government of India and had come to Allahabad on tour on a date about the middle of September. As was usual with him, moving from place to place on foot, which made him extremely tired when he returned home in the evening. After sometime, when it was past midnight, he got so restless that his wife feeling alarmed at his condition, enquired of him if she should inform the Civil Surgeon. Wishing not to disturb the latter at that odd hour, he told her to wait till the morning. Fortunately for him, his Personal Assistant, who happened to be in the premises, called the Doctor, acting on his own initiative. The latter found Sri Lal Bahadur in the throes of a massive heart attack and he did what he could to give him temporary relief, besides sending and S.O.S. to

Lucknow and another to Delhi, to summon the best heart specialists from there. On their arrival by plane early next morning, they had him removed to hospital, where he remained as a bed patient for some ten weeks, before returning to Delhi. After this incident, any one in his position would have taken sufficient care of his health but not so was Sri Lal Bahadur. Such was his devotion to duty that he never spared himself even at the risk of inviting a second attack.

Among his other qualities, his industry his high idealism, his sincerity and his personal magnetism distinguished Sri Lal Bahadur from all others. Often during his tenure as Home Minister of U.P. did any one find him glued to his seat, till late in the night, poring over papers calling for his attention, while strings of visitors of a nondescript type sat outside his room, awaiting their turn for interview, which he denied to none. He had no regular hours for his meals and at times missed them altogether under the pressure of work.

Sri Shastri had two other qualities, which stood him in good stead. One of them was his fine sense of humour, once, when he was asked to give a speech on family planning, he blurted out shamefacedly that he had really no claim to do so, being the father of as many as six children, a remark which made the audience burst into peals of laughter. On another occasion, when a news paper correspondent from a foreign country sought his views on non-violence, promptly came his reply "What else can you expect of me." This he said against the back-ground of his diminutive size.

The other quality which he possessed was his acute political sense, for he knew when to quit office. This he did as Railway Minister in the wake of two train disasters in each of which hundreds of passengers were killed. Incidentally, as Railway Minister, he gave me an opportunity to meet him, at least once a month on an average, to allow me time to discuss with him my problem as Inspector General, Railway Protection Force, which enabled me to put through my reorganisation proposals more speedily than would have been otherwise possible. This was largely because from the experience he had previously acquired as Home Minister of U.P. he had a keen insight into the requirements of a Force.

The highest tribute that can be paid to Sri Lal Bahadur Shastri is that he started life as an humble citizen and remained so at heart, even when he adorned the office of Prime Minister of India. He had a smile of recognition for all those who had ever served under him. In their turn, they took him for their best well-wisher. His politeness left everybody gapping. He always got up from his seat to greet a visitor or to bid him good bye. This and similar other signs of his greatness marked him out as one of God's own good men.

In fact, if ever there was a man who rose to the pinnacle of power and the height of glory through sheer force of his character, it was Lal Bahadur Shastri of hallowed memory.

* * * *

Chapter 63

Not Tired but Retired

The heading of this chapter would suggest that after retirement one is apt to be tired. But this need not necessarily be the case, with all. One may have to retire from service at 55 years of age, as I did or at 58, 60, 62, 65 even, depending upon the category of service to which one belongs. This only shows that the retirement age is arbitrary and has nothing to do with one's physical or mental fitness. For instance, although I retired from service some 40 years ago and will be 95 next April, I feel as fit as ever. Let us take the case of Sri Morarji Desai. He was nearing 98 but I believed he still walked straight as an arrow and was capable of doing much hard work.

Talking of Morarji, I am reminded of a meeting I had with him at Pune in October 1953, some months after my retirement as I.G. Police, U.P. He was then Chief Minister of Bombay (now Maharashtra), while I was working as Security Adviser to the Indian Railways after my re-employment. My visit to Sri Morarji was simply in the nature of a courtesy call. The interesting thing about it is that in introducing me to him, the moment I told him that I had retired as I.G. Police U.P. some time ago, he took a start and abruptly said, "Mr. Lahiri, what is the secret of your youth? I was taken aback at this question. So, after some hesitation, blurted out, "Sir, I think it is because I have always taken delight in my work."

He said vehemently, "You are perfectly right, you are perfectly right" and, thereafter, we started discussing other things.

Although I gave my reply to Sri Morarji's question on the spur of the moment, I can say there is much truth in it. For, if one is interested in one's work, then, there is no question of one's feeling of looking tired whatever one's age may be. It is said, one is as old as one feels. In fact, there is nothing wrong with old age by itself. "Grow old with me, the best is yet to be, the last of life for which the first was made," so said Browning in one of his poems. I feel proud of my age, because, for one thing, taking advantage of it, I can pontify, assume air of infallibility. I can tell others, do this or do that.

I recall Browning's tribute to his grammarian, who was decrepit and old, but remained young in spirit:

"Calculus racked him:

Leaden before, his eyes grew dross of lead:

Tussis attacked him.

"Now master, take a little rest!" - - not he!

(Caution redoubled,

Step two abreast, the way winds narrowly!)

Net a whit troubled

Back to his studies, fresher than at first."

In my own case, I must say fortune had favoured me in that I have had something or other to do ever since my retirement in Jan. 53. In the first instance, I was re-employed as Security Adviser to the Railways. This took me on to 1957. In the interval, apart from creating the Railway Protection Force, I had a wonderful opportunity to tour the entire country by rail and that, too in some style, with an eight-wheeler coach at my disposal. I made friends during this period. One of them was Mahadevan, Chief Security Officer, Southern Railway, who alas is no more. Endowed with much go, combined with suavity of manners, he was a jewel of a man rarely to be seen.

During this spell, I was particularly struck by the magnificence of the temples of South India that I saw, their colossal size and wonderful architecture recalling the greatness of Ancient India.

The sea beach of Madras, the lagoons of Kerala, the Back Bay of Bombay (also known as the Queen's necklace because it looks like one when lit up at night), the Pamban Bridge connecting Rameshwaram with the main land, the Rock Caves of Ajanta and the Kailash temple of Ellora are among other sights that stand out in my memory with some vividness. If the Taj of Agra is one of the wonders of the world, I must say the Kailash temple is another. Carved enmasse, out of a hill side, it is indeed a marvel of human ingenuity. Its enormous gateway, its spacious platforms, its spires and pinnacles, its life size images of gods and goddesses, one and all give the impression of having been built from the ground upwards and not carved out of solid rock from the top downwards, as they actually are. Whosoever conceived this Temple was, without doubt, a Master Craftsman.

Coming back to the point I was making, that though retired one need not be tired, I might refer to the spell I had between 1959 and 1962 as Security Adviser to Hindustan Steel. That was another experience that gave me some insight into the great strides India has taken in the field of heavy industry, since Independence. It is no wonder that the area covered by the industrial towns of Asansol, Dhanbad, Durgapur, Chittaranjan, Jamshedpur, Bokaro and Ranchi, with their teeming mills, in now generally known as the Ruler of India. Incidentally, it was during this spell of my service that I conceived the idea of an Industrial Security Force and at the same time gave concrete shape to it in respect of the giant Steel Plants at Durgapur, Rourkela, Bhilai and Bokaro. I am glad there is an All-India Industrial Security Force today on the same pattern.

With the ending of my tenure as Security Adviser to Hindustan Steel, I had another assignment for a year and a half as Director-Civil Defence-cum-Secretary to the Government of U.P. This was a challenging job of a pioneering nature, which kept me frightfully busy till April, 1964. The Homeguards Organisation of U.P. happens to be my creation.

From 1966 to 1969 I was member of a High Powered Committee on Security and Policing of the Railways, set up by the Government of India. This meant another spell of Bharat Darshan for me in luxury, as we had an air-conditioned coach at our disposal and an

Officer of the Catering Department of the Railways in attendance, to look after our creature comforts.

Later on, as a member of a study group on road safety set up by the Government of India in the Ministry of Shipping and Transport, I had an opportunity, for a second time, between 1969-72 to travel from Srinagar in the North to Rameshwaram in the South and from Shillong in the East to Jaipur in the west. Our task was to examine in depth the problem of an ever increasing number of fatal road accidents in the country in recent years and suggest appropriate remedial measures for promoting safety on the roads. I took an active part in preparation of reports of both the High Powered Committee and the Study Group, for submission to the Government of India. But I have no idea about the extent to which our recommendations have since been implemented. I only hope that the reports are not gathering dust in the archives of the Government of India, as is the case, with most of such reports.

These were my activities on the official side after my retirement. On the non-official side I was actively associated with the Bharat Scouts and Guides, U.P., till a recent date. During this period I helped to put up at Allahabad, for this organisation, a number of buildings of which the Bajpai Smarak Bhawan and the Mahamana Madan Mohan Malviya Bhawan deserve special mention. I also founded in 1958 the Bharat Scouts and Guides, Higher Secondary School at Allahabad, which is regarded as one of the best Schools of this place.

In December, 1964, as Chief Director of the All India Jamboree of Scouts and Guides held at Allahabad, I had to make arrangements for the reception of some 12,000 Scouts and Guides, who came from all corners of India. The dates for the Jamboree were from the 27th to the 31st December. But from September onwards I had to remain almost glued to the site chosen for the Jamboree, to make all the necessary bandobast for it in good time. It was a case of putting up a regular township with market square, providing for 72 shops of various types of goods and edibles. The most formidable part of the arrangements was tackling of the problems of lighting, supply and sanitation of the camp. I remember, the night of the 25th December which was harrowing one for me in that I had to keep awake for the whole of it, to get some leaking water mains put right. By the grace of God, the Jamboree was a great success, far and away the best held in India till then. Some of the demonstrations given by its participants were superb. The Oddisi dance of Orissa, the Bhangra of the Punjab and the Rasleela of Uttar Pradesh were adjudged to be the best.

Between the years 1963 and 1971, at the invitation of the U.P. S.C., I worked for several years as an associate Member of their Interview Board for the selection of Personnel for various Services. This was an experience I would have been sorry to miss.

My interest in gardening has helped me spend my time profitably, I have a fairly extensive garden around my residence in which, I have planted hundreds of trees of all varieties since my retirement. My eucalyptus trees, which I planted some 40 years ago, are joy to see by me. So are a number of other fruit and flowering trees. They all form part of my creation. Hence I derive immense pleasure from watching them grow up. On the other hand, it grieves me to see one or the other of them die. Life and death are like brother and sister who go hand in hand.

Of late, I have been distributing biochemical medicines to a limited number of persons for minor ailments and it makes me happy to see them respond to my treatment. There is indeed no greater joy in life than the joy one derives form giving joy to others.

Although, I am no professional coach, it gives me pleasure to give occasional coaching in English, History and Geography to odd students, preparing for the High School or higher examinations. I have a particular liking for Shakespeare's Plays.

I take delight in the company of children. Currently I have a girl friend, a pretty little child, a little over four years of age, whose name is Ruby. She is a veritable chatterbox and often comes to me to exchange small talk and gossip. One day she floated into my study and said, *"Lari chab"*, I want you to remove my shoes. I said, "whatever for!". She said, "I will dance on your sofa." I felt alarmed and it took me some time to dissuade her from her dire intention and thus save my sofa from ruin. I know that Ruby, when she grows up, will forget all about me. Alas! such is the way of the world. I have a grand daughter who was extremely attached to me when she was a kid and never left my side for sometime in her waking hours. But now that she is grown up, she barely recognises me. It is indeed tragic how most children if not all, when they grow up, are prone to forget their own parents even, regardless of the extent to which they had been dependent on them in their infancy, for their very survival.

One's health largely depends upon one's habits. Some of these are of positive, others are of a negative character, which I believe in and practise. On the other hand, there are certain habits one must avoid, to keep fit. In my own case, the fact that I do not drink or smoke, nor eat pan or take tea, has presumably helped me to do so. Of these habits, pan chewing is the one I detest. It is not only unhygienic but filthy. If I had my way I should ban it by an ordinance, if necessary.

I have found that two things add zest to life. One is creation, about which I have already made a mention. This composition itself is in the nature of creation. The other is challenge. Since my retirement I have been given to the reading of religious texts such as the Bhagwat Geeta, the Upanishads and the Balmiki Ramayan. Having been ignorant of Sanskrit, I took this up as a challenge which I have enjoyed. Here is a secret. I read a chapter of Valmiki's Ramayan at night before going to bed. Apart from the pleasure this gives me, it acts also as soporific.

The Geeta, I find, contains gems of thoughts, without a parallel. Here is one of them relevant to the subject of this talk:

> He whose mind is not shaken by adversity, who does not hanker after pleasure and is free from attachment, fear and anger, is a sage.

Here is another:

> The enjoyments that are born of contacts of the senses are only generators of pain, for they have a beginning and an end: O, Arjun, the wise man does not rejoice in them.

What all this matter boils down to, is that, for one physically fit, mentally alert and usefully employed, there is no such thing as retirement until death.

Before I close, let me quote the ensuing lines from Tennyson's

"In Memoriam", which portrays to a nicety the type of death, which I should welcome when I shall have run my course:

> Sunset and evening star;
> One clear call for me;
> May there be no moaning of the bar,
> When I put out to sea.

* * * *

Index